Discerning the Way

Discerning the Way

A THEOLOGY OF THE
JEWISH   CHRISTIAN REALITY

Paul M. van Buren

A Crossroad Book
THE SEABURY PRESS / NEW YORK

1980
The Seabury Press
815 Second Avenue
New York, N.Y. 10017

Printed in the United States of America

Library of Congress Cataloging in Publication Data

Van Buren, Paul Matthews, 1924-
Discerning the way.
"A Crossroad book."
Includes bibliographical references and indexes.
1. Theology, Doctrinal. 2. Christianity and
other religions—Judaism. 3. Judaism—Relations—
Christianity. I. Title.
BT78.V28   230   79-27373
ISBN 0-8164-0124-1

Contents

Discerning the Way

Introduction to the Way

Death stands at the end of every human life, however diverse the paths we travel. To look death in the eye, as we shall if we look up and see where we are going, is to confront the insignificance of our own part in the human enterprise. Death, the great equalizer, seems to deny the particularity of each journey, and the thought of death not only "wonderfully concentrates the mind," as Dr. Johnson said, but punctures our modern confidence in human autonomy. Are we anything more than the product of chance and necessity? Since this is the end (*finis*) of us all, was it perhaps our end (*telos*) all along? Is death the last word?

Yet death, which surely marks our end, is the starting point for reflection on the Way in which we find ourselves, for therein we see who and where we are: creatures, not the Creator; our feet in the dust, not on the clouds. If death is not the first word we admit, it will become the last word said over us. For the vast majority of humanity, life itself is but a living death. The rest of us owe them the admission that "in the midst of life we are in death" and that "from the dust we are and to the dust we shall return."

In view of that certain and universal end before us, and as an act of faith of a fundamental order, we turn our attention to the uncertain and the particular: the Way on which we travel. I say the *Way*; but, given our particularity in history, ought we not rather speak of the *ways* which we in our diversity walk? We must do that too. Yet, for those of us who try to digest what Franz Rosenzweig called "the offensive idea of revelation," there is no escaping the conviction that a path has been shown us. This Way is one because it is provided and enlightened by One, even though it is given to different peoples to claim as their own and to walk in their respective manner. A particular stretch of this Way, we believe, is ours to walk here and now. It would be a faithless refusal of our particularity to think that we could walk this stretch only as others before us walked theirs, or to insist that everyone now must walk just as we are trying to walk. Such pretensions overlook the fact of death.

The Way which we believe to have been shown us, however, is one which we discern only with difficulty. It is far from obvious and it diverges from and is crossed by many other paths which have their own attractions. Not least of these is one called the "American (one may substitute British, French, German, etc.) way of life," which is surely *a* way to walk. There are also other and more subtly attractive roads, such as those of "modernity," "the cultural spirit of the age," "the modern scientific world-view" and secularity. Finding the Way as it weaves through these others is the particular challenge of the stretch assigned to us in these days.

I shall argue that the Way we have been shown has been opened to us precisely as one we ourselves must find and walk with our own feet. *Coram deo* we must walk *esti deus non daretur* (even were there no God), as Dietrich Bonhoeffer put it. The Way which we half-sense and seek to discern seems to be a gift, whenever we find it, and some appear to be quite sure about the Giver. Many more, however, are almost certain that there is no giver. Most of us hope, wonder, half-believe in a Giver in whom we try to trust. Given the horrors of this century, we can walk at best by faith, not by sight. We must proceed today under thin but endless clouds of burned children, mostly Jewish children. Under that cloud it is hard to strike up a conversation.

Silence might be easier, but conversation is essential to walking on this Way which we seek to discern. Because we sense from time to time that this road is a gift, wonder, joy and also doubt are constituent elements of our walk and these press us to converse. Something has to be said about the Giver of our Way or else we could not go on walking it as His. Or better, because we believe it is

His, then, trusting who He is, we grasp it really as ours. The Way we walk demands our conversation.

To walk on this Way is already to acknowledge that it is a genuine gift, ours to walk in all our created diversity. Since our diversity is created and not merely our own doing, we may conclude that the Giver of the Way loves us in that diversity, in our concrete historical particularity. He evidently loves our different feet which walk His path in different ways and therefore wants us to do what we must because of our diversity: talk together about the Way and how we are to walk it together.

The Way on which we find ourselves was there before we were born. It first opened up, so our oldest stories have it, in ancient times as the path for one man, a father of many peoples. It became in time the Way of a people who kept alive the story of the ancient father. In the present volume, which describes only the first of four stages which we hope to travel, we shall not come far enough to even retrace the steps of the road walked by that one people. That will be done in Stage II, *The Way of Israel*—a Way continuing in our day. If we can discern the Way in this our first stage and follow, at least with our heads and hearts, *The Way of Israel* in the second stage, we shall be ready to enter upon the third stage — *The Way of the Church*—which is of course the actual road that Christians walk. By then we shall be more aware of the fundamentally significant fact that, as we look about us, we of the Christian church see almost no Jews within our company. Our Way began among Jews and was first walked only by some of them but, within a remarkably short piece down the road, the Jews were to be found walking the Way in their own manner and we Gentiles were left to find a distinctive path. Therein lie matters to ponder for Gentiles walking a road which they are certain is the Way for them of the God of Israel!

Finally, in Stage IV we shall have to come to terms with the fact that only some Gentiles walk the Way under the sign of the cross. We shall need to consider the fact that father Abraham had a son named Ishmael for whom a Way was also promised. If breath and courage remain to continue our walk and its accompanying conversation, we shall want then to consider yet other ways in which it has been given other peoples to walk, peoples of other and ancient civilizations who yet walk today and for whose walking we should also be thankful. Since human beings tread such diverse paths, which many of them believe to be the Way of One who loves and cares for His whole creation, we must turn eventually in our conversation to talk of *The Way of the World.*

These four stages of "The Way" could have been conceived as four volumes of what used to be called "systematic theology," for theology is and has always been, as I understand it, a contribution to—in the form of critical reflection on—a conversation *in ipso itinere* (while walking) among members of the Christian church concerning the Way on which they have found themselves. Since the definition of theology is an essentially contested one, itself a matter of theological discussion, I have used it only in the subtitle.

The projected four volumes could, after many more years, be written and published as one book for they have been conceived as a whole. Understanding theology as a contribution to a continuing conversation, however, I prefer to offer what I have to say a piece at a time. A monologue is not a conversation and the Way must be walked in the meantime. The matters which we should discuss warrant more than can be said in one volume. The four-stage format is more appropriate to this enterprise.

Theology is part of the conversation which takes place among all those who walk together. There may come moments, however, when some more or less professional talkers want to stop and settle a detail between themselves before proceeding. So as not to break the flow of conversation, I shall insert these more technical digressions into the text in smaller print. Those who are finding the walk difficult and prefer to confine their attention to the main thread of the conversation should feel free to skip such passages. The inclusion of these digressions together with the style of the major argument reflect my concern to address the full range of thoughtful Christians seeking new sign posts in these strange times.

The purpose of this volume is not to defend the Way on which Christians walk, but to contribute to the conversation that is itself a part of our journey. Those who are actually walking could hardly care to defend their walk, whatever that might mean. What they may well desire is to see the way more clearly and then to walk it more joyfully and more responsibly. To meet this proper concern for walking, step by step, these words are offered for what help they may provide.

The more immediate occasion of this book is an important change taking place in the mind of the church. Under the impact of certain events in this century, we have begun, starting with the decisions of the Second Vatican Council, to reverse our traditional understanding of and behavior toward the Jewish people. Other changes are also taking place, but I know of none that has led to a comparable reversal of our teaching. Other changes may also be important; this one certainly is, for it has profound implications for our understanding of ourselves (ecclesiology), God (theology in the strictest sense) and the foundations of our faith (the Bible and revelation). This book is an attempt to encourage fresh thinking about these matters and to search out the ground for theological reflection in our new situation.

In both form and content, this volume is shaped by the historical character of this particular change. Rather than develop a metaphysical or cosmological framework for our reflection, I have felt impelled to set the discussion in the context of our temporal existence. The whole book and especially its early pages will stress this context by emphasizing a figure of speech or metaphor: We are on a journey, a path through history; we are on a Way. If the figure seems at first to be overworked, the reader is asked to bear with it and absorb the picture, for the metaphor is itself the content of what I wish to say. It is not *like* our situation; it *is* our situation. The style and content, in other words, are meant to "fit." The titles of the whole and each part reflect this intention. The metaphor which shapes them all is itself the message.

The change occurring in the mind of the church with respect to that most significant other — the Jewish people — has been brought about by events in the public realm which find their appropriate intellectual home in the field of history rather than philosophy or theology. This should surprise no one influenced by the Bible, for that book invites and challenges us to see ourselves in history, albeit a history which we dare to call that of God with His creation. As familiarity with the Bible can lead us to read the newspaper with an eye for "the signs of the times," so the events of our day, when so apprehended, can help us to see the Bible in history — the product of successive reinterpretations of a tradition under the impact of new events. The Bible thus invites our fresh reinterpretation not only of itself in the light of our own history, but also of ourselves and our world in its light. Our situation is that of the apostolic authors, whose use of the Scriptures Norman Perrin described so well, in spite of his incongruous use of the present tense: "The text

is reinterpreted in the light of immediate experience and imma-
nent expectation,"[1] resulting in "a long and constant process of interpretation and reinterpretation."[2] We too are part of that historical process.

To see the Bible in this way is to reject alternatives. The Bible
cannot be read as history in the modern sense of the term. Its authors were often responding to and sometimes recording events
which historians can investigate, but they also present themselves
as responding to that which defies the categories of modern
historical research. More importantly, the Bible is not a
sourcebook of doctrines or theological truths. Those who assert
that "the Bible says. . ." forget that the Bible has no mouth; what
the Bible allegedly "says" comes always from the lips or pen of
someone interpreting it. The church has often supported its
teachings and what it conceived to be theological truths by citing
biblical verses, but to treat that book as a collection of prooftexts is
to disregard its historical character. For the same reason, I reject the
all-too-extensive use of the Bible as a sourcebook for theological concepts. Such a use removes the Bible from the historical "process" or
flow, of which our existence as well as its various books and layers
are a part. The Bible was no more written to provide concepts than
it was to be a sourcebook of types and symbols.

Redaction and canon criticism, which focus on the historical circumstances that gave shape to the individual books and their
larger groupings, have helped us to see the Bible as consisting of
layered reinterpretations of a sacred tradition occasioned by successive events in Israel's history. That structure is evidently open-
ended: It invites further reinterpretation in response to further
events, even up to our own times, as it continually challenges our
self-understanding and our reading of our own history. The
hermeneutical task is therefore dialectical in effect: The Bible
itself leads us to interpret its story so as to show that our story is
part of it, that our history continues its history. Our very effort of
interpreting it in this way results in our being interpreted by it.

This dialectical hermeneutical exercise has theological implications which were nicely expressed a generation ago by E. Hoskyns
and F.N. Davey: "The Old Testament writers, be they historians,
prophets, psalmists, or wise men, see each situation confronted by

---

[1] *The New Testament: An Introduction* (New York, 1974), p. 35.
[2] Ibid., p. 34.

the Word of God. They are driven to do so, of course, by history—the history behind them which illuminates their own experience, and their own history which unveils to them the meaning of the experience behind them—but what is always of primary importance to them is the analysis of history, not in terms of itself, but in terms of the truth of God, to which, so they believe, it bears witness, and which dignifies it as the revelation of God."[3] Seen in this way, the Bible leads us to do theology historically ("what is always of primary importance... is the analysis of history") and history theologically ("in terms of the truth of God to which... it bears witness"). Such a theology will, therefore, consist to a large extent in an analysis of the history in which it is set and of which it is part. That history, in turn, will always be history-as-told, there being no other possibility. History may be told ("interpreted") in more ways than one, of course; history untold ("uninterpreted") simply does not exist. The resulting conception of the theological/historical task is that of reinterpreting the story that begins with Abraham, Isaac and Jacob, continues with Moses, David and the prophets, and then includes Jesus of Nazareth and Peter and Paul, so as to show that our history continues theirs, not in spite of but specifically in the light of all that has happened in the intervening nineteen centuries.

Theology so conceived is addressed to those who read the Bible as *their* book, the story of *their* past, and so are open to reconsider their present identity and situation in its light. Such readers, however, live today among many on whom the Bible has no such hold. We shall be neither arguing nor trying to find common ground with these "unbelievers." The framework for our reflection will be historical and therefore particular. It does not follow from this that we intend our claims to be only relative or subjective. Of course the truth we seek must be the truth as we can see it, but we seek the truth of God, Creator of heaven and earth. We claim that a Way has been shown us and that we are called to walk this road for the sake of the whole of creation. We cannot pretend to establish to the satisfaction of all enquirers the grounds for this claim, for the grounds of truth themselves are in dispute. What we can aim for is to so present our claims that anyone who wishes can at least see how we understand them and possibly why *we* hold them to be true.

[3]E. Hoskyns and F.N. Davey, *The Fourth Gospel* (London, 1947), pp. 114f.

Having indicated why and how I shall proceed historically, I shall say only a brief word about the metaphysical and cosmological consequences of this approach. Consistent with a historical understanding of reality, cosmology would begin "in the beginning," with Creation. *Creation* (capitalized) is our word for the beginning—in every sense of the word—of "creation" (lower-cased) or "the world," which stands for everything there is, other than God. "Everything there is" does not include God, but is the result of God's intention or purpose. We can speak of God only as creatures speaking of our Creator and only of Him as He who has become Creator. If creation came to be because of an intentional beginning (of course, we cannot prove the intention; it is our unavoidable starting point, inseparable from seeing reality as the history of God with His creation), so also God became the Creator in that same "beginning," and this is the only God we can presume to know. However God may have been before "the beginning," He is now the Creator and, by His own intent, He has an other—creation—over against and distinct from Him. Creation (and God's becoming Creator) is conceived as an act of love which posits an other and confers freedom. Creation is grace—*ex nihilo* or, as I would prefer to say, *ex amore.* The result—creation—is free to develop and grow. It is good, but it is only a beginning. In time creation came to include beings who could respond to the love that confers freedom. The story of that response is the story of the Way. In the following conversation, I intend to display whatever case can be made for our basic commitment to a historical framework for all our reflection. The great theme of Creation, although important in this book, will receive fuller discussion in the second stage of our journey.

I have many to thank for help with this project: Temple University for a study leave; the Episcopal Divinity School for an invitation to give the Kellogg Lectures where an earlier version of three chapters were exposed to helpful criticisms; and the Boston University Institute for Philosophy and Religion, where another chapter had a first exposure. I am grateful to David Burrell, C.S.C., Stanley Hauerwas and Dietrich Ritschl for having read the penultimate version and offering encouragement as well as thoughtful criticism. My special thanks go to James Wharton for extended remarks which helped me reconsider, if not always change, my arguments and conclusions. Above all, I wish to thank the graduate students in my seminar who were the first to hear the whole project and whose criticisms, questions and encouragement were invaluable. Since I care more about the subject of this work than that of any I have published, I dedicate it to the person for whom I most care.

TO ANNE

In the Way:
The Context of Theology

WALKING AND TALKING

As people on a voyage talk over their experiences and the purpose of their trip, the church engages in conversation on its journey through history. We talk as we walk, and theology is a part of such a conversation.

The authors of the King James Bible used the word *conversation* to translate *derek*, the Hebrew word for a trodden way, a path or road, and also to translate *anastrophe*, the Greek word for behavior or way of living, a sense which the Hebrew word can also and often does carry. The conversation of which theology is a part takes place on the road.

Theology is only part of our conversation. One could say that all of our talk is theological, since it centers on God and His Way for the world. Since the eighteenth century, however, theologians have increasingly restricted the term *theology* to the critical review of our conversation for the sake of its integrity. Theology, then, is that part of our conversation in which we reflect upon what we have been saying, try out more adequate ways to speak and clarify the criteria for making such corrections.

It is important to observe that, whether the conversation flows or flags, the walk goes on. The conversation of which theology is a part is always accompaniment to the sound of walking feet, even when we forget that we are talking while walking or pause by the wayside to settle some difficulty in the conversation before running to catch up with the others. One can read notes on our past conversation that sound as if they had come from people sitting down for good or from pure spirits untouched by the dirt of the highway. Common sense tells us, however, that for every theologically thinking mind there have been two feet walking, stumbling or running, whether that mind was conscious of this fact or not. The more theologians have been aware of their feet and where they were walking, the more helpful their contributions prove to be for the conversation of those who walk after them.

Tillich argued that theology takes place in what he called "the theological circle." The figure is useful in reminding us that our conversation is carried on within a continuing community of those who walk by faith. The figure of a circle, however, is static, whereas in fact we are on the move, whether we walk well or poorly, purposively or uncertain of the path ahead. We therefore prefer the figure—the historical reality—of a conversation among those who move along a road.

It has also been said that theology should be seen as the theory of praxis, a Marxist model. This has been a contribution coming primarily from South American theologians such as Gustavo Gutierrez and Ruben Alves. The model has the merit of placing the emphasis on praxis, the walking. Certainly the "marching orders" which laid out our Way put a maximum value on walking and a minimum on talking. A certain man had two sons (Mt. 21:28ff.) and clearly the obedient son was he who in fact went, not the one who only said he would go.

The relationship between our conversation and our walking, however, is more complex than can be captured by the pattern of theory and praxis, for we have matters to speak of which cannot be put into practice. Much of what we must discuss concerns others than ourselves, and even more has to do with One quite other than ourselves. One might stretch the terms and say that respect or even sheer wonder is the praxis of the former and prayer or silent adoration the praxis for the latter. Rather than force the model, it seems simpler to use another: Theology is related to Christian life as conversation is to walking.

Because the subject of our conversation is serious, we take seriously the subjects of our conversation. We walk a Way that began long before we joined it. We could not engage in this particular conversation if we did not both remember and respect those who kept it alive and are no longer with us. We would do those earlier conversationalists no honor, however, if we refused to take full responsibility for carrying on the conversation as a living occurrence, a fact of the present, not just a remembrance or repetition of words of the past. We talk as we walk, and the steps we have to take today are on ground not covered yesterday.

The flow of our talk depends on the movement of our feet. If we stumble over rough terrain, we cannot pretend that this does not cause gaps in the conversation. If we are out of breath from the steepness of the Way at some moment, we may have to walk a while in silence. The concrete humanity of our conversation is brought home to us by such limitations. There are other activities as human as is theology, but there is not one that is more human, including the pause by the roadside to relieve ourselves. That little act is also necessary to the continuation of our walk and our conversation.

Because our conversation is thus embodied, it is better not to call its context "Christianity." Christianity is a religion and the trouble with the concept "religion," apart from the lack of consensus in its definition, is that it leads us to ignore sprained ankles and blisters. The term *Christianity* itself lacks specificity of time and place. It becomes definite only when spatially and temporally qualified, as in, e.g., "Western Christianity of the fourteenth century." It is better, therefore, to call the context of our conversation the Way, as did those who first set out upon it (Acts 9:2, 19:9, 22:4), before others began to call us "Christians" (Acts 11:26). There is also early precedent for saying that our whole business is a matter of walking (Paul wrote in Romans 6:4 that Christ had been raised in order that we might walk in a new way).

There can be no question, however, of going back to our beginnings or any other stage of our voyage, such as the so-called "Consensus of the First Five Centuries," or the supposed renewal of our walking tour in the sixteenth century. A longing to go back, to be anywhere but here or in any time but now, is not merely a failure of nerve. It is a failure of obedience to One who is calling us to walk here and now in the Way. If the trip is to continue after we have died, we are responsible for walking today.

That is not to imply that we have no need of those who have walked this way before us. On the contrary, without their walking in this Way as they understood and talked about it, we would not be here to continue their journey. So we have every reason to listen to what they have left us in print of what they said as they walked. We can read them with deep interest or high irritation, rejoicing in what help they can offer us and refusing what we find hinders our walking our own assigned stretch. We also may be able to learn from what we take to be their mistakes, such as their bitter denunciations of those they were charged to love (e.g., the *adversus Ioudaeos* literature) or their gullibility in following false road signs that took them on long detours out of the Way (e.g., the Crusades), for we may be making just as serious mistakes as we walk along. We need all the help we can receive, and those who spent their lives walking along this same Way can assist us. They cannot be, however, more than helpers, for we are called to do our own walking and carry on our own conversation. Our responsibility cannot be fulfilled by appealing to "the faith once for all delivered to the saints."

This expression occurs in one of the late Apostolic Writings — the Letter of Jude, whoever he may have been. His letter seems to have been written in a time of trial and strife and his word to his readers was to hold fast, to keep walking with courage and perseverance in those difficult times. His exhortation (in verse 3) carries the sense of "be faithful in walking in that Way which has been walked by God's holy ones from of old." By "the saints" he meant the faithful of Israel.

It would be irresponsible to interpret this verse so as to imply or make explicit the thesis that there is a body of sacred formulas that we must repeat, rejecting any variation or alternative. To put the issue in terms of our Way through history, there is not a definite step over a specified piece of the road that each generation, beginning at the same starting point, has to make, proving itself by walking just that stretch in just one way.

George Foot Moore argued that both the "legalism" of the rabbis and the "creedalism" of the church fathers expressed their common acceptance of the idea of "revealed religion embodied in divinely inspired Scriptures. The conception of historical development is equally foreign to both, and as irreconcilable with the finality of the Mosaic Law as with the finality of the 'faith once for all delivered to the saints' (Jude vs 3). The idea of development is the germ of dissolution for legalism and creedalism alike."[1] As Moore put it in another place, "the idea of development involves, consciously or unconsciously, a complete change in the idea of revelation, a change which orthodoxy, whether Jewish or Christian, has resisted with the instinct of self-preservation."[2] I believe that this analysis is substantially correct and the identification of Christians as those moving along a Way through history has at least this in

---

[1]*Judaism in the First Centuries of the Christian Era* (New York, 1971 [1927]), vol. I, Notes, pp. 60f.

[2]Ibid., p. 250.

common with Moore's conception of historical development: It is willing to surrender orthodoxy for the sake of something else — namely, our living responsibility here and now to a living God. As the conversation proceeds, the consequences of such a self-understanding for how we are to speak of God, the Bible and Revelation will become clear.

We are responsible to those who have walked before us to find our own way. There are two reasons for this. First, new events have taken place along the Way which we must take into consideration, as did our forebears with respect to events of their time. Had they not found new ways in which to walk and talk in the face of new challenges we would not have had a gospel of a crucified messiah, a church open to Gentiles, a decision to claim the Hebrew Scriptures as our sacred texts, a Nicene Creed, the formation of monastic communities, the founding of schools and universities, the new awakenings of the sixteenth century and much more that documents the long story of the people moving along the Way. We forget how radically unconventional were those whose new steps now pass for classical. Those people were confronted by new circumstances and they walked ahead in a new way because of them. Loyalty to their steps demands a like newness of walking from us.

Second, we have an obligation to the future, to those who will follow us and who will have to pick up the journey when we have walked our days and have been buried by the wayside. The journey began before we came on the scene and will be continued, we trust, by others after we can walk no more. The story, of which we take our present to be a part, is not over; we find ourselves in the midst of the history of God's plan for His creation. We dare not, in loyalty to Him, assume that His greatest words and works already have been spoken and performed. If we believe in Him at all, then we must believe in Him as a living God, whose ways with His creation are not closed to novelty. For this reason above all there can be for us no "going back" and no staying put.

WALKING BY FAITH

In locating our conversation as that of walkers in the Way, we define the conversants as walkers. Is it not, however, a more basic and prior self-definition for us to understand ourselves as believers?

Properly understood, it may also be said of us that we are believers, but the dangers of misunderstanding are so great at this point that it seems far sounder to define ourselves as walkers.

The danger of designating Christians as believers may be seen in Martin Buber's misunderstanding of Christian faith as a case of acknowledging something to be true, in contrast to faith as a case of trusting someone, which he took to be typical of Judaism. More specifically, Buber defined the Christian meaning of faith as "acceptance of the truth of a proposition and of unbelief as the opposing of it."[3]

It should be said that the tone of Buber's book from which this distinction is taken is irenic. Buber was not being tendentious. On the contrary, in spite of all that has been written in theology in the twentieth century, not to speak of earlier times, to show that this is just what faith cannot mean for Christians, Buber had excellent grounds for his understanding of Christians. Surely passages from the Apostolic Writings, such as Rom. 10:9 ("if you confess with your lips that Jesus is Lord and believe in your heart that God raised him from the dead, you will be saved") and John 3:16ff., have been taken by many Christians to mean that it was essential to believe certain things to be true. The line may not be direct, but it has surely seemed possible to many to move from such texts to that of the *Quicumque vult*, the so-called Athanasian Creed. It begins, "Whosoever will be saved, before all things it is necessary that he hold the catholic faith...." This is then defined with some logical precision in the succeeding list of propositions and it concludes: "This [i.e. this long list of propositions] is the catholic faith, which except a man believe faithfully, he cannot be saved." In the light of such a document, one can hardly be surprised at John Locke's definition of faith as "the assent to any proposition not... made out by the deductions of reason, but upon the credit of the proposer, as coming from God, in some extraordinary way of communication."[4] We must conclude that Buber understood quite accurately what many Christians have said.

On the other hand, St. Paul spoke of the obedience of faith (Rom. 1:5) and of walking by faith (2 Cor. 5:7), and the great parable of the last judgment in Matt. 25:31-46 says nothing about what anyone believed to be true but only what they in fact did. A theologian of as much logical rigor as John Calvin could insist that faith is more a matter of the heart than the head[5] and would clear-

[3]*Two Types of Faith* (New York, 1961), p. 41.

[4]*An Essay Concerning Human Understanding*, bk. 4, chap. 18.

[5]*Institutes*, III, ii, 8.

ly have found acceptable only Buber's conception of faith as trust, never the idea which Buber understood to be that of Christians. Perhaps more than on any other point there would be a consensus among Christian theologians today that the primary meaning of faith is trust, and that belief in the truth of propositions is a derivative and minor aspect of what it means to be a "believer."

The distinction between believing certain propositions to be true and trusting in someone has only a limited value in this connection, and a sharp separation of the two senses rests on a superficial analysis. To trust someone and to believe that something is true are not the same, of course, but they are not so separable.[6] If I trust someone, then I do so, usually, because I believe that that person is trustworthy. Generally, trusting my doctor is only possible if I believe that he or she is a competent physician. To "acknowledge something to be true," to believe that such and such is the case, will therefore always be implied by belief in the sense of trust.

Trustful walking in the Way implies that the world and human life is such that there is a Way for persons to move through history, given by God, although made both by God its giver and by human beings who walk it. It is possible, as a logical exercise, to analyze a person's trust into propositions implied by that trust. This is, however, an exercise in abstraction which, from the walker's point of view, is a move from the primary and important to the secondary and much less important. Propositional reduction abstracts from the actual walk and the actual Way. Logical difficulties which may arise from considering such propositions (e.g., the great difficulties in clarifying how the word *exist* can work in the assertion "God exists," or the genuine puzzles in explaining whether or how *God* is a referring expression) are far less of a problem than the actual difficulties of walking in the Way. The so-called believer, therefore, is uncomfortable when his deeper concerns are set aside by the logically minded who want to talk about these other problems. He is uncomfortable because he is being asked to see as his chief problem one which seems so disincarnate. He is more or less content to live without clear answers to these logical difficulties because he has bigger worries on his mind. This decision about priorities does not settle those difficulties by any means. It only puts them in their place. They will, therefore, only receive

[6]The philosophical literature on the distinction is extensive. For a criticism of its use by theologians, see R. Hepburn, *Christianity and Paradox* (London, 1958), especially chaps. 3 and 4.

consideration at a later point in the conversation.

Faith is not primarily a matter of thinking, but of walking in a certain Way. Does this way of looking at the Christian enterprise blur a distinction that has been drawn sharply by some of our company who have walked before us? Some of those who have gone before us made a distinction, which they took to be of prime importance, between faith and works.

The classical texts for the distinction are, among others, those of Paul in Galatians 2 and 3 and Romans 3 and 4. The distinction was developed primarily by Augustine in his anti-Pelagian writings and then by Luther.

Faith and *works* have become code words which stand for a larger complex of realities not immediately suggested by the words themselves. What was at stake for those who used these code words was nothing less than the matter of our relationship to God, the question of salvation. The code word *works* stood for a claim that, by the way in which we walked, we could earn the right to reach the end of the Way. *Faith* stood for another view: The path leading to life was already ours as a completely free gift, so the only appropriate response on our part must be simply one of thankful walking in the Way provided.

The more clearly one states the alternatives, the more improbable it becomes that anyone ever seriously maintained that how we walked was the only thing that mattered. It seems unlikely on the face of it that anyone walking in *this* Way could ever have thought salvation, the ultimate realization of God's plan, could be anything other than the fruit of God's own love, His free gift to His creation. It may sound as if Paul at moments thought he heard from some people some such notion, but such an idea is unlikely to have arisen among Jews, those who bless God every day for His gift of instruction in walking in the Way, and who thank God daily for His mercy and forgiveness.[7]

As we hear overtones of that old debate by those who walked and conversed before us, we must have the courage to put the issue in our own way rather than rely on code words of the past. The issue is not whether any human being has a claim on God (as if we could

---

[7]The *Siddur*, the standard Daily Prayer Book of the Jews, is full of such blessings. See P. Birnbaum's translation (New York, 1949), especially pp. 18, 24, etc.; Moore's *Judaism*, vol. I, pp. 507ff.; and chap. 9 of S. Schechter's *Aspects of Rabbinic Theology* (New York, 1961).

in any way put Him in our debt)—for we are on a Way freely given to us, a miracle at which we can never be too astonished—but, rather, how we should walk, what pattern our trust should take, as an appropriate and responsible way of moving. If God in His love has given us a light for our feet and feet with which to walk and called us to this walking, how can there be any conflict between trusting and walking, as if there were any place here for an either/or? The author of the Epistle of James saw this clearly (2:18); I see no reason to suspect that Paul would have disagreed with him.

If Paul was not fighting for a claim upon God by means of trust, as opposed to establishing a claim by means of walking, if for Paul there was no place for talking about establishing claims at all, then what was his concern? In this matter Krister Stendahl's reading of Paul is helpful.[8] Paul, as Stendahl sees it, was concerned about the relationship between the church, with its new Gentile membership, and the Jewish people. He was concerned about how his own calling to go to the Gentiles fitted in with God's plan for His people Israel. The point he hammered home in his defense of Gentile membership in the church was that there was now the possibility for Gentiles to be in the Way that did not require that they become Jews nor walk God's path in a manner commanded of Jews. Gentile access to the Way had been opened up by God through the one Jew Jesus, and that opening was therefore the reflection of the very heart of God Himself. That such an issue should be reduced to a controversy over faith versus works is a pitiful devaluation.

The issue of faith versus works is also associated with the contributions of Augustine and Luther at differing stages along the Way. What was it that concerned them? Again, we may learn something from the Lutheran Stendahl: Augustine was the great father and Luther the great example of what Stendahl calls "the introspective conscience of the West." They were, for reasons not unconnected with their own historical circumstances and personal background, quite different in each case, profoundly troubled by a sense of their own unworthiness of God's love. For them, then, the question on which all else turned was, as Luther asked it, how can I find a gracious God. For those who are deeply troubled in a similar way, these two voices will remain among the most helpful that have contributed to our conversation. We must be wary, however, of generalizing and universalizing from those who suffer from an in-

[8]*Paul Among Jews and Gentiles* (Philadelphia, 1976).

trospective conscience. There are other petitions in the Lord's Prayer than "forgive us our sins," for example, "thy will be done on earth"; and there are those who pray this petition with even more urgency than the first. If Augustine's and Luther's question about a gracious God proceeds from a sense of unworthiness before God, the question of how we are to cooperate with our gracious God proceeds from a sense of our responsibility to Him. We are called to live answering lives; to live this answer is our greatest joy just as it is God's greatest gift. This I take to be what lies behind Calvin's turning to a discussion of "justification by faith alone" only *after* he had discussed at length the meaning of true repentance, the Christian life and the place of self-denial in it, bearing the cross as an aspect of this, meditation on the future life and the proper use of this life.[9]

OUR IDENTITY

The need to attend more to difficulties in our own conversation and walking than to problems which bothered our predecessors will become clearer if we recall who we are. We may begin by noting that we are on a journey and are therefore embodied: We have feet. Second, we converse and are therefore social persons. Third, as we put one foot in front of another, we walk in history. We are, then, embodied, social and historical conversationalists.

These three general aspects of our identity may be further specified. As embodied, we are mortal. Our conversation is therefore fallible and subject to change. Those who preceded us in the Way did not see things just as we do, for the landscape has changed as the journey through time has progressed. We will not say just what our forebears said, nor will those who follow us want to repeat our words, for a living conversation is "made up" as we go along. This conversation may at times become tense; it is by its nature always *tensed*. To speak of what Paul *says*, or of what Aquinas or Luther *says*, is to misunderstand the reality of the Way as history. If one listens to the echoes of this conversation as it has developed over the ages, one will notice interesting and important shifts in the ways in which Christians have understood not only themselves, but also the world and God. On other stages of the Way, when change was thought to be a sign of death, shifts in our

[9]Reference is to the interesting order of the crucial and original Book III of Calvin's *Institutes*, chaps. iii to xi. Cf. the author's *Christ in our Place* (Edinburgh, 1957), pp. 107-24.

conversation were either not noticed or else denied. Today when we consider change to be a sign of life, we can rejoice in this evidence of a living conversation. This in itself constitutes no small change in our self-understanding in the Way.

We are not only temporal beings; we are ecclesial. Whether we get along or not, we are in the Way together. There is no Way for us simply as individuals, for we have been called in the Way together and as a church. Our talking therefore takes the form of conversation, not monologue. Theology is only a contribution to this ongoing conversation.

A contribution to a conversation may be intended as such and yet have no "uptake." It may call forth no response but drop as it were like a stone into the water to sink silently. Then it does not in fact become a contribution, not part of the conversation, and so not part of the theology of the church. Sometimes an offering only awakened a serious response after some time, as was the case with that of Thomas Aquinas. Other offerings have been taken up at once and have awakened a considerable response, only to die out of the conversation in short order. We have seen much of this in recent years, but perhaps this has always been the case and we notice the recent examples because we are present for their short lives. Again, there have been offerings which have awakened an immediate response and continued for centuries to be heard in the continuing conversation of those in the Way.

On our journey through history, we have carried in our hands a certain book whose contents has always marked our conversation. The church's particular book consists of the Apostolic Writings, usually know as *The New Testament*; but we have also carried the book of the Jews, the Hebrew Scriptures, and the Scriptures together with the Apostolic Writings have been regarded as authoritative whenever we have come to serious disagreement in our conversation. In addition, however, it is a matter of record that walkers in this Way have also managed to carry other books by such Gentile authors as Plato, Aristotle, Kant and Hegel and, whether acknowledged or not, these too have been turned to as authorities. We shall return to these matters at a later step along this stage of the Way, but we mention them now because each of these three bits of reading material has left its mark on our historical character in the Way and each of them has played an important part in our conversation.

At this point, however, we must say something further about the first of these books — the Apostolic Writings — for it constitutes, in a special sense, *our* book. This one was not borrowed; we wrote it ourselves. It is essential to a clear understanding of our own historical identity, however, that we take note of the fact that "we" (in the Way) are not today who "we" were when "we" wrote that book. The "we" who wrote the book were all (possibly only "almost all") Jews. They wrote for fellow walkers who were mostly Jews, although gaining more and more Gentile fellow walkers.

Unlike those authors, we are today almost all Gentiles. The phenomenon of the Jewish-Christian has become so rare that the term is no longer usable without clarification. There are a few Christians who have joined our walk whose background is Jewish. We must note, however, that there are also those who have joined the walk of the Jewish people whose background is Gentile Christian. This second and corresponding phenomenon is usually ignored when the significance of Jewish-Christians is discussed. We shall in the course of time consider them both together as proleptic signs of the goal of the Way. As matters stand now, however, the church is an almost purely Gentile enterprise. Since the Apostolic Writings were composed before this was the case, we shall have to reflect on this fundamental aspect of our identity with minimal aid from what their authors said. Our obligation to them is to be as responsible to this further development as were those authors to the events which forced them to reinterpret their own tradition.

Our historical identity may be further defined by recalling that we are Gentiles whose walking shaped a culture and civilization called "the Christian West" or Christendom. Those before us in the Way lived to see that culture dominate the world as their forebears had dominated the West. Their manner of walking provided an example of universalism and imperialism for the "Christian" West, so the theology which informed and justified it is a matter which we shall want to discuss. Our conversation cannot ignore the universalism — "triumphalism," as some have come to call it since Vatican II — of its past, for the rest of the world, and our fellow walkers and conversants of the Third World, want no more of Western domination. Since our Gentile identity and our relationship to the rest of the Gentile world are at the root of all these developments, we need to consider with new attention this aspect of our historical character.

Our Gentile identity is a strange fact. A Gentile is by definition anyone who is not a Jew. It is, however, notoriously difficult to identify exactly who is a Jew. Why then do we define ourselves by reference to that which is itself indefinable? We do so because the authors of our Apostolic Writings force us to do this. We define ourselves by reference to the Jews because our Way has no starting point and no possible projection except by reference to the Way in which the Jews were walking before we started and are walking still. So said the first walkers in the Way and so have said all since who have not forgotten where and how our walking conversation began.

Those first walkers who produced the Apostolic Writings were convinced that our Way could be walked only with the help provided by carrying with us the book that Jesus and all his apostles had understood to be their one and only Holy Scriptures—the Hebrew Scriptures, which St. Jerome liked to call "the Hebrew Truth." That book, backed as it is by the continuing vitality of the Jewish people, most of whom at least hear it still in its original tongue, reminds us that we are Gentiles, not Jews, although Gentiles who worship Israel's God.

Finally, our identity as Gentiles must be further specified by the fact that we are not all the Gentiles but only a small minority from among them. Most non-Jews have no interest in the path we try to walk. Yet along with the Jews we trust in a God whom we have always thought to be the God of and for this whole world. We have come and are coming to know Him whom we call "our God" always as the God of all humanity, yes and of nature too, the God of His whole creation.

The Daily Prayer Book of the Jews, which certainly addresses God as the God of Israel, also addreses Him innumerable times as King of the Universe: *melek ha-olam.*

After two thousand years on our part and over three thousand on theirs, however, the ways in which Gentiles and Jews have walked in the Way have not yet turned out to be the Way for the world. Never before in our history have we seen this more clearly and been more aware of the rest of the world. The vast worlds of Marxists, Muslims, Hindus, and Buddhists confront us as other ways in which great numbers of Gentiles walk. How shall we evaluate and respond to this fact? Does it represent some great mistake or is all this also part of God's way with His creation? Could these be other ways which He has offered to other Gentiles to walk His Way? Our historical identity as walkers in the Way opens us to such questions and we shall have to discuss at some point the criteria by which we can make a judgment in these vital matters.

Our particular identity as Gentiles in the Way, however, implies at least that we have been given a Gentile way in which to walk, as the Jews walk in their own way. Our heritage, then, appears to be a double one, part of it being Jewish, part of it pagan. So we have been called from the beginning and so we have made our way these many centuries. Unless this whole enterprise has been a mistake, it must be that the particular stresses that mark our walk and reveal themselves so clearly in our conversation are themselves characteristic of the dual aspect of the peculiar calling of the church. On a path that branched off from that of Israel and has criss-crossed numerous pagan paths, the church lives and walks stimulated — and sometimes confused — by the multiplex route that is hers.

Franz Rosenzweig suggested that the church's special calling is to live in God's plan in a perpetual and creative tension between Israel and the world.[10] For our conversation the consequence is that we are neither as "biblical" as our Jewish beginning demands of us nor as pagan as our origin and context imply. As Rosenzweig pointed out, for Jews being "in the world but not of it" is simply a fact of their existence by birth and nature; for Christians it is always a calling and a struggle. The ways of the world are of course a temptation for both and perhaps in the American setting at least it is almost — but not quite — as easy for a Jew as for a Christian to fade into the landscape. The Christian can in any case drift back into his or her pagan background in a passive rather than an active way. For Christians to remain in the Way, however, and for our conversation to be appropriate to this particular walk, the tension between Gentileness and being in the Way of Israel's God will remain central to our identity and mark our conversation. How it does so we shall begin to discuss as we take our second step.

[10]Rosenzweig's contribution on this matter may be found in his *The Star of Redemption* (Boston, 1972), part three, especially pp. 278-83 and 337-79, and in his letters and shorter essays, some of which appear in N. Glatzer, *Franz Rosenzweig* (New York, 1961), especially pp. 271ff, and 341ff. His early letters on this subject may be found in his correspondence with Eugen Rosenstock-Huessy, who edited part of it as *Judaism Despite Christianity* (New York, 1971); see especially pp. 107ff.

Our Conversation:
The Subject of Theology

INTRODUCTION

We talk on our journey because we are human beings. For those who walk in the Way, however, conversation is essential as well as natural, for our very walking raises the questions of how we came to be in the Way, where we are going and how we are to proceed. "Shall two walk together unless they be agreed?" (Amos 3:3). We seek agreements about the whence, whither and how of our journey. I say agreements, in the plural, because there can be no once-and-for-all agreement about our walking, since the road is never the same and because those who walk this bit of the road today are not the same persons as those who walked that other bit yesterday. We walk a road through time and history, not a squirrel cage. Yesterday's conversation can never suffice for what we must say to each other today.

These issues arise from reflecting critically on our conversation. There is a place for such reflection, for at any time we may forget from whence we came and where we are going or even misunderstand the whole nature of our walk. Until we reach the end of the Way there will remain this possibility of confusion and, therefore, the need for critical reflection on our conversation. Our traditional name for this reflection is theology. Walking is our first business and conversation a necessary accompaniment, but theology is also essential for our journey.

THE SUBJECT OF OUR CONVERSATION

As we walk, we talk primarily about the Way in which we find ourselves. Conversation about this particular Way, however, touches on another subject at every point. Our conviction that there is a road for us to walk rests on the further conviction that this Way is of God. Because we believe that God has provided this path and set us in it, we cannot say much about the Way without speaking of God. God is not our experientially first subject of conversation, nor even the subject about which we must do most of our talking, but talk of Him is inevitable among those who walk this road.

What does to speak of God mean? What do we mean with the word, indeed the name, *God*? "When we mean something," Ludwig Wittgenstein remarked, "it's like going up to someone, it's not having a dead picture (of any kind). We go up to the thing we mean."[1] Wittgenstein was resisting a theory of meaning which would indeed make it difficult to grasp how the word *God* has been used by those who began this walk before us. We do not have ideas or concepts stored away somewhere (a dead picture) to which we then refer when we use a word to mean that thing. A storage bin of dead pictures of tables and chairs, persons and places and, yes, God is a patently absurd idea. By such a theory—and we are all a bit influenced by it—in order to say table and mean table, I have to have that dead picture of a table stored away in some invisible black box. Is the box supposed to have dividers for storing such disparate pictures as those of dining tables, time tables and water tables? Equally absurd is the notion that, in order to say and mean God, I must have stored away some picture or note which I can produce on demand from out of its mysterious nowhere.

Wittgenstein's suggestion is especially appropriate for understanding what we mean by the word *God*. It is, he said, like going up to someone. It is a movement, for which the appropriate grammatical subject is a proper name. It is the movement of a person and, in the case of speaking of God, it is a movement of a person toward a person. This is the essential feature of the way in which God has been spoken of by those in the Way. Speaking of God is personal speaking and knowledge of God is personal knowledge.

[1]*Philosophical Investigations* (Oxford, 1958), par. 455.

There is, of course, no knowledge that is not personal in one sense. All of our coming to know and then being in that relationship which entitles one to speak of having knowledge, all of our getting into a knowing relationship to things is always the movement of persons.[2] This is as true for the most abstract matters, such as mathematics, as it is of our knowledge of each other. In mathematical notations we also go up to the thing we mean.

Our knowledge of God, however, is personal in a second sense: Our words work here as they do when we speak of knowing another person. To speak of Tom, we can say, implies that I know Tom, if by "implies" we mean that, if I do not know that there is such a person, I would not speak of him at all. But if I do know Tom, it can still be in order to ask, "Do I really know him?" One answer would be that I may not know him all that well, in spite of this, that and the other situation in which we have been together. The word *knowledge* is not a receipt indicating that we have acquired and stored away a dead picture of *any* sort. Knowledge of another person is a movement, a becoming, and so always a matter of more or less. And its having become more at one time is no guarantee of its remaining so. It can and frequently does become less. It is no misuse of our language to say, "I really knew him well back then, but I couldn't tell you much about him now." Nor would this be due to forgetfulness. Knowledge of persons by persons is always a coming to know, a being in the act of knowing, a happening whose life depends upon being in motion. Do I know Tom then? In some ways and at some times I think I do, but there are other periods when I must frankly admit that I do not. This is how our language works when persons speak of knowing persons. So it works also when we speak of knowing God.

In this connection it is worth noting that, along most of the road which we are walking, those before us found *The Song of Songs* an excellent guide for speaking of our relationship with God.[3] Knowing God is like (that is, the workings of our language is the same as in the case of) a lover knowing his or her beloved. At its most intimate and personal, it always includes a large element of not

---

[2]William H. Poteat has sharpened my vision here; cf. also M. Polanyi, *Personal Knowledge* (London, 1958).

[3]For a fascinating post-critical critique of nineteenth-century attempts to provide a merely secular interpretation of the *Song,* see Franz Rosenzweig, *The Star Redemption,* pp. 199-201.

knowing, of sensing the distance, the otherness of the one we know so closely. There is no contradiction in this realm between the closest knowing and the highest sense of strangeness. Knowing in this realm is full of movement back and forth. It has nothing to do with a dead picture of any sort. It is always a coming-up to the one we mean. It is a grasping, a risking, always an attempt. Only with such active terms can we catch something of what it means for persons to know persons. This is how we speak of God and of knowing Him.

Speaking of God takes place in our conversation along the Way, and its root is this history in which we find ourselves. We come to speak of God because we learned from our parents and others of the linguistic community to pray and so to speak of God. By earliest association with that community (or in some cases by later voluntary affiliation), we came to walk with them and thereby to enter into their conversation. There was good sense, then, in Augustine's remark that without the church he would not have believed in God. Apart from the fact of the Christian community, whatever our individual reservations about one or another aspect of it, it is unlikely that any of us would speak of God.

The community in the Way makes it possible to speak of God, and its conversation makes it necessary; but some of us find this harder to do than others. For those who find it uncommonly difficult, we would point out that simply to take part in the conversation will make it somewhat easier, especially if they will remember that most of us who do speak of God are acutely aware how minimal is the distance we have covered in going up to the One we mean. It has often been said that faith is a necessary condition for taking part in our conversation, but serious talk of God does not depend upon a particular experience such as people have in mind when they speak of a religious experience. What is required is that one join the walk, that one accept with one's feet the shared movement of those in the Way and thus find oneself in the midst of their conversation. Just this trudging along in solidarity with those who walk in the Way is the prerequisite for taking part in this conversation, whether one has received such "extras" as faith or an experience of some special sort.

This is by no means to denigrate the special experiences of some of our number or the faith of many more. Any of us may be grateful for having shared in some small measure in such faith and such experiences. But those among us who have had a special warming of the heart (John Wesley), or even felt fire (Blaise Pascal), or seen visions (St. Paul, St. Theresa), or received the stigmata (St. Francis of Assisi), have of their own confession received these special extras not for themselves but for the rest of us. Their warmth or fire can warm us a bit too, even if we have never felt it first hand.

In reflecting on these matters, we can hear echoes of a bit of conversation that was a matter of bitter dispute some four hundred years back in this walk. Back then the matter was called "the problem of implicit faith." The issues, deriving in large part from its even earlier formulation by St. Thomas Aquinas, was of course set up rather differently at the time. On the assumption that faith was to be defined as assent to teaching, St. Thomas had argued three centuries earlier that people need not assent to matters beyond their understanding. On the contrary, he argued, they should indeed assent to the essential doctrines, but it would be sufficient if the simple agreed to go along with the wiser conversationalists in matters too complex for them to understand.

In the sixteenth century, Calvin was faced not with St. Thomas, but with corruptions of his thesis that held that a Christian need only obey without question the teaching authority of the church. Thomas would have shared Calvin's objection to this. Simply doing what the church hierarchy said would never have passed muster for Thomas, for even implicit faith depended for him on the faithfulness of the wise, the leaders of the walk, to a proper understanding of where they all were going and Who was giving directions.[4] (True doctrine, Thomas called it, but not, we may presume, without a sense of true leading.)

But I want to suggest that the concept of "implicit faith," once lifted out of the narrow conception of faith within which Thomas developed it, is not without its merits. We do indeed depend on each other in just about every area of life, from making love to quantum mechanics, from casting our vote to going to work in the morning. None of us ever really has a grasp on all the complexities of life in the Way. Someone always has something to give us and something we could well use. What we do need, what is necessary to our participation in this venture, is a desire to be part of it, or even simply our finding that we have been drawn to be part of it, only to discover that it matters to us, that we care about how this enterprise proceeds.

Whence this being drawn and this caring? I see no reason to think that the specifics of what may have led people to the Way and to caring about this walk need be any less various than the variety of personal histories of all those who have come to share in this conversation. No matter how

[4]*Summa Theologica*, II, II, qu. 1, art. 2f.; qu. 2, art. 5-8. Calvin's objections may be found in his *Institutes*, III, ii, 3.

they may tell their own stories, I suggest that we shall find them all, in one way or another, having come to a conviction that there is, after all, a Way through life and history, a path on which to walk, and that this path seems as if it had been given, marked out and set before and under our feet, as it were, that a goal and a direction have been made possible for us.

Those of us who find we can speak of God are also aware that there are great difficulties—cultural, logical, even moral—in speaking of God today. I am neither going to define these difficulties nor attempt to respond to them at this early step of our journey, for it seems to me that the weight to be given to these difficulties can only be properly assessed after we have gone a good way farther in clearing up just who it is that we are trying to go up to.

THE GOD OF ISRAEL

No agreements on other matters could hold us together in the Way if we could not agree on one point about the One of whom we speak when we use the word *God*. The person of whom we speak is the One designated in the Scriptures as the Holy One of Israel and the God of Abraham, Isaac and Jacob. We mean the One who is said to have spoken to Moses in the wilderness, but who did not give His name. God's name occurs in the Scriptures only with the Hebrew letters *Y-H-V-H*, yod-he-vav-he. When the word appears in the Hebrew Truth, the Jews say *Adonai*, which means "Lord." This is the One Jesus of Nazareth called *Abba*, Father. We mean always and only the God of Israel. Since He is the Living God, let us be more concrete: We mean the God whom faithful Jews, including Jesus and his followers, have always prayed to and called upon. Regardless of how the word *God* is used or meant elsewhere and by others, for those on the Way it has always meant what it meant for Jesus: the LORD, the God of Israel.

I am rejecting the habit of certain students of what they call "the Old Testament" of inserting the surmised vowels into the tetragrammaton (the four consonantal YHVH) to give a pronounceable "Yahveh." Certainly Christian scholars of Hebrew Scripture must work within the framework of the church's claim upon these writings as its own tradition. But this can be done in such a way as not to deny that these same writings are also the primary and sacred scripture for the Jews. Surely a Jew can become a scholar of our Apostolic Writings without sneering each time the name of Jesus occurs; so can we have the humility and grace to concur in Jewish respect before the divine Name. It is appropriate for Gentiles to write or say "the LORD."

It should be noted that it is *our* (Christians') claim that the God of whom we speak and whose Way for us we believe ourselves to be walking is the LORD, the identical One whom the Jews love as their God, the God of Israel, who loves them, in whose Way for them they themselves walk. We claim precisely this One, *Israel's* LORD, as *our* God. The assertion that the church adores Israel's LORD is fundamental for all its conversation and all its theology, and every further theological point can be only an unfolding of this one claim. Consequently, any theological affirmation, any proposed contribution to our conversation that cannot be shown to be derived from or rooted in this one key sentence, is to be regarded with the gravest suspicion.

The statement that the church adores Israel's LORD as its God seems at first to have an element of contradiction in it, not so much on the level of logic as on that of history. We could bring this out by underscoring the present tense of the verb, a historical present: Today, as in its past, the church adores and trusts in the God of the Jews. That is, both the Christians and the Jews have been saying all along and of precisely the same One, that He is *their* God, not as a possession, not in an exclusive sense (for both have believed their God to be the King of the Universe), but nonetheless theirs by reasons of a special relationship of love and concern. Consequently, both the Christians and the Jews have been convinced that the Way in which they walked, differently as it has been understood by each, is God's Way. Both the church and the Jewish people, then, each in its own way, have made parallel claims which both have mistaken as mutually exclusive.

The church, throughout its history, has felt the force of the contradictory element in its claim to which I am calling attention. It has maintained, without audible dissenting voice until well into the present century, that it worshiped the one who *was* Israel's LORD but had called them to replace the Jews as His people. The long and often bloody history of this teaching, with its consequent teaching of contempt for Jews, has been documented by Christian as well as by Jewish scholars.[5]

The shameful history of the relations between the church and the Jewish people is the result of one way of seeing this contradiction. The church asserted its worship of Israel's God by denying Israel its identity and reality as Israel and so its own worship of its God. The Jews, in response, could only allow at most that the church worshiped Israel's God in a perverted, distorted manner. From at least the second until the middle of the twentieth centuries only four serious voices interpreted the claim that the church worshiped the God of Israel in a manner which might have overcome the contradiction: Jehuda Halevi, Maimonides, Menachem Ha-Me'iri and Franz Rosenzweig. I am not aware of a single corresponding voice from the side of the church.

In spite of this history, and in the light of singular changes presently at work in the church, we would maintain that the claim that we worship *Israel's* LORD as *our* God is fundamental to our present conversation. Moreover, it could lead to quite different relations between the church and the Jewish people if we also said that the church is *out* of Israel, but not *of* Israel, for a purpose larger than both Israel and the church together: the redemption of this world. To say that the church is *out* of Israel would be a short way of summing up the history of the origin of the church, the beginning of our Way. To say that the church is not *of* Israel would be a summary of the historical development of a Gentile church alongside a vigorous Judaism. And to say that the purpose of Israel and the church lies beyond them would be to affirm with both that the One they adore in their respective ways is the Creator and the Redeemer of the whole world.

A fresh understanding of our claim would be a contribution to the conversation within the church. If our claim that we adore Israel's LORD is not a contradiction, it must define the central fact of our own identity as the church and indicate the primal ground

[5]James Parkes led the way with his *The Conflict of the Church and the Synagogue* (London, 1934; paperback, New York, 1977), *The Jew in the Medieval Community* (London, 1938; paperback, New York, 1976), and many shorter essays (bibliography, Southampton, 1977). Malcolm Hay's 1950 study, *Thy Brother's Blood* (New York, 1975), is selective but powerful. From the Jewish side are Jules Isaac, *The Teaching of Contempt* (New York, 1964), and Jacob Katz, *Exclusiveness and Tolerance* (New York, 1961). Any Christian wishing to think seriously about the whence and whither of the Way should be familiar with at least this minimal selection as well as with R Ruether's more recent *Faith and Fratricide* (New York, 1974; paperback, 1979).

for our claim that our Way is indeed of God. A reinterpretation of our claim will have consequences for Jews as well as Christians, Israel as well as the church, but it can only be offered as church theology, theology that takes its ecclesial identity and location as indispensable. In no sense can a Christian presume to speak from some no-man's-land between the church and Israel or presume to engage in Israel's conversation.

We cannot help but consider, however, that what we say in our conversation may be overheard by the Jews, the people of God, as they walk in their Way. For better or worse (and it has on the whole been for the worse), they have all too often been forced to overhear what we say. More important, they have had to take account of what we do, of how we walk. Since what we say is part of our walk and affects our walking, they (or at least some of them) may hear what we say and will be concerned how our conversation develops.

The explicitly ecclesial character of our claim should not be offensive to Jews, for this very feature should assure them that we are speaking from the heart, trying to be most truly ourselves, not pretending to some superficial if well-meaning alternative to our real identity as Christians.[6] By being explicitly ecclesial, we are being ourselves. To do otherwise, especially in this matter, would be to deny ourselves, our Way and, so finally, Him who has called us into the Way. Since we confess Him to be Israel's LORD, such a denial could only end in denying the reality and identity of the Jews. The last thing they should want from us — or should have from us — would be a denial of our own identity. They never suffered so much as when the church did just that in so many ways from 1933 to 1945.

Our identity as a church lies in the fact that we adore, and so speak to and speak of, Israel's LORD. Therefore, it makes no sense to ask, "Israel apart, what do we mean by *God*?" This is to fall back into an epistemological superstition of the modern age which we owe so largely to the genial inventiveness of Réne Descartes. That is to say, we are supposed to abstract not only from our particularity, from our actual *use* of the word *God* which we learned from the Scriptures, but also from the people who have worshiped this God all these centuries and apart from whose continuity there could never have arisen the church. Are we to believe that, in setting all

[6]This is the judgment of an orthodox Jewish theologian, Michael Wyschogrod, in his "Why Was and Is the Theology of Karl Barth of Interest to a Jewish Theologian?" in *Footnotes to a Theology: The Karl Barth Colloquium of 1972* (Toronto, 1974). For a similar judgment see F.-W. Marquardt, *Die Entdeckung des Judentums für die christliche Theologie* (Munich, 1967), pp. 105ff.

that aside, we come closer to our subject in the clean air of pure
and distinct ideas? How could we ever have been beguiled by such
a procedure? Yet beguiled we have been these past three centuries,
and the attractiveness of falling back under the spell of this
superstition is there to meet us whenever we turn again to read
Descartes's *Rules for the Direction of the Mind.* The way out of this
trap is to reject the question. Apart from Israel, God can be
anything or nothing — an abstraction, an idea, a hallucination, what
you will. The God we wish to speak of, however, is just the One we
do speak of in a quite specific way, namely, as Israel's LORD.

These considerations imply something more. If, in order to
understand what we do in speaking of God, we cannot abstract
from our actual speaking, then our personal selves are essential to
this speaking. From this it follows that, when Christians speak of
God or when they speak of knowing God, this must be at least to
some extent different from Jews speaking of and knowing God. In
other words, the Christian's way of knowing God and the Jew's way
of knowing God are no more the same than the Christian and the
Jew are the same. Of course they are both human beings, but in
relation to God they are different, for the *church* adores *Israel's*
LORD and the relationship between Israel and the church is
nonreversible.

The nonreversibility in question is first and most simply temporal or
historical. But, since our conversation is rooted in, dependent on and
part of this continuum, the nonreversibility is also theological.

It does not follow from this nonreversibility, however, that the
one knows better or more than the other. Here we must revert to
our example of personal relationships and consider how two sib-
lings know their mother or father. Each child knows the parent in
his or her own way, just as what the parent is for the youngest son,
for example, is quite different from what she or he is for the oldest
daughter. It is the difference in similarity that needs to be kept in
mind here, so that we may see the difference without being led to
think of a more or a less, a better or a worse.

The progress of our conversation, and so of our journey in the
Way, requires an agreement that the God of which we speak is
Israel's LORD. From this central affirmation, our identity, the way
we follow and our relationship with the Jewish people will all have

to unfold. As our conversation develops, we need to remember that any question about our talk of God can only be properly considered if we are clear that it is talk of this God, the God of the Jews. Much more may and must be said of God. This, we must agree, comes first.

CONCERNING REVELATION

The conviction that there is a Way given by God has been said to be grounded on revelation. The Way is God's gift, not our invention, and its Giver is known because He has given Himself to be known. Why then has there been, even at this early stage, no mention of revelation? It is true that the word has not been used; but, in speaking of the Way, we have been discussing the substance. I shall return at length to the topic, but at this point a preliminary definition of the term, with sufficient elaboration to make it clear, may be helpful. Revelation, we have always believed, comes from God; but it also reaches us. Divine revelation, therefore, always has a creaturely shape. A preliminary definition of this creaturely shape of revelation could run as follows: The word *revelation* is sometimes used by those in the Way to refer to *an acknowledged reinterpretation of their tradition in response to Jewish history.*

Revelation is *an acknowledged reinterpretation of the tradition.* Not every reinterpretation of the tradition comes to be called revelation. Only those reinterpretations are so called which have come to be accepted by the community as it walks the Way through history. It walks conscious of its past, its tradition. As long as the tradition is received unchanged, more or less as it stands, there is no cause to speak of revelation except as another name for the tradition so received. Revelation is a term specifically for the occasions when the tradition is not simply received, but received in a new way—reinterpreted. Both a past and a change in how the past is perceived are necessary for us to speak of revelation. If a proposed change in how the tradition is to be received does not eventually win the agreement of most of us in the conversation, the term, of course, will not be used. Only when a reinterpretation of the past becomes *our* interpretation do we speak of revelation.

This definition of revelation is derived from the two cases in our tradition that have been central to the conversation of those who have gone before us. I refer to God's revelation to Moses in the wilderness and especially in the giving of Torah from Sinai, and to the claim of the Apostolic Writings that God has revealed Himself in Jesus Christ. Moses is presented as standing in a tradition. He identified himself with his people, and the voice that he heard from the burning bush was that of the God of his fathers—of Abraham, Isaac and Jacob. But now the God of ancient times becomes the present redeemer. The God of the ancient promises is now the God of their fulfillment.

When we move to the revelation of Sinai—the gift of Torah—then the reinterpretation of the tradition becomes more pronounced. The God of the patriarchs became the God of the people and His promises took on the character of a covenant. God was not only to be their God; they were to be His people. He had not only His plan and purpose: His people were given a plan as well, a way in which to walk into the future.

These elements are equally evident in the documents of our own beginning. The Apostolic Writers were also heirs to a tradition: They were Jews. They gave this tradition, however, a radical reinterpretation. The whole of the tradition was now reinterpreted to point ahead to the coming of Jesus, his death and resurrection, and then to the new community of Jew and Gentile that soon resulted. Above all, the promise that Israel would be a light to the Gentiles was seen to have had an unexpected fulfillment through him. Through him, the whole tradition was reinterpreted to point to the new phenomenon of Gentiles coming to adore the God of Israel as also the God of the ungodly. Here too the event of revelation consisted for those who so saw it in the reinterpretation which they accepted of Israel's tradition.

Revelation is the reinterpretation of the tradition *in response to Jewish history*. Revelation has not come in a vacuum. It has always happened in the context of history; indeed, as a historically identifiable reinterpretation of a historical tradition, it would have to. Moreover, it has generally come in response to historical events in or bearing heavily upon the history of the Jews (or their ancestors, the Hebrews). Events having political and social dimensions, not ideas, generally have been the occasions of what we have called revelation. Some event in Jewish history has led one or more of the people in the Way to see matters in a new light. The event reoriented some individual. When this reorientation then worked its way upon the community, the result was that communally acknowledged reinterpretation of the tradition which we call revelation. In the case of Moses, the historical occasion that triggered the great story of revelation was the oppression of his people in Egypt. The move from the oppression in Egypt to God as the Liberator was hardly direct, but we can say that the historical situation, capped by his own violent response to the violence being done to his people, was the occasion that drove Moses to the wilderness and brought him back to lead his people to Sinai and a radically new conception of the Way of God.

A formally similar sequence lies in our own beginnings. For the disciples of Jesus, the historical occasion of revelation was his death by crucifixion under a messianic title. Easter marked the realization that this title was to be believed, that Pilate had written truly. The Easter event was understood to be God's confirmation of Jesus as His totally faithful servant, exalted by God and lifted up precisely as the crucified one. A crucified messiah was as unexpected as the Exodus from Egypt, or for that matter as the Babylonian Exile and the return. The events in Jewish history which have been the spurs to reinterpretation, which have ended up by reorienting the community, have not been expected on the basis of the tradition. That is perhaps why they have led to reinterpretations of that tradition.

In each case, as I shall argue later (Step 8), the events, however insignificant on the scale of world history, have been part of Jewish history. Events in other parts of the world and among other peoples may play a larger role in our history books. A review of the evidence will show, however, that only those events happening among or to the Jews have been at the roots of the shifts of view which we have called revelation. Clearly, we shall in due course have to consider with care more recent events in Jewish history which have begun to exercise a reorienting effect on the mind of the church. Since a reinterpretation of our tradition is beginning in our time, we may be living in another stretch of the Way which will warrant our use once more of the term *revelation*.

It should now be clear that to talk of the Way is already to talk of revelation. When revelation occurs, be it from Sinai or from the cross and Easter, what is revealed if not the Way? If we ask to whom revelation occurs, the answer again must be "to those in the Way." And as to how it comes about, there is no way to describe this other than to describe our movement in the Way.

It was strongly maintained and widely accepted during the second quarter of this century that revelation as a term in our conversation referred primarily to God's self-revelation, so that the content of revelation is not doctrines or information, but God himself.[7] Revelation, it was argued, is self-disclosure. The merit of this view was to stress the personal aspect of God's work and ways with His creatures, at least from His side. In the way in which it was developed, however, it does not seem to do justice to the fundamentally mutual aspect of personal knowledge, the ineradicable role of the knower in his or her movement of coming to know another. But the more serious objection to this personal model of revelation, it was argued, is that it does not do justice to the fact that, when God unveils according to biblical traditions, He unveils something—either His will for His people, or a warning or promise of what is going to happen, or something about Himself, e.g., that unlike human beings He is going to act in different way or judge matters by different criteria.[8] The richness and variety of what God has had to say, as the biblical writers presented it, is overlooked or abstracted into something that in fact never quite happens. Normally, God does not unveil Himself. He remains almost always veiled. As a hiding God, He nevertheless discloses some important things to those who obey Him, both about Himself and about His world. Above all, He made known to His people that Way in which they were to walk and how they were to walk it. And then He disclosed a way for "a people who are not my people," a way for some drawn from many peoples, another way in which to walk in His Way. For both His people and for those who are not His people, the "content" of God's revelation has been the Way. To talk of the Way, therefore, is to talk of revelation.

THE JEWS AND OUR CONVERSATION

These preliminary reflections on the concept of revelation as the ground of our conversation has brought into prominence the crucial place of the Jews and their history in our conversation and for the life of the Christian church. The most casual acquaintance

[7]On the Christian side, this view was urged by Karl Barth and others. On the Jewish side, Franz Rosenzweig and Martin Buber presented similar views.

[8]Cf. Rolf Rendtorff's essay in Wolfhart Pannenberg, ed., *Revelation as History* (New York, 1968).

with the history of our relations with the Jews, however, reveals that these have not been good. Since revelation forces our attention to the Jews, we need to know and understand them and their history aright for, in everything that has to do with our future movement along the Way, we are profoundly dependent upon them.

One of the most decisive if least noticed ways in which the Jews are important to our walk is the fact that we carry on our conversation by means of a predominantly Jewish vocabulary.[9] When we Gentiles in the Way wish to speak of those things which most concern us, we speak of the Law and the prophets, creation and covenant, sin and repentance, holiness and the sabbath, judgment and resurrection. Each of these is a Jewish concept, a translation or merely a transliteration of a Hebrew word. Without the vocabulary of Israel and Judaism, we could hardly have begun this conversation in which we are engaged.

A Jewish vocabulary on the lips of an almost totally Gentile church reflects the church's worship of Israel's LORD. It is a mark of the givenness of our conversation and the vocabulary on which that conversation depends. Not we but God's dealings with Israel made our talk possible in the first place. It marks the Way as made for us, not by us, something for us to receive.

This feature of the Way might not seem worthy of such attention, for it could be said merely to express the fact that the church was an offshoot of Judaism. That fact, however, is extremely complex. We shall have to deal with it at length, but even here something should be said, for we are engaged in a conversation which, from at least the second century until the twentieth, and still among many of us today, has been conducted in a manner that has denied the validity of Israel's manner of walking in the Way. The movement that came to be called the church may have begun within and among Jews but, within a generation, it began to gain numerous Gentile members. By the second century it had broken fully with Judaism, a break mutually encouraged, and had begun to see the Jews as no longer God's people, no longer God's Israel, but a rejected and accursed people. The increasingly Gentile church seemed to take no comfort in its Jewish roots or in any remaining Jewish members. Rather, it saw itself increasingly as the true people and Israel of God, totally displacing a dead Judaism. The view of those early developers of our conversation was summed

[9]I am indebted for this observation to Michael Wyschogrod (see note 6).

up by Adolf von Harnack years ago and his summary has stood the test of further scholarship. Their view, he wrote, was that the Jews "stand in no favored relationship with the God whom Jesus has revealed; whether they formerly did is doubtful; this however, is certain, that God has cast them off, and that the whole Divine revelation, so far as there was any revelation prior to Christ (the majority believed in one and looked upon the Old Testament as Holy Scripture) had its end in the calling of a 'new nation' and spreading of the revelation of God through his Son."[10]

We have already had occasion to mention this traditional "teaching of contempt" of the Jews. Events in our present century, however, the Holocaust and the founding of the state of Israel have brought forcefully to the attention of many the fact that the Jews have been around all along and that they have continued their long walk through history, still faithfully in the Way, still carrying on their walking conversation, still praying to and praising their God, the LORD of Israel. Have we not grounds then for questioning whether in fact God has cast them off? Moreover, have we not grounds now for seeing that our millennia-long conversation, by assuming the rejection of the Jews, is involved in a contradiction? If God is not faithful to His people, if He does not stand by His covenant with Israel, why should we think that He will be any more faithful to His Gentile church?

Morever, the books which were from the first the sacred Scriptures of the church, namely the Hebrew Scriptures, have the people of Israel as their protagonist. This people has been not only the bearer and author of these books, To read these writings is to read of that people, what they said and did, and what happened to them. *That* history of *that* people, we have generally agreed, is what we have in mind when we speak of God's revelation in history. But the history of that people has continued and continues up into our own days. In fact, that people has gone through events in this century which have been as shaking as any it has endured. We do not have to decide whether the events of 1933 to 1945 in Europe or those begun in 1948 in the Land promised to their fathers are of greater or lesser importance than other reorienting events of their past. We need only observe that they appear to be exercising a comparable reorienting effect upon the church, leading us to read the book which we carry with new eyes. When the people whose

[10]*Outlines of the History of Dogma* (Boston, 1957), p. 42.

history the church has held to be revelatory are again figuring so centrally in events of our days, we have, on the face of it, at least an occasion to ask whether we do not see today something of the ways of God with His people and of the Way in which His people walk. Consequently, we have grounds to consider afresh the Way the church is to walk. The alternative, if we would be honest, is to stop speaking of God as the Lord of history and agree that He stopped being that centuries ago. It is one thing to make mistakes about the signs of the times. It is another to refuse to see that there are signs of our times about which we may be right or wrong. Surely, if Israel's LORD is rightly thought to have been detectable in and through the weavings of events up to 30 C.E., it seems fair to assume that He might possibly be detectable in and through further events up into our own days. If He was understood to have been leading and guiding, yes and chastising, His people in the Way up to 30 C.E., surely the very book which we carry warns us not to think that this has come to a stop.

Both Israel and the church have been resistant to any suggestion of new revelation since biblical times. Israel and the church have both had their fingers burned by messianic and millenarian movements which have raised and then dashed hopes. Each in its own way has instead preferred to believe that revelation is complete, that nothing new needs to be or can be seen until the end. Indeed, as one Christian theologian has put it recently, history as revelation is only known from its end, but "with the resurrection of Jesus, the end of history has already occurred, although it does not strike us in this way."[11]

Well, in all frankness, no, it does not strike us in this way. Perhaps we must say that in the resurrection of Jesus something about the end has been shown us; but to say it "has already occurred" is to sweep all following history, including the history in which we now live, into the bin of insignificance. That is a high price to pay for protecting the importance of the history of Jesus as revelation. Surely it can be done in some other way.

On the other hand, there are serious reasons for raising the question about events in the history of the Jewish people since 30 C.E. as potential occasions for revelation. The first would be the desire to take seriously the Way which has been walked by so many for all these centuries. Were they really only marking time, their move-

[11]Wolfhart Pannenberg, *Jesus: God and Man* (Philadelphia, 1968), p. 142.

ment really of no account, because "the end of history has already occurred"? Do we really want to say that all that history, including our own, is of no account? Has it all been a meaningless pause between the already-occurred end and its final unveiling? Can we really learn nothing from it at all?

The ongoing historical existence of the Jews and their continuing relationship with God are conspicuous by their absence from our conversation over the centuries. Having ignored their history, it is not surprising that we have found it difficult to take any history seriously. Because we either ignored or ridiculed their walking (*Halachah*), we have weakened our own will to move responsibly through time and history. Forgetting about the Jews has contributed to our forgetfulness of the fact that we are Gentiles who have been called to walk the Way of Israel's God in a new way. With our back turned on God's first witnesses, no wonder that we have become confused about our own witness, to the point of thinking we were supposed to persuade them to abandon their calling from God and join us!

When we remember the Jews, when their history and present existence take their appropriate high place on the agenda of our conversation, we shall discover the proper order for the rest of it. Because we are Gentiles, we have a number of peculiarly Gentile questions and concerns to consider. With an eye on the Jewish people, we shall see that these concerns must be ours always as Gentiles who have been called into the Way of Israel's God. It is right that we wrestle with Gentile issues, for we have a responsibility for the rest of the Gentile world and its concerns, including the world that is now called secular. It cannot be a matter of serious contention among us, therefore, whether we should discuss these concerns at all. The only question which we can raise is when and where to discuss them. Some are saying that they must come up in the beginning. I intend to put them off, assigning to them a lower order of priority, not because I take them less seriously, but because I think their full seriousness can best be brought to light after we have discussed other matters. We are indeed responsible to the world, but I believe we can only meet that responsiblity by being answerable to those in the Way, those who preceded us, each other, and those who will continue to walk after us.

Together in the Way:
Theological Responsibility

Having located our feet in the Way and acknowledged our identity as Gentiles who adore the LORD, the God of Israel, we have begun our reflection on the conversation which takes place as we walk. Given the variety of our backgrounds and circumstances, we should not expect uniformity in our various contributions to our continuing discussion. How could there even be a conversation if we all said the same thing? On the other hand, there will be no conversation if each of us feels free to say whatever he or she pleases. The question arises, therefore, about the limits of our conversation or, better, about our responsibility for what we say. We shall begin this step by considering to whom we are responsible. Then we shall discuss the best way to deal with mistakes when they occur among us and differences of opinion as they arise in our conversation. We shall then be prepared to consider some of the principal mistakes which we have made in the past and which we may be tempted to repeat now, wandering off to the left and to the right, forgetting to walk or that we have been set in the Way and, of course, the terrible mistakes we have made about the Jews that has caused them much suffering and many deaths.

THE RANGE OF OUR RESPONSIBILITY

What we say to each other is part of our walking together in the Way. Responsibility in our conversation, therefore, is an aspect of

our response to the Giver of the Way. We are answerable first and
last to God. The great commandment for our journey, therefore, is
to love God with all our heart, soul and mind (Mt. 22:37). A responsible conversation will consequently be conducted among us as lov-
ers, as people in love with Him who has set us together in the Way.
Responsible conversation and therefore responsible theology will
always be an act of love not only when we agree, but also when we
disagree with one another. Bitterness and animosity have been present all too often, but they have no proper place in our discussion.

As a matter of experience, we know that we fail again and again
to respond to the God who is love with a corresponding love. We
need God's forgiveness at every step and with every word. Because
forgiveness is part of God's love, the conversation of that other people in the Way reiterated a word that can encourage us: "It matters
not whether you do much or little, so long as your heart is directed
to heaven" (*Ber.* 17a).[1]

We should realize, however, that in the rabbinic tradition directing the
heart is no mere "good intention" but a movement of the whole person.[2]
The words of our mouths and the meditations of our hearts are also part
of our walking.

We are set on this journey together and so the second commandment is inseparable from the first: "You shall love your neighbor as
yourself" (Mt. 22:39). Responsible conversation, therefore, will be
that which helps those near us to walk well. We are answerable to
each other for our moving along in the Way together. We cannot
meet this responsibility, however, unless we are also answerable to
those who walked before us and for those who will follow us.

First among those who were before us and to whom we are
responsible are those saints to whom the Way was first shown, the
faithful of ancient Israel to whom the author of our Letter of Jude
referred. We owe them faithful following and a responsive conversation in which they have a distinguished place; but for them we
would not be here at all. We carry their writings with us and we
will surely go astray if we do not listen to them, learn from them
and make them a living voice in our conversation.

[1]Cited in C.G. Montefiore and H. Loewe, ed., *A Rabbinic Anthology* (New York, 1974), p.
272.
[2]Ibid., pp. 272ff.

After those saints of ancient Israel come those other Jews, the ones who first tried out a way to walk that made it possible for us Gentiles to join them. The fragments of their conversation which we carry with us — the Apostolic Writings — also deserve to be answered by us and, therefore, warrant a place in our conversation. Because of the special attention we have given them along the Way, we shall have to consider with care in Steps 6 and 7 the character of our responsibility to and for them. For the moment we shall say only that they have a central place in our conversation; but that is not the same as letting them dominate the talk or always have the last word. We owe it to them to take responsibility before God and each other for finding our own words.

We cannot stop there, however; others also have walked before us, up to our own day. If they walked well and stuck to the path, then we owe to them too the fact that we are still in the Way, rather than wandering off in the brush. On the other hand, when they stumbled or missed a turn, we have had to bear the consequences. They therefore deserve our careful if critical attention. We can learn much from following what they have left us of their conversation. If, however, we find that one and another of them — not to mention whole generations — have gone astray in some respect, walked in the wrong direction or sound as if they had stopped walking, then we should first be sure we hear them as they themselves wanted to be heard and understood. Only when we have understood them in this way should we feel justified in taking issue with them. Responsibility to those behind us calls for us to treat our predecessors as we would be treated by our successors.

We are likewise responsible to those who shall come after us. We owe it to them to think through carefully the possible consequences of what we say and do, for they will have to bear these as we have had to live with what we have inherited. John Chrysostom in the fourth century, for example, or Martin Luther in the sixteenth, never conceived that their vile words on the subject of the Jews would help significantly to produce a climate which a later pagan ruler would take advantage of in order to destroy six million of God's people. We must shoulder our own responsiblity for our failure to have offered more than a token resistance to this horror, but our forebears are also answerable. The steps we take and the words we say today could someday mislead or desensitize our followers to become accomplices to evil. If there is that in our conversation—whether the inherited part of it or that which we add in our day—which can lead to harm to any of God's creatures, then our responsibility to those who come after us is to correct what we say to each other. If, for example, we leave unchallenged and do not wipe out the tradition of anti-Judaism which we have inherited, we shall have failed those who will follow us. Whatever we may say about the roots and rise of that tradition, we today—after 1945—can no longer continue it.

This immediate task for our times brings us then to our responsibility in the present, to one another. We who walk together owe to each other the mutual help and encouragement that befits companions on a long journey. No detailed surveys are needed to tell us that all is not well with this company. Many of us walk more from habit than conviction. The rapidly changing landscape through which we have made our way over the past century or two has caused much disagreement about which direction we should be headed. We need from each other, therefore, all the help we can get, and so we owe to each other all the support we can provide. Because we are on a road that leads to God's purpose of wholeness and peace for His whole creation, that same wholeness and peace stands as our guide as well as our goal in our relationships and in our conversation in the present. Paul's words to the Phillippians are in place here:

> If then our common life in Christ yields anything to stir the heart, any loving consolation, any sharing in the Spirit, any warmth of affection or compassion, fill up my cup of happiness by thinking and feeling alike, with the same love for one another, the same turn of mind, and a common care for unity. Rivalry and personal vanity should have no place among you, but you should humbly reckon others better than yourselves. You must look to each other's interest and not merely to your own. (Phil. 2:1-4)

Finally, we have a responsibility to the world, the totality of the human enterprise of which we are a part. Our movement along the Way, together with Israel, is for the sake and itself part of God's plan and purpose for His whole creation. We can only fulfill our responsibility to the world indirectly, therefore, by being faithful and responsible in all the other ways which we have mentioned. Our responsibility to the world is not one which we should expect it to understand. Our concern for the world is not that it become like us, which is what would happen if the rest of the Gentiles were to become Christians. That would put neither us nor the world any closer to creations's completion.

The author of the Gospel of Matthew did conclude by having Jesus command his followers to go make disciples of all nations (28:19), but he also had Jesus say at an earlier point that they would not have time to go through even the towns of Israel before the Son of man came (10:23), just as the very last words of the book speak once more of "the close of the age" (28:20). The author can hardly have intended the command to make disciples of all nations in a literal and all-inclusive sense. Perhaps we could say that we are ordered to make some disciples from out of any or all nations, from among the Gentiles, in contrast to Israel. The requirement to convert everyone to Christianity could make sense only on the assumption that the church was itself the Kingdom or God's ultimate purpose for His creation. We have generally along the Way been at least realistic enough to recognize that, whatever the church may be, it is not the Kingdom of God.

God's purpose for the world, which we have frequently called redemption, is greater than simply adding to the number of those in the Way. His purpose is the completion of that good thing which He began in the beginning. Indeed, as the apostle Paul saw it, that completion of creation would involve a final self-realization within God Himself, in which God would become what He apparently is not now: "all in all" (1 Cor. 15:28). Our responsibility, in the hope of this coming completion and self-realization, is to do our assigned task of walking faithfully in the Way. There are therefore no conflicts in our responsibilities since, with respect to the world as well as to those in the Way, we shall be properly answerable when we answer to God.

WORRYING ABOUT WANDERING

The discussion of the range of our responsibility sets a framework within which we can begin to be more specific. If we can be right about the Way, then we can also be wrong. We can wander from the path by forgetting or taking too lightly those who have gone before us in this Way, a failing which invariably makes our conversation anemic. Or we can forget that we are walking as we talk, with the result that our conversation becomes ethereal or abstract. It is all too easy to go wrong, so a bit of worrying about wandering from the path is quite in order, as is a bit of admonishment when we see each other starting off in the wrong direction.

In past times there has been perhaps too much worrying and too loud warnings, which have appeared in the form of heresy trials and excommunications. The canons, or decisions, of the old councils of the church often took the form of citing declarations judged to be destructive of our continuing conversation, sayings which should be excluded. "If anyone says thus and so, let him be accursed or cut off — *anathema*," is a typical formulation. It would be best to leave to God who is or is not accursed and for what, but if we translate *anathema* as "cut off," then we rightly catch both the tautological reality in this formulation and its seriousness. If anyone so speaks as to disrupt the conversation or speaks in such a way as to deflect us from walking ahead, he or she has already broken ranks, has already cut him or herself off from us. How can we continue together unless we have some agreement on the most important matters we discuss? Yet, for all that, it would be more in keeping with the Way into which we have been called and with our conversation as an act of love if we were to rephrase it as a question put to the one we think to be in error: "How can you speak as you do and still want to be part of this conversation? In what way can what you say be a contribution to our conversation?" Such a form of addressing serious disagreements among us will lead less to charges of heresy and more to earnest conversation, and it might save us from foolish actions. As William Gladstone wisely observed, "To be engaged in opposing wrong affords, under the conditions of our mental constitution, but a slender guarantee for being right."[3]

The wandering which is perhaps the greatest cause for worry at this stage of our journey is that of incoherence. Questions about the coherence of our understanding of God have been raised recently by some of our company as well as by others who have been listening with some care to our conversation and find they can make no sense of it. We shall address these logical problems in due course. Before we worry about logical problems, however, we need to face a far more serious threat of incoherence, one which can have the gravest consequences for whether we are cohering, sticking together, in the only way that matters — by holding to the Way

[3]*Homeric Synchronism* (London, 1876), pp. 7f. I owe this reference to John Turnbull.

of the LORD, the God of Israel. No other mark of incoherence can match that of our trusting in the love of the God of the Jews while at the same time denying God's faithfulness to His people. Our centuries-long bitter tradition of contempt for the very people whom God first chose for the Way, from whom came one to make a place for us alongside them, our pretense that the Father's prodigal love for us means that He no longer loves the people who are His first-born son and our elder brother (Jer. 31:9; Luke 15:31f.), is surely a case of incoherence beside which all others pale. Nor was the consequence of this a merely logical or conceptual difficulty; our historic contempt of the Jews helped us to quietly look the other way when a full third of God's people were slaughtered. To worry about a possible incoherence in our idea of God when we have this larger matter before us would be like someone worrying about an untuned piano in the band aboard the Titanic or about whether or not Adolf Eichmann underfed his cat. By all means let us aim for coherence and clarity in our conversation about the Giver of the Way, for the world may overhear us and we have no wish to mislead or confuse; let us only not consider this our most serious problem.

It is not our conversation that we owe to the world, after all, and so neither its clarity or coherence. What we owe the world is the Way itself and our walking in it. Our conversation is for the sake of our walking, so it has only an indirect relationship to our obligation to walk in this world in a certain way. According to the prayer of Jesus as presented by the author of the Fourth Gospel, the mission of the church and its fruitfulness in the world depend not so much on what we say to the world as on our sticking together, our coherence in the Way (John 17:23).

To define our mutual relationships within the church and our fidelity in walking, on the one hand, and our responsibility to and for the Jewish people, on the other, as the primary forms of coherence that should concern us, is to take issue with a widely-held view that places the emphasis on the conceptual coherence of our talk, and especially its coherence with the thought and according to the standards of our contemporary academic institutions. The force of this view derives from the fact that, increasingly in the modern period and especially in recent years, the location and employment of theologians has moved more and more to the modern university. From the beginning of the development of universities, of course, theology was taught and was indeed at first held to be the highest branch of learning in them. To this day, in some of the older universitites of Europe, the theology faculty leads the others in academic processions. In the United States, however, theologians generally taught in divinity schools of universities or seminaries established by the various churches. More recently, there has been a considerable move of theologians from divinity schools and seminaries into religion departments of universities, both public and private. These religion departments are within faculties of arts and sciences. A natural consequence of this move has been for many theologians to see their field as one of the branches of the humanities, with the same norms and requirements as any other discipline.

The further consequence of this shift has been for theologians to think that their primary responsibility was to the university rather than to the church, for it is the university which employs them. The standards of scholarship and the relationship they have to students are all set by the charter and character of the university. In sum, in this view and under these circumstances, theology appears as one discipline among others, devoted to the critical pursuit and dissemination of knowledge, as this is defined by the explicit and implicit standards of the academic community of the modern university. The most convincing case for this view has been offered by Van Harvey. The most whole-hearted acceptance of it is manifested by David Tracy.

Now it ill behoves anyone to bite the hand that feeds one, but there is no need to lick it either. We can accept the fact that universities provide a place for theologians to work as an unexpected token of the world's Creator having so shaped His creation as to make room for some of those on the Way to reflect with more care and concentration than is possible for most. That creation's Lord thus finds a way for sustaining those in the Way is a matter for thanksgiving. It is not, however, grounds for idolatry. If theology exists to serve the Way, and if the Way exists for the sake of the world—a part of which is the university and all of humanity's intellectual pursuits—then, obviously in a manner which the university would not recognize, theology serves the university. But it can only serve it if it does its own business, which is to serve walking in the Way. As Israel has had to accept the fact that it has been called all sorts of things by the world—a people, a nation, a religion, a race—so theology can live with being called a discipline by the university. What, however, is a discipline? There are disciplines which are defined primarily by the subject matter which they investigate (i.e., chemistry), whereas others are defined by an agreement in method or procedure (philosophy). But how can theology be forced into one or the other group, or some combination of the two, without distortion? Our subject matter has no limits, even if it is focused on the Way and its Lord, and our methods are as diverse as are all those that serve a continuing conversation.

As long as the universities of this world offer us room and time, let us enjoy it. But we only serve the university by setting our own agenda. And for the carrying out of our agenda, what is essential to theology is not that it be a discipline, but that it be disciplined. For the sake of the disciplined character of our conversation, then, we need all the clarity and all the coherence we can muster. But clarity begins at home! We owe it only indirectly to the university; we owe it directly to each other who walk in the Way.

LIBERAL AND CONSERVATIVE WANDERINGS

The desire to share a blessing which we have received can only be commended. This is one of the more attractive ways in which to define the missionary motive that has always been strong among Christians. So the desire to show other Gentiles that there is a Way through the mess of this world is appropriate.

It would be a total denial of our own Way if we even pretended to try to show it to the Jews, for they already have their way of being in the Way and, indeed, our way of being in that Way presupposes the validity of the Way in which their ancestors were traveling before we came along and in which they continue to walk. All we can show them is how some Gentiles have come to a manner of walking in the Way in which they already walk. To ask them to come walk as we do would be a denial that, along *with* Israel's way, there is *also* a way for the Gentiles. The only "call to faith" that is proper for us to give to a Jew would be the call to a fully secularized Jew asking him or her to be faithful to the walking of his or her own people.[4]

The desire to invite wandering Gentiles to come walk with us is fully in order. What calls for care is the consequent temptation to present our Way in a manner which the world can easily grasp and accept. I call this a temptation because it is a test of whether we understand that we have been called into a Way, rather than to a world-view or a conceptual scheme. "As Christ was raised from the dead," said Paul (Rom. 6:4), "so we too are to walk in a new way," not merely to have some new thoughts. The desire to appeal to other Gentiles too often has taken the form of shaping our thoughts to theirs. At its best, this would conform their minds to ours, whereas God's concern for His creatures is focused on their feet and how they walk.

This apologetic concern has characterized primarily the tradition of so-called liberal theology, especially in the modern era. The danger for every apologetic theology—and every theology has at least some apologetic elements in it—is, as Rosenzweig noted, to take the world too seriously and theology's own enterprise too light-

---

[4]Cf. D. R. A. Hare and D. J. Harrington, S. J., "Make Disciples of All the Gentiles (Mt. 28:19)," *Catholic Biblical Quarterly* 37 (1975): 359-69.

ly. This happens when, for example, we present ideas, bits of our conversation, as a better philosophy, as though that were what we had of value to offer. A more responsible apologetic would be to present our Way and our conversation as something which only makes sense within, because it only takes place as an aid to, our walking.

Some apologists have gone so far as to try to convince the world that it already has what we have to offer. Some (Friedrich Schleiermacher, for instance) have said that the church presents what the culture already values as "highest and dearest."[5] Others have claimed that what we present is only a better expression of what the world already believes.[6] More than one has attempted to present our conversation as the answer to questions which the world implicitly asks.[7] In all these there is evident the weakness detected by Rosenzweig. More importantly, they reflect too little sense of what our Western culture has proved itself so far to be. They assign to the world, or to our culture, or to its intellectual leaders, a self-confidence, a trust in the ultimate significance of human actions (the Catholic theologian David Tracy) or the ultimate worth of ourselves (the Protestant theologian Schubert Ogden), which is conspicuously absent and which none of us has any reason to expect. We no longer live in the confident nineteenth century (which manifested worries enough). After the slaughter of World War I, the rise of totalitarian regimes of the Left and the Right, the horrors of World War II, especially those perpetrated on the Jews, the nuclear devastation visited on Japan and the assorted other nightmares inflicted on the Vietnamese and Cambodians more recently, with our world in danger of death by pollution and international peace maintained by a balance of terror—after all this, what earthly reasons can there be for this supposed confidence in our culture which our liberal apologists seem to have?

Given the rationality of control, exactitude and total articulation which we have already considered and found wanting, how can we bow down and worship before the standards of this culture? I do not propose for a moment that the Christian enterprise has proved able to offer a better or more workable rationality. Nor does our own history—when we were more in control of affairs than we have been for the past few centuries—give us any grounds for pretending to be superior in these matters. I only contend that,

[5]Friedrich Schleiermacher, *Über die Religion* (Berlin, 1799; Hamburg, 1958), p. 11.

[6]David Tracy, *Blessed Rage for Order* (New York, 1975), p.8.

[7]Paul Tillich, *Systematic Theology* (Chicago, 1951), vol. I, p.8.

if anyone is to argue the merits of secularity as commanding our allegiance, then, in the light of the history of this century, the burden of proof is squarely on his or her shoulders.[8] Watering down what we are doing with our feet or with our lips needs better justification than some broad appeal to the accomplishments of the natural sciences, impressive and scary as these have been over the past century.

In avoiding the missteps of liberal and apologetic concerns, one can also wander from the Way by being too conservative, too concerned with orthodoxy. One cannot walk while sitting down and maintaining a fixed position. One cannot walk if one constantly looks back. The conserving that is needed on this walk is that of carrying ahead into ever new situations a confidence in the Giver of the Way and a joy of having the Way to walk in continuity with those who came before us. The issue is faithful walking, here and now. For that we need all the help the past can give us. But the walking and the conversing that is right for us must surely be that which will be right for taking new steps on the particular stretch of the Way which has been given us to walk. If we do not walk our assigned stretch of the Way with new steps, then we shall surely have betrayed those who came before us, as we will unquestionably do harm to those who shall walk after us. What is to be conserved, then, is the newness of walking which the past has bequeathed us.

Orthodoxy, a right conversation for those on the Way, can be nothing other than holding to that which has marked the Way from its beginning: an impressive ability to innovate, to take new steps in new circumstances. Indeed, this was the mark of him who became the door to the Way for us, for he is reported to have taught that fresh interpretation of the Way was available. "You have heard it said of old, but I say to you . . ." — and in this he was himself being true to the spirit of what was "said of old."[9] Likewise, as our path was beginning to appear, the apostle Paul saw this new development as an astounding novelty occurring, as it were, before his eyes. What past was he conserving when he proclaimed an entry of Gentiles into the Way? For Paul, orthodoxy, "right teaching," was as novel as the radically new events of a crucified messiah and a resurrection from the dead.

[8]Irving Greenberg's opening essay in E. Fleischner, ed., *Auschwitz: Beginning of a New Era?* (New York, 1977) should be read in this connection, expecially pp. 14ff.

[9]The rabbis continued this tradition. Leo Baeck gives a number of Talmudic examples in his *The Essence of Judaism* (New York, 1961), pp. 26ff.

Precisely those to whom one would most naturally appeal as definers of orthodoxy were themselves highly original in their contributions to our conversation. Time lends a more stately luster to their name than they ever enjoyed in their day, for we may recall that Athanasius found himself at one time almost without friends in the leadership of the church and Thomas Aquinas died while on the way to defend his writings against charges of irregularity. Indeed, Thomas's daring attempt to reinterpret the Augustinian tradition in the framework of the new rationality of his time stands as a monument to an originality and creativity to which any serious right teaching at any time could well aspire.

So it was with the originators of the monastic movement, and also that other reform movement that broke out in the sixteenth century. Reformers along the Way have consistently claimed that they were restoring the original meaning and direction of the Way, and those who have led the way toward the ecumenical movement of this century were taking courageous new steps as their responsibility to right teaching.

Right teaching for us in our time, therefore, must reserve the right to take issue with some of those that have gone before us, insofar as past teaching has led to a situation which in our century has come to light as intolerable. A teaching of contempt of the Jews, to be specific, in which our whole tradition has taken part with a painful consistency, cannot be excused from having developed a climate which facilitated Hitler's fearful work. That some of our outstanding canonized figures of the past should have contributed in this way to the slaughter of one-third of God's beloved people is surely grounds for seeing to it that we come to a right teaching, a real orthodoxy, in this matter, no matter how seriously we depart from what has been said of old.

Such a departure was enacted by the Pastoral Council of the Roman Catholic Church in the Netherlands in 1970[10] in declaring null and void a passage in its own canons which read in part: "Relations with Jews must be avoided. . . . Moreover, the faithful must take care — according to the warning of Benedict XIV (Enc. *A quo primum*, 1751) — never to need the help or support of Jews." That canon, it must be noted, had been adopted as recently as 1924! One can marvel at the reversal of "right teaching" in only forty-six years, but one must shudder over the price paid by others to bring this about.

[10]*SIDIC*, vol. III, no. 2 (1970), cited in *Stepping Stones to Further Jewish-Christian Relations: An Unabridged Collection of Christian Documents,* compiled by H. Croner (London and New York, 1977), pp. 55 and 48 (referred to hereafter as *Documents*).

OTHER WAYS OF MISSING THE WAY

Of other ways of missing our footing, I wish to single out two for special attention: spiritualization, which results in irresponsibility to God, and secularization, which leads to a failure of responsibility to the world. The word *spiritualization* requires careful definition, for there is certainly a right spirituality, a directing of the spirit or the person, that is surely to be encouraged, and of course *Spirit* is one of the names or functions of God. Spiritualization, however, rests upon a distinction between the material, physical or visible, and the immaterial and unseen. This distinction is not in itself a problem if it entails no evaluative judgments, for God is Creator of heaven and earth, things visible *and* things invisible. All are His creatures and so all are our companions, to be lived and walked with in God's given coherence, or to be misused and abused and turned to some other purpose than God wills.

Spiritualization, however, consists in a further movement of the imagination that places a higher value on the unseen than on the seen, turning toward the immaterial and away from the material. It seeks to defend itself by appeal to a quite different distinction which can be found in our Holy Writings, usually translated as that between spirit and flesh. But this distinction, as made for example by Paul, has to do with whether any thing or person serves God's purposes. A dollar bill used to facilitate that wholeness to which the Way points, for example, would in Paul's terminology be spiritual. Used to hurt or fragment any part or aspect of creation, it would be fleshly. A thought or idea can be fleshly as well as spiritual, depending on its aim and our intent.

This Pauline distinction has been clarified by fairly recent historical study; for most of our history, however, and even among many of us in the Way today, Paul has been read as an authority in support of the distinction of spiritualization. Nowhere has this misunderstanding done greater damage than in its application to our understanding of the Jewish people. *We*, the church, seek the spiritual, invisible realities, we have said, whereas *they*, the Jews, seek only fleshly, earthly goals. The spiritual is the real, in this understanding — e.g. a heavenly, invisible home — in contrast to the earthly, physical hope of Israel for the actual Land of Promise. It is ironic that our forewalkers, especially beginning with Origen in the third century, learned this allegorical interpretation of God's concrete promises to a flesh and blood people from a Jew! It was the Jewish thinker Philo who more than a century earlier developed this spiritualization of the Scriptures that was picked up and developed by Christians, to the eventual deep hurt of the Jewish people.

The time has come to say No to this whole tendency. If we believe and trust in God as a real Creator who created a real world, giving it genuine existence in autonomous freedom, for better or worse, then we must take the physical consequences of God's act seriously and thankfully. If we do that, we shall be able to see that God's promises and so our hopes are really for men and women such as we, for creatures—not for such invisible entities as our souls, in contrast to our bodies. No, we are addressed and called and will be redeemed by the God of Creation as persons, and so presumably as embodied beings. Spiritualizaton—which has difficulty with creation and which cannot digest a God who called an actual people out of real slavery to a historical journey into a promised area measureable in square miles—constitutes a failure of trust in and responsibility to the only God of whom we know anything at all—the LORD, the God of Israel.

In a reaction to this otherworldly wandering from the Way, there has arisen, particularly in our century, a move to secularize the Way. As spiritualization can often arise from the sound urge to distinguish the Way of God from the ways of the world, so this opposite tendency arises from the perfectly laudable concern to underscore the fact that our way is really in and through this world, to be traveled with our feet firmly on the ground. When our cultural two-dimensionality is taken uncritically as normative (as in my *The Secular Meaning of the Gospel*, 1963), however, when the patterns of our culture are gloried in as though they were themselves the norms of the Way (as in Harvey Cox's *The Secular City*, 1965), when indeed the faith of our secular culture is taken to be essentially identical with our own (as in David Tracy's *Blessed Rage for Order*, 1975), we have surely reached a point of unhappy confusion. The Way to which we have been called is not the American way of life, nor the way of Western civilization, nor any of the other ways by which our path is criss-crossed. It is no service to the world we know in this century to offer it only a reflection of itself. We have better things to say to this world than merely to echo back what it is already saying without us. By this move of secularization, we fail utterly to fulfill our responsibility to the world for the very sake of which we have been called into a Way that is not that of the world.

An important variation on these concerns for our worldly involvement is sounded by those who call us to identify our Way with that of the poor, or at least to walk in such a way that the poor find us helping them rather than those who oppress them. Francis of Assisi could be the model for this call, but the voices of Latin American liberation theologians are the ones which ring most forcefully in our ears these days. They are calling our attention, as have others before them, to the fact that there is a prejudice in favor of the poor in the biblical story. The Way of God's servants, therefore, must lead them to a special sympathy with all who suffer and are oppressed. It does not follow, however, that we should identify the Way of God with the way of socialist movements, as liberation theologians tend to do. The socialist way has only to a limited extent proved itself of benefit to the poor. Where in some countries it has, there is every reason for Christians to want to support it. But to support the socialist way uncritically, to offer it no alternative, would be to fail in our responsibility to both socialism and the poor whose cause it may champion. It is worth noting that many Jews and Christians have not only been driven by the Way in which they walk and by biblical insights to agree with the analysis of our world made by socialist thinkers, but they have then also drawn from the socialists their ideas of what to do about it. At least one who has taken the first step, however, has seen that the Way itself offers alternatives, some of which are every bit as radical and all of which are more person-building than the blueprints of socialism. The "institution" (whether ever actually realized historically) of the Jubilee (Lev. 25), for example, has been seen as a model of decentralized, family-oriented redistribution of wealth which offers the basis for a critique of the centralized, bureaucratic proposals of socialism for solving inequality in land and its use.[11]

From a distance (i.e., from North America), liberation theology appears to be a response to the world in which it has arisen. More fundamentally, however, it seems to be addressed to and intended as a contribution to the conversation of those in the Way in that place at this time. It is not our place in our rather different situation on another conti-

[11]Arthur Waskow, *God-Wrestling* (New York, 1978), pp. 110-27.

nent to direct their conversation. We would point out, however, that from here there do seem to be problems in their conversation arising from a tendency to accept uncritically the spiritualization of our traditional theology, especially with respect to the concrete and continuing history of the Jewish people. If Gustavo Gutierrez may be taken as a spokesman for this movement, the "Old Covenant" has been rendered "invalid" and its promise has been "fulfilled" in Christ,[12] yet at the same time history and God's concern for history is to be taken with the utmost seriousness. Thus an antispiritualization intent is undermined by the oldest spiritualizing features of our conversation, an unfortunate fate for a theology which wants to be worldly in the best sense.

Given our past treatment of the Jewish people, given a many-centuried history of teaching our children to despise them, it is understandable that one of them has written, "All we want of Christians is that they keep their hands off us and our children."[13] One might hope that that little could be granted but, if it were, it would not exhaust our special responsibility to the Jews, for they have laid upon them, for better or worse, the election and the obligation to sanctify the Name of Him who has prepared for us a Way and called us into it. Indeed, our own calling, and so our Way, would make no sense at all apart from that of the Jewish people. St. Paul, back at the beginning of our Way, wrote to the believers in Rome, of whom perhaps most were Gentiles, "In the spreading of the Gospel [i.e., among the Gentiles] they [the Jews] are treated as God's enemies for your sake; but God's choice stands and they are his friends. . ." (11:28). In other words, God has kept the Jews out of our path and given them their own instructions to continue in the Way so that we Gentiles might find our *own* manner of walking in the Way. But for all that, they remain God's beloved people, ever before us as evidence of God's faithfulness. The answer we give concerning our responsibility to and for the Jewish people, however, must be made against the background of the story of nineteen centuries of ignoring or misunderstanding what Paul said. That story does not give us an answer, but no answer would be responsible that ignored that past.

How to answer responsibly depends on where one finds oneself along the way, and as the situation has changed, so what constitutes a wrong answer has changed. In the very beginning of the

[12]*A Theology of Liberation* (Maryknoll, N.Y., 1973), p. 167.

[13]Eliezer Berkowitz, in F. E. Talmage, ed., *Disputation and Dialogue* (New York, 1975), p. 293.

Way in which we find ourselves, the apostle Paul identified the answer of those we call the Judaizers—whoever they may have been—as a wrong answer. That answer, whether proposed by legalistic Gentiles or Torah-true Jewish Christians, was that there was only one way in which to walk the Way and that was the Jewish way. If anyone was to walk in the Way, then that person had to become a Jew. Paul's response to this was that God was showing that there was a new way which God had opened by means of Jesus Christ, available to all, Gentiles as well as Jews, to continue on in the Way which Israel had walked since Abraham and leading to the day of redemption; if one were not a Jew, one did not first have to become a Jew to walk in this new way.

In the course of a few generations, however, the young church of Jews and Gentiles became increasingly, predominantly and, finally, almost entirely a Gentile enterprise and also, unhappily, increasingly hostile to the vast majority of Jews—those who had never even heard of and those who had heard of and chose not to walk in this new way, but to walk more faithfully in the Way as they had known it. The hostility was mutual and understandable. Two groups appealing to the same tradition could understandably, if regrettably, see themselves as rivals and competitors, regarding each other as apostates from the truth and wanderers from the one Way of the One God of whom they both claimed to be beloved. The result was that the false answer of the Judaizers was displaced by its equally false opposite. The Judaizers had claimed that only as a Jew could one walk in the Way; now it was claimed that only as a Christian could one walk in the Way. The judgment that this opposite answer is also false follows from the conviction that in the historical development of a continuing and thriving Judaism and a growing and thriving Gentile church, side by side, and in spite of each other, God's hand is to be detected.

It is a matter of historical fact, however, that the Christians saw the prospering of the Gentile church as the work of God, but not the prospering of the Jewish people. The question which confronts us now is whether we shall continue to see the one and not the other and thus continue to give our traditional answer that the church has displaced the people of Israel as God's people and we alone are those whose manner of walking is the only one in which God's Way can be walked.

That theology of displacement has its roots in apostolic times and can appeal to the Apostolic Writings for support. Out of the early period of misunderstanding, competition and rivalry, words were spoken and written that have had fearful consequences. Whether they are Paul's words or, as seems more likely, the addition of a later editor, the Jews are said to be "heedless of God's will and enemies of their fellow-men, hindering us from speaking to the Gentiles to lead them to salvation. All this time they have been making up the full measure of their guilt, and now retribution has overtaken them for good and all" (1 Thess. 2:15-16).[14] (The last sentence sounds suspiciously like a response to the destruction of Jerusalem, which came five years after the generally accepted date of Paul's death.) With such things being said, whether earlier or later, many Jews must have seen this new movement and its opening to the Gentiles as a denial of the reality and validity of the faithful walking of the Jewish people. Was it not clear to them from fairly early in its development that this new movement was calling in question the very identity of the Jew and his people?

Other and more venomous words appear in the parable of the vineyard, as the author of the Gospel according to Matthew wrote it (21:33-43), which concludes: "Therefore, I tell you, the kingdom of God will be taken away from you, and given to a nation that yields the proper fruit." And yet more vitriolic is the passage in John (8:44) in which the "Jews" are said to be the children of the Devil, not God. Another passage which could support a theology of displacement is that found in the letter to the Hebrews, of unknown authorship: "By speaking of a new covenant, he [i.e., God through the prophet Jeremiah] has pronounced the first one old; and anything that is growing old and ageing will shortly disappear"(8:13). This strange interpretation of Jeremiah's eschatological hope, recast in the terms of a historical process, became a commonplace in the centuries of conversation that followed. Yet none of those conversants stopped to look that historical process in the face, to notice the fact that the so-called "old" was being called new every morning by those who walked in it. Only the church, not God or Israel, had pronounced it "old." In fact it did not "grow old or age"; it grew and was renewed with ever fresh interpretation and living devotion. So of course it not only did not "shortly disappear," it has not to this day disappeared and

---

[14]For the argument that this is a later addition, see B. Pearson, "1 Thessalonians 2:13-16: A Deutero-Pauline Interpolation," *Harvard Theological Review* 64 (1971): 79-94.

shows no signs of doing so in the future, so far as the human eye can see. And, of course, we can see only the human side of the covenant. The facts of the historical process within the terms of which the church had erected its theory of displacement, therefore, have contradicted the theory. After what many judge to be the most devastating blow in all its history, at the least one of the greatest, the Jewish people lives, badly shaken surely, but determined and once more in control of its own land. Given these facts, we dare not continue repeating the answer we thought we heard from the Epistle to the Hebrews.

I shall put off to a later step an answer to the question much discussed in recent years of whether the Apostolic Writings are anti-Judaic. There is a difficulty with the question which a straight Yes or No answer ignores. The Apostolic Writings have always been a book read and interpreted by the church and only as read and interpreted is it a reality for the church. As this interpreted reality, from the second century until now, it clearly has been anti-Judaic. Whether it will continue to be so read and interpreted, whether it will continue to be anti-Judaic, is the great question before us at this time. My whole contribution to our conversation is offered as an attempt to help change this reality so that in the future we shall not find this book to be anti-Judaic.

We should touch upon, at this point, some of the difficult questions arising from concrete relations between the church and the Jewish people. If there truly is a way for Gentiles to be in the Way, as our historical experience confirms, does it follow that for a Gentile to become a Jew constitutes a violation of God's plan? On the other side, is it necessarily disobedience to God's purpose if a Jew becomes a Christian?

The possibility of giving a general answer is limited by the special circumstances of particular cases, which can vary considerably and yet which ought to be taken into account. Nevertheless, there are two premises from which we can construct the beginnings of a tentative answer. First, the continuing reality of both the Jewish people and also a preponderantly Gentile church forms an important part of God's plan. Second, there is a profound difference between these two entites: generally—and according to Jewish law—a Jew is a Jew by birth, by the fact of having a Jewish mother (although even this is not without its problems as the famous case of Brother Daniel reminds us);[15] a Christian, on the other hand is a Christian by baptism and so with some degree of personal choice (although the unsettled debate about infant baptism and the undeniable ambiguities in the relationship of confirmation to baptism remind us that this too is no simple matter). On these two premises we can propose the following theses for our further conversation.

1. Traditionally, Judaism has put a low priority on proselytism. The

[15]See Solomon S. Bernards, ed. *Who Is a Jew?* (New York, undated).

passage in Matthew (23:15) about Pharisees who cross sea and land to make a single proselyte is a consideration, but it has little support from later rabbinic sources. This much is history and we should consider whether it is not also part of the history of God's dealing with His people. We must add, however, that there is, from the perspective of their tradition, no theological reason for Jews not to proselytize. Be that as it may, there have been Gentiles who, with or without encouragement from Jews, have found that the church did not provide for them an adequate way to walk in God's Way and so have become Jews. Surely, in the light of Rom. 11:20-22, we must allow that God can do a new thing and such conversions may be a warning to the church to take its manner of walking more seriously.

2. For most Gentiles in the Way, however, the church has served as their entry into the Way *as* Gentiles. This much is also history and we should consider whether it is not also part of God's dealing with His church. From its beginning, the church has been deeply concerned to carry out its mission to preach the gospel to all the Gentiles. There have been some Jews, however, who have heard this preaching and found that the church, Gentile though it be, has offered them a more compelling way in which to walk in God's Way and so have become Christians. Here too we must allow that God once more can do that new thing which He did with the beginning of what became the Way for Gentiles, and such conversions may remind the church that it would not be had there not been Jews who heard the gospel gladly.

Any proselytizing from either side must therefore satisfy two requirements. First, it must not be undertaken in such a way as to encourage anyone to deny the reality of God's continuing concern and love for His people and His church. The special circumstances of particular individuals must not blind us to the larger historical fact of God's dealing with His creation up to this moment: He has provided two ways for walking in His Way, one for the Jews and one for the Gentiles. Second, due to the loss of one third of God's people in the Holocaust, special care must be exercised by the church for the foreseeable future not to weaken the Jewish people. In sum, all care should be exercised by the church—and we can also hope by the Jewish people—to make ours a cooperative competition in the more faithful service of God's purpose for His whole creation.

With respect to the special case of the Hebrew Christians, Jews for Jesus and other such communities, two things must be said. First, surely *one* way to be a Jew is to be a Christian Jew. This possibility, however, flies in the face of the history of the past nineteen centuries. Second, and without any qualification, it should never be claimed that this is the *only* way to be a Jew or, more guardedly, a "full" or "fulfilled" Jew. Such a claim would be an attempt to turn back the clock of history to the late first century and take again the false turning made at that time. It would constitute a breach of the requirements which we have recommended.

One further point should be made about our relationship with the

Jews. Surely the modern form of Judaizing is as wrong for us now as its old form was in Paul's day. The modern form, arising out of improved relations between Christians and Jews, is that of Christians taking Jewish traditions into the practice of their church or family. So some churches have begun to include the Jewish Passover seder in their calendar and a few churches have even patterned their services of worship after that of the synagogue. In its mildest form it appears in the claim that "we are all spiritually Semites" or that "we are honorary Jews."

It is one thing to join as an invited guest in a Jewish Passover seder or a synagogue service; it is quite another to rob the Jews of precious acts of thanksgiving which reaffirm their special identity. It is one thing to claim that we worship the God of the Jews; it is another to presume to elect ourselves into their company on *our* "spiritual" or "honorary" terms, rather than actually to join them on their own Halachic terms.

Such forms of Judaizing are to be rejected on two grounds. First, they rob the Jews, however politely intended, of their own identity and reality. They are therefore a breach of the commandment "Thou shalt not steal." Second, they imply the denial of the theological validity of the development of two different ways in which to walk in God's Way and thereby deny God's hand in the history of the Way up to this day. They therefore imply a denial of the God of the Way, making light of either God's Way for Israel or God's Way for his Gentile church or both.

If we dare to trust that God's hand is to be detected in Jesus Christ and so in the beginnings of our being in the Way, then we must dare also to trust that He has had much to do with the history which has come since. Certainly other hands, sometimes all too painfully evident, have also been at work in that history, but that is the price that God was willing to pay for calling actual people into cooperating with Him in completing His creation. It is a risky business to see history as the location of God's work, and both the Jewish people and the church have been hurt by false readings of its signs. Yet to reject this risk is to close ourselves to any living relationship to the God of this world. If God is a living God, then we must accept the risk of living with Him and under Him, *hic et nunc.*

One of the apostolic writers contributed a challenging suggestion to an early stage of our conversation, one that has been picked up and repeated in our generation. The author of the letter to the Ephesians proposed, as an image of his hope, that the Jewish people and the Gentiles in the Way would in time, perhaps at the end of time, be united as one people. In the first generation the image must have seemed right, for a church of Jews and Gentiles was in fact taking shape. But, over the longer run, the image has not been sustained. It ignored the vast majority of Jews, who had never felt called to or had never even heard of the new Way. What has in fact developed are two peoples, not one—Jews there and Christians here (in each perhaps a precious few having crossed over, which may be a sign of the eschatological possibilities of the Ephesians image). What unites these two is not Jesus Christ, as Ephesians had it, but the fact that they worship the one God, the LORD. Or perhaps we could say that Jesus unites us Christians to his people by having opened a way for us to worship their God. This was hardly the point of the author of Ephesians. It is, however, what has in fact happened.

What then is our final hope in this matter of the relationship and conversation between the Jewish people and the Gentile church? That they may finally be one? If so, then certainly not by the fact of one having been assimilated into the other; not by Jews giving up their way of being in the Way to join the Christians in theirs, nor the opposite. But it is at least imaginable, as a possible subject of hope and praying, that a time will come in which we will find ourselves, the Jewish people and the church, walking along in such close proximity that each could see the other and see indeed that both were walking in the same direction, and that the conversation of each should be understandable and seem right to the other. The day of this experience may be far off, but when and if it does come, then Christ will surely have completed an important part of his work and God will be that much nearer to being "all in all."

That expression occurs in 1 Cor. 15:28; it is the final word, as far as Paul could utter it, of the fulfillment of God's redemption and purpose. Christ the reconciler no longer appears at the end of this vision. So it would have to be, for he reconciled the Gentiles to God; but the historical result was divisiveness between the Jewish people and the church. That divisiveness was our own corruption of the divine plan, but as a further fact of history it now has to be taken into account by God. For Christ to be the ultimate reconciler, therefore, he must as it were step out of the picture into the background for he is there as the word of his Father, not as an independent word that must have its own day.

It is food for thought that, in the vision of the consummation of God's plan with which Paul concluded his last great wrestling with the issue of the Jewish people and the church (in Romans 9 through 11), there is again no explicit mention of Christ. The deliverer who will appear is Israel's God, as proclaimed by the great prophet of the Exile (Isa. 59:20f., cited by Paul in 11:26–27). From there to the end of Romans 11, with its great doxology, there is mention of none but the LORD, Israel's God.

This, then, is the beginning of our proposed answer to the Jewish people. It is the only answer that seems coherent with the fact from which we began: The church, all those upon the Way, for all their Gentile background, adore the LORD, Israel's God.

The Provider of the Way:
The Triune God

THE DOCTRINE OF THE TRIUNE GOD

The church adores the LORD, the God of Israel. This is the beginning and the end of our being in the Way, because He, the LORD, is the beginning and the end of the Way itself, the one from whom, with whom and toward whom we walk. Since it is we Gentiles who do this walking on this road, our conversation about this most central and decisive of all matters will be carried out, appropriately, in our own Gentile way. This is precisely what we do when we adore the LORD, the one God of Israel, with the words Father, Son and Spirit. Our next step is the critical examination of this confession.

Apart from a brief flirtation with the ideas of Marcion, we have had little doubt that the God we adore is the LORD, Maker of heaven and earth, the God of Abraham, Isaac and Jacob. When the church has tried to account to itself for this adoration, however, when it has tried to find its own words with which to make clear that it is indeed this God and no other whom it worships and in whom it trusts, the words it has found are *Father, Son, Spirit*.

If the doctrine of the Trinity expresses the church's immediate apprehension of God, then in it we are saying that we do not first know of God, worship Him and confess His holy Name, and then add the doctrine of the Trinity as an elaboration of our understanding. If that were what we meant, then we should say that the doctrine of the Trinity does not express our immediate apprehension of God; it only sums up a series of three distinct apprehensions of God. If the church first knows God as Father, apart from knowing Him as Son and Spirit, and then comes to know God as Son, and thirdly comes to know Him as Spirit, then it could confess that God is sometimes one, sometimes another, or perhaps changes, being first one then another. One or another of us has said such things, but that is clearly not how most of our conversation has gone. Indeed, we have expressly excluded such a teaching under the label of Sabellianism. What we have said is that God *is* triune, in Himself and in all His ways, that every experience of God, every apprehension of God to which we dare lay claim, is of the one triune God.

The main line of our conversation implies that this doctrine is primary in character, not secondary or derivative. The doctrine of the Trinity reflects one not three apprehensions of God. If that is what we mean, then this doctrine quite properly comes at the forefront of our teaching, not at the end as a summary of other things that the church has to say. From early in the Way and still today, I would judge, the central line of our conversation has been a confession of God as triune.[1]

The necessity for this confession becomes clear if we recall who we are and how we got to be where we are, especially if we recall that our feet are on the ground, walking. We are Gentiles, preponderantly, who worship the God of Israel. It is one thing for the Jews to call upon God as Father and to know Him immediately and always as their God. That is their right and their duty because of their election, because they are called to precisely that immediate relationship by God himself: "I will take you for my people, and I will be your God" (Exod. 6:7). For Gentiles to call upon this God is another thing, a strange thing, which can only happen because God has made toward them a further movement and has drawn them to Himself in a further way. Just this way in which God is Himself in reaching out to us Gentiles and drawing us into the Way in which we know and worship Him, just this reality of God —and so our apprehension of Him directly in this His reality—is what we express with the doctrine of the Trinity. With those words —One God, Father, Son and Spirit—we express our apprehension of the one God, the God of Israel, who by His Spirit and through

[1]Karl Barth, in his *Kirchliche Dogmatik,* I/1, §8, 1, provided a wealth of sources on the issue and arguments in support of the contention that this doctrine is primary in character.

His Son has drawn us to Himself. It is the only adequate way for the Gentile church to confess the God of Israel. This is just what the God of Israel is for us, what He is in Himself in the miraculous fact of being also the God of the church. Both the mystery of Israel's God also being God for the Gentiles and the miracle of Gentiles being in the Way and worshiping Israel's God are expressed in this teaching. That is why we can assert that the doctrine of the Trinity is the distinctive doctrine of the church, the absolute center of all our conversation. It is, in short, *our* doctrine of God. It is how we share our joyful understanding that God is God for us, really our God, the Father, precisely in what He has done for us in Jesus Christ. And God is God for us in what He has done for us in Jesus Christ in no other way than as He who has drawn us as Spirit to worship Him. That is the only God we know, indeed the one LORD, truly one, who in the unity of His love and being has been also for us Gentiles in the Jew Jesus of Nazareth and has drawn us into His Way for us on our way to becoming fellow citizens with His beloved people—the Jews—in His coming Kingdom.

Although it is correct to say that the doctrine of the Trinity expresses our Gentile apprehension of the God of Israel, it would be inadequate to say that it expresses only our apprehension. Insofar as we understand God at all, we mean with this doctrine to speak of Him. We confess and worship Him as triune because that is how He has been and that is how He is with us and for us. We worship Him because we trust Him. We trust that His move toward us was really a self-determination, a self-expression, in a word, His own act. We are speaking of Him in his Self-disclosing activity, then, not about ourselves, when we speak of God as triune.

I said that the doctrine of the Trinity is primary doctrine. There have been those who have argued that it is secondary or summary doctrine. Friedrich Schleiermacher only discussed the doctrine of the Trinity at the very end of his influential contribution to the conversation in the early part of the nineteenth century, and in this he has had his followers, most recently Paul Tillich. Schleiermacher saw our whole conversation as being about our walk, about a special sensibility that led us into and was produced by being in the Way. What we talk of in the Way is what he called our religious self-consciousness, so that whatever we say about the Giver of the Way is itself an expression of that self-consciousness. It followed from this approach that, since the doctrine of the

Trinity did not express that self-consciousness itself but only combined three different expressions of it, it could only come at the end of his discussion, almost as an appendix.

The reason why we take issue with Schleiermacher and Tillich on this matter is that we take our point of departure from the historical reality of the church. Our starting point, not to be forgotten, is that we are Gentiles who have been drawn to worship the God of Israel. The historical component of our consciousness of who we are and who we worship is awakened by the historical existence of the Jewish people, of Israel before our eyes and within our hearing, still worshiping and sanctifying the name of their God. With our eyes on the Jews, we can do nothing but identify ourselves, on the whole and in overwhelming majority, as Gentiles, non-Jews, who nonetheless worship Israel's God as ours also. Thus our own history, which is the context of our knowledge of God, forces us to deal with this doctrine early in our discussion.

The doctrine of the Trinity, as the central expression of our apprehension of God, has become part of our worship. If we worship the God who is triune, then our worship will naturally reflect these words. Yet there is a danger here. The language of worship and praise is the same language as the one in which we reflect and carry on our conversation. Yet the use is not the same, however closely related. What we do with words when using them doxologically (to praise) is not quite what we do with words when we use them doctrinally. Unless handled with the greatest care in liturgical formulations and hymns, the trinitarian doctrine can lead to something close to tritheism. Such traditional ideas as attributing creation to God as Father, redemption to God as Son and sanctification to God as Spirit, without the equally traditional correction that this is only a manner of speaking—since *opera trinitatis ad extra sunt indivisa* ("the triune One is indivisible in His actions")—is liable to further distort worship. The fact that we apprehend, know and worship God as triune should never obscure our realization that in this way we worship *God,* the one Lord, the God of Israel. He whom we know as the triune God is no other than He whom the Jews know simply and immediately as Father, as the one God confessed in the Shema: "Hear, O Israel, the Lord our God, the Lord is one." The Jews can say this, but we Gentiles, drawn by the Spirit through the son to worship this same and only God, must find our own words.

THE SPIRIT OF GOD

As Israel opens its confession with the words *Shema Yisrael* ("Hear O Israel"), so the church begins its confession with the words "We believe." If we acknowledge and begin with the historical facts, then the most utterly amazing wonder of the church's confession is that it should be made at all by such a community. The wonder is that Israel's God has drawn us Gentiles to Himself and placed us in His Way. The very first thing we have to say of this God, then, is that He is the God who has done this. He is God the Holy Spirit.

I am of course aware that by beginning with the Holy Spirit, rather than with the Father, I am reversing the traditional order of trinitarian theology. Karl Barth remarked, some years ago, that he would have liked to develop a theology of the "third article," that is, a theology leading off from the third article or paragraph of the creed, which affirms the Holy Spirit and the church. This is what he felt Schleiermacher had done in an invalid fashion, interpreting the third article as an article about human experience. He felt, however, that Schleiermacher's influence (which he regretted) had not yet been sufficiently overcome to take the risk. Barth clearly saw the third article as being not about human religiosity, but about God's making human beings available to Himself.

Whether Schleiermacher is sufficiently behind us is an open question. I choose the doctrine of the Holy Spirit as the proper way to open this discussion, not because I think the time is right—who can judge that?—but because the facts require it. The facts in question are not new. They are only new in the consciousness of the church insofar as it has become aware of what has been a fact for centuries, but one unacknowledged in its conversation and so in the way in which it has walked. I refer to the fact of the existence of Israel, the reality of the Jewish people, the preservation of God's own people of His love. In the face of that reality, the church can only acknowledge the strange fact of its own existence as Gentiles who worship the God of the Jews. When this fact of its own identity is acknowledged, it must follow that the primal mystery of the God it worships is that this God has reached out and drawn this collection of Gentiles into the Way, into a task and a part in His plan and purpose. These are the facts, Schleiermacher and Barth aside, which force us to take the doctrine of the Spirit as the proper starting point for our reflection on the church's conversation about the God it worships. We begin, then, not with some idea of a prime cause, an origin of all things, some supposed universal experience of limits, or any such abstraction, but instead with the utterly mundane mystery of our concrete identity as Gentiles who worship the God of the Jews and therefore with the doctrine of God as the Holy Spirit.

The church's confession and worship of God is of Him who has made that confession and worship possible. It worships Him first of all, therefore, as the God who has taken this strange new step beyond, if on the basis of, His covenant with Israel, the Jewish people. Because of that covenant, there are human beings, the Jews, who know and love God and seek with joy to walk in His Way for them. Now there appear other human beings, a company drawn from many peoples—from the Gentiles, who also worship Him and who dare, as the Jews have always dared, to say *our* God, Father. They can dare to say this not on any presumption of their own doing, but solely because this same one God has reached out to them and drawn them into His Way. God Himself has moved toward them to make it possible for them to move toward Him.

As a result of this movement of theirs, which is nothing other than a response to His being the God who has first moved toward them and so moved them, they confess him as Father, their Father too. The church prays, "Our Father"; that is the beginning of its own prayer. But when we stop to reflect upon this fact, when we take up our conversation that becomes possible as the fruit of this fantastic fact, then we can only begin by saying to each other and also to Him that we believe God is the Holy Spirit. Luther spoke for most of us in the Way when he wrote in his shorter catechism: "I believe that I am not able by my own reason or strength to believe or come to Jesus Christ my Savior; rather, the Holy Spirit has called me by means of the Gospel.[2] Precisely. Faith in God the Spirit is trust in God, trust and thanksgiving because of an event in which God showed us who He is by reaching out to us Gentiles and drawing us to Himself, so that Gentile though we be we dare to call upon the LORD, the God of Israel, as our God as well as of the Jews. The ground of this confession is not our religious sensibility, but the historical fact of Gentiles having come to worship the God of the Jews. This event of a Gentile church worshiping the God of the

---

[2]*Die Bekenntnisschriften der evangelisch-lutherischen Kirche* (Göttingen, 1952), pp. 511f.

Jews, which in no way detracts from the special relationship which He has always had and continues to have with His people Israel, demands of us that we begin our confession of trust in Him by confessing God as Spirit. If this event is really God's doing, then God is for us first and foremost the doer of this thing, God the Holy Spirit.

From this beginning we can now see that, when we speak of the gift or sending of the Spirit, we are referring primarily to the self-giving of God Himself. Insofar as the story of the gift of the Spirit at Pentecost is accepted as an appropriate representation of this event, it is rightly called the "birthday of the church." For the immediate result of this gift was the community, the church on its way to becoming a Gentile enterprise alongside God's continuing Jewish enterprise. The author of the Pentecost story, therefore, had to tell further stories—of Peter's being sent to a Gentile house and, of course, the great theme of his book, the mission to the Gentiles centering in the work of Paul. Much is said in the stories of Acts, as well as in other Apostolic Writings, of the gifts of the Spirit, but these are all fruits of the self-gift of God which we adore when we worship God as the Spirit. Insofar as we are touched by the Spirit, then, we are touched by God himself.

> For all who are moved [or led] by the Spirit of God are sons of God. The Spirit you have received is not a spirit of slavery leading you back into a life of fear, but a Spirit that makes us sons, enabling us to cry 'Abba! Father!' In that cry the Spirit of God joins with our spirit in testifying that we are God's children; and if children, then heirs. We are God's heirs and Christ's fellow-heirs, if we share his sufferings now in order to share his splendour hereafter. (Rom. 8:14-17)

What is it to have "received" the Spirit when the Spirit is God? It is to be led, to be moved along in the Way (v. 14). And the Way is contrasted with that wandering in the dark in the fear and confusion, or maybe simply blind complacency, that is so characteristic of our age as well as Paul's (v. 15). No, there is a Way and it is of God, so we need not fear. To have the Spirit is to be joined with Christ. Paul, a Jew, set aside his Jewishness, so to speak, in order to address a church of Jews and Gentiles together. And now that whole company of the church in Rome, Gentiles as well as Jews, can call God "Father" with all the familiarity and trust of the Jew Jesus for, by being united with this beloved son of the Father, we too may cry "Father!" We Gentiles who were far off are now part of God's affair. We have been brought near, so near that the cry to God which we utter, said Paul, is God's own cry in us (v. 16).

> Up to the present, we know the whole created universe groans in all its parts as if in the pangs of childbirth. Not only so, but even we, to whom the Spirit is given as firstfruits of the harvest to come, are groaning inwardly while we wait for God to make us his sons and set our whole body free. For we have been saved, though only in hope. . . . In the same way the Spirit comes to the aid of our weakness. We do not even know how we ought to pray, but through our inarticulate groans the Spirit himself is pleading for us. (Rom. 8:22-24a, 26)

On the one side, as it were, is God, from whom we must and do await redemption, the liberation of all (vs. 19, 21). On the other side are we, in the midst of the whole unfinished, unredeemed, unliberated creation, groaning as in childbirth (vs. 22, 23), and also, strangely, God as Spirit too (v. 26). Yes, God is on this side too, dwelling with us, the promised comforter (John 14:26). Although the Spirit is really with us, a token, a pledge, a firstfruits, we are not yet sons and daughters of God (v. 23). We have only this strange promissory note, said Paul, the Spirit who groans with us.

As God is with His people in the Way as what they call the *Shekhinah*, so God is with His church in the Way as what we call the Spirit. The Jewish tradition has developed the idea of the *Shekhinah*—the Presence of God, one of God's emanations—as God's way of being in exile with His people and sharing in their suffering. When the messianic age comes, then will come not only Israel's redemption, but also the time of redemption, so to speak, for the *Shekhinah*, the time of God's own reconciliation with Himself. (The Jewish tradition, mystical as well as rabbinical, has made generous use of the expression, "so to speak," in full awareness of how feeble are our words to capture the mystery of God.)

The church has acknowledged God's presence with us in the Way by adoring Him as Holy Spirit. As the *Shekhinah* in Jewish thought has been the consoling, mothering, feminine aspect of God, so the church may reflect on the mothering character and work of God the Spirit. Creation, we ourselves, and God the Spirit groaning together in childbirth is not exactly a masculine image.

The Spirit, in words hammered out in long conversations in the past, "proceeds" from the Father. This cannot mean that the Spirit is an agent or emissary of God, for the Spirit is God Himself. What the Spirit does is God's doing. If the Spirit is with us, God is with us.

When we speak of the Holy Spirit, we are speaking, for example, of God's way of hovering over the waters of creation as a mother hen hovers over her brood, of His comforting care of His creation. The Spirit proceeds from the Father, also, as His maternal reaching out and gathering to Himself, as has happened to us Gentiles in the Way. This gathering was accomplished through that strange event in history and in the very life of God that is bound up with the things concerning Jesus of Nazareth. That man was the occasion and so the means and therefore the mediator between the LORD, Israel's God, and us Gentiles. God gathers us—that is His reality as maternal Spirit—to His son, so that we are now on our way to becoming sons with him, sons and daughters of God to be adopted by the strange procedure of being made into younger brothers and sisters of that one son. "For God knew his own before ever they were, and also ordained that they should be shaped to the likeness of his Son, that he [Jesus] might be the eldest among a large family of brothers [and sisters]" (Rom. 8:29).

Those who first set out upon the Way for us Gentiles were convinced that Jesus was the normative image and likeness of God, doing only what He willed. They could therefore say that the Spirit of God was also the Spirit of the Son, that the reaching out of the one was the reaching out of the other. So at a later stage there crept into our confession of faith the little clause *filioque:* The Spirit proceeds from the Father *and the Son.* Those who walk over on the Eastern side of the broad path that constitutes the Way—our companions of the Eastern Orthodox churches—have objected to this Western addition. Western Christians, in return, have feared that to say the Spirit proceeds from the Father alone, or from the Father through the Son, would imply the subordination of the Son to the Father, a strangely typical concern of the West's about rank and power! When we consider which Son we are speaking of, however, we must realize that the equality of the Son with His Father, a matter to which we have not yet given due attention, can only be that of obedience, service and so precisely of subordination! For we are speaking of God, not of ourselves. The humility of God,

His lowering Himself to accomplish His will, His power which works through weakness, are recurring themes in Paul's letters.

Gregory of Nyssa expressed this insight into God's character beautifully in chapter 24 of his *Address on Religious Instruction*: "God's transcendent power is not so much displayed in the vastness of the heavens, or the luster of the stars, or the orderly arrangement of the universe or his perpetual oversight of it, as in his condescension to our weak nature. We marvel at the way the sublime entered a state of lowliness."[3] And again, "The one thing which really befits God's nature [is] to come to the aid of those in need."[4]

God the Spirit is the Spirit which proceeds from the Father concretely to gather us Gentiles to His Son so that we may be His sons and daughters, for he or she who is with the Son of God is with God. Surely this can be said without the *filioque* clause, for it is no derogation of the Son to stress the obedience, the submission of the Son to the Father.

Let us recall our feet and the dirt on which we walk. How is it with us, how is it with our feet, since we "have" the Spirit? Do we in fact have Him? We can assure ourselves at least that He has us, to the extent that we are here walking together. Placing one foot in front of the other is our consolation and our grounds for conviction that God is with us as Spirit. The Spirit, we believe, empowers our walk and so enables our talk. Our own walking, our own feet, are the best evidence we have, weak as it is, that Israel's LORD has truly reached out to us, that God really is God the Spirit.

It follows from God's reality as Spirit that the gifts of the Spirit are those which aid us in walking together. These will not always take the form of our talking, of the use of our tongues. Might not the gift of silence be of incontestably more value to our progress? Is not one of our chief failings in the Way that we have talked so much that we have sometimes forgotten to walk? We have often seemed incredible to those who heard us because lips that speak unconnected with feet that walk are just that. Perhaps, then, we should value that gift of the Spirit that leads the feet of some just to walk, without saying much, as much or more than we value the gift of ecstatic utterance ("tongues"). The greatest gift of all, as Paul said, is a way of walking that concerns itself primarily not with how

[3]*Library of Christian Classics*, vol. III, p. 301.
[4]Ibid., p. 306.

we are getting along, but how our fellow walkers are coming along. If this walking in love, this loving with our hands and feet, an embodied love, does not take place, all other so-called gifts of the Spirit are as nothing.

A silence of the Spirit, however, could not be simply not speaking, merely negative. As a gift of Him who is, it must have its positive form: expectation, silence as waiting. It will correspond to the fact that the presence of the Spirit is felt often as absence, as not being available. The silence of the Spirit is then an eager but patient waiting, listening for a Word not yet heard, not yet spoken, but one for which we long. The absence of the Spirit for those in the Way will take the form of a presence missed and longed for. That too is the LORD, whose presence missed and longed for is as much a part of our experience under His leading as is a presence felt and a Word heard.

Above all, we confess God as Holy Spirit as the Spirit of the God of all creation, present at its birth, and ever since groaning for its redemption. The *Shekhinah* or presence of the LORD, the God of Israel, is leading His Gentile church, we believe, to walk eagerly and patiently until the day in which God's presence or Spirit, together with His Son, return into the fulness of His unity when God shall be "all in all."Whatever the apostle may have meant by that strange figure, the final vision which it can reflect is one of the perfect wholeness and unity of the LORD, the God of Israel, when God's purposes shall have been realized and His creation completed according to His will. The Spirit, in the meantime—and it is very much a question of a meantime, an interim—leads us to walk in a Way, the walking of which is itself part of what leads to that End. And the End, the destiny of our Walk, of the whole creation and even of God Himself, is that which guides the Spirit, for that End can be no other than the *telos* of the Lord, the God of Israel.

THE SON OF GOD

The church worships the LORD, the God of Israel, as *its* God, as He has made Himself available to it through the Jew Jesus of Nazareth. This Jew was and is for the church the one in whom it is confronted with God as He who chooses to be also the God of the church. Because of and by means of Jesus Christ, then, the church is drawn into the Way of God.

Because Jesus of Nazareth has and continues to play this essential role for the church, its confession of God as the God who did this thing—who made us to be fellow-citizens with the Jews and, therefore, able to call on God as our Father—has centered from the beginning on him. This is true of the earliest writings of those in the Way; it has marked our major agreements in crucial conversations of the past (the creeds) and it has marked our ongoing conversation down through the centuries.

It is essential to remember not only that Jesus was a Jew and that his ministry and teaching fall well within the range of Judaism of his time, but also that all of his disciples and followers were Jews. Those who were drawn to him by his teaching, works or person were all Jews who saw or sensed in him the sign of an approaching crisis which they could not but have understood in wholly Jewish terms; the coming of the reign of God, the restoration of His people and with them the whole earth, the promised Day of the Lord was at hand.

Whether they called him the Messiah is not certain; if they did it is also uncertain how they would have meant the title. Whether Jesus understood himself to have been God's messiah, perhaps as in some way the inaugurator or initiator of the age of redemption, is even harder to decide from the limited documents we have, coming as they do from the church that was shaped by the decisive events of Jesus' death and his appearances to his disciples beginning on Easter. What is incontestable is that Jesus was charged by Pilate with being a would-be messiah, for the title of execution read "King of the Jews." It may be that Jesus did in fact not deny the charge when it was made. It is as sure as any historical conclusion from so long ago can be that he was crucified by the Romans as a messianic pretender.[5]

There no doubt the matter would have ended, as it did for others crucified under the same or similar charges. The Easter appearances changed everything. The Jewish disciples who claimed to have seen Jesus after his death, the first witnesses of the resurrection, took this utterly unexpected event to be God's confirmation of the crucified messiah. The crucified one was God's anointed, the figure of the end of time of which Jesus had spoken. He was for his Jewish disciples Israel's messiah. Searching the Scriptures, struggling to make sense out of the tradition in the light of this new and

[5]See Nils Dahl, *The Crucified Messiah* (Minneapolis, 1974).

astounding event, his disciples interpreted it in such a way as to lead up to this new development. In a typically Jewish move—as the prophets, the Deuteronomic editors, the authors of the books of Chronicles had done before—these Jews retold the story in such a way as to include this last chapter, the one that had been written before their very eyes. This too was part of the story; this too must therefore have been implicit in the story of God's dealings with Israel.

All this they did as Jews for, as Jews, how else could they have reacted? So they seized upon Jewish concepts and categories to speak of what had happened. Within a short time, perhaps within only a year or two,[6] they fastened on the term *son*: Jesus was the son of God. That designation expressed the intimacy or closeness of the relationship between Jesus and God, but it also put that relationship in the terms of another: the intimacy and closeness of the relationship between Israel and the LORD, the God of Israel. It is to be noted that the central themes in the opening chapters of Montefiore and Loewe's *A Rabbinic Anthology* are "God's Love for Israel" and "Israel's Love for God." This is the relationship of Fatherhood and sonship in the terms of which Jesus, a true Israelite, was designated son.

Israel, and with Israel then also Jesus, was designated son of God by God's own choice of His people. For us Gentiles, however, the focus is on Jesus as son, since it was and is because of him that we too dare to claim that we are on our way to adoption as sons and daughters of the same one God. That cannot be our only focus, however. The church cannot let Israel itself out of view for, without Israel, there could have been no Jesus and so there would be no church. The church's claim to relationship with Israel's God depends on Israel's prior relationship, for that alone provided the historically essential context for the existence of the one Israelite through whom the church has a claim to sonship. We must say more than this, however. Israel remains today the foundation of the church's claim to sonship for, if Israel were to cease to be, then the historical embodied reality of divine sonship would have died. If God were to abandon His sons and daughters, of what value would sonship be? When the church calls Jesus the son of God, therefore, it must also confess Israel to be God's sons and daughters. Because this one son has claimed and loves us Gentiles

[6]See Martin Hengel, *The Son of God* (Philadelphia, 1976).

as his younger brothers and sisters, so we are called to love the Jews as also our elder brothers and sisters.

It has been said that Jesus is what separates us from the Jews. In point of fact this was not true for the first two generations of the church, and it is only superficially true today.[7] The author of the letter to the Ephesians, however, saw Jesus as the one who united Jews and Gentiles (Eph. 2:13ff.). A triumphal church has tended to read Ephesians as though it claimed that there was no longer any validity in a Judaism that did not accept Jesus as the only way to the Father. But Ephesians is not that explicit. Its author addressed our precursors as "you, Gentiles. . . . who were without God." Jesus, he claimed, had now brought them near who were far off. In our terms, they had been drawn into the Way; in Ephesians terms, they were "no longer aliens in a foreign land, but fellow-citizens with God's people." This new gathering, which we call the church, was by the author's time made up of Jews and Gentiles. It had begun only with Jews. Then came the Gentiles and "in Christ" (that is, in the church) the distinction Jew/Gentile was unimportant. But within another generation or two, Gentiles far outnumbered Jews in the church. Not long afterwards, the church had become an almost completely Gentile enterprise. All that while, however, God's people, the Jews, were still there, still God's people, still those whose citizenship alone makes sense of our "fellow-citizenship." The historical root of the fact that there came to be a Gentile way, alongside of Israel's way of being in the Way, is Jesus, God's only son to bring about this strange new development.

The son of God, in scriptural usage, is clearly not God Himself. He (she, they) is one called and chosen of God, beloved of God and faithful to God. Israel is God's son (Exod. 4:20, Hos. 11:1). Solomon is God's son. So is the King (Ps. 2:7). So is every faithful Israelite (Hos. 1:10). In the early movement of the Way, however, Jesus was called God's son in a special sense, which we can begin to mark with a capital: God's Son.

In Martin Hengel's words,

> Jewish thought and language concerned with a mediator of revelation and salvation at the beginning and the end of time almost forced Christianity to interpret Jesus' preaching and actions, his

[7]Our different understanding of Torah and of redemption have been, in fact, more fundamental.

claim to be God's eschatological messianic ambassador, his unique connection with the Father, the imminence of whose salvation he announced, his shameful death and his resurrection...in a concentrated form as a unique, eschatological saving event.[8]

"Almost forced"? Well, Hengel has shown that it was consistent, a likely historical development, for he has shown that such ideas as preexistence, mediation at creation and the idea of "sending into the world" were all "typically Jewish."[9] Clearly the earliest followers of the risen Christ wanted to say, as we still want to say, that this event was truly God's doing. Did Jesus have a unique connection with the Father? Yes, in the precise sense of being the one Jew through whom salvation came to the Gentiles, providing entry into God's Way ahead in the history of His creation. Jesus as Son was indeed unique as God's effective call to the Gentiles. Whether this event was eschatological, however, is another and complex question. It surely has to do with God's final end, his ultimate purposes, if it has anything to do with God's will at all. For if this event was God's doing—and so we claim—then it must reveal God's will that there be already, before the end, a way for the Gentiles to be in His Way.

Hengel, however, then goes on to argue:

It was impossible [in the earliest years, immediately after Easter —i.e., probably before Paul joined the movement] to stop at a simple adoptionist Christology...because this would have continued to give God's action...with his people Israel under the old covenant an independence from his conclusive, eschatological revelation in Jesus. . . . The whole revelation of God, the whole of salvation in Christ Jesus...could not remain one 'episode in salvation history' among others.[10]

To this interpretation we must object. I agree fully that an adoptionist Christology, simple or otherwise, is inadequate—that is, it constitutes a radical break with the way in which our conversation started—but hardly for Hengel's reason. Adoptionism constitutes a break because it sets the man Jesus, rather than God, as the initiator or his significance, an idea which is contrary not only to all of the known writers of the apostolic communities, but also to what they present as the teaching of Jesus himself. Such a break in the conversation is not thereby ruled out. It would have to come, however, with an argument for its acceptance. What happened in the event of the life, teaching, actions and death of Jesus, as confirmed by the resurrection, is, the church claims, the manifestation of God's will that there be a Way for the Gentiles. He opened for us Gentiles a way to the Father and so a Way into the future with God. What happened in him, therefore, cannot be "just" or "merely" one episode in a string of others. It marks a genuine *novum*, a new beginning, a step out from and beyond the circle of God's living covenant with His people Israel. But it surely cannot annul or detract from that

[8]*The Son of God*, p. 72

[9]Ibid.

[10]Ibid., p. 90.

covenant. God was not double-crossing Himself in the cross of Christ. This new move toward the Gentiles fulfills in part one of the promises of His covenant with Israel: The God of Israel was known by Israel and is known by Israel to this day as the God of the whole universe.

To question, as Hengel does, whether the covenant is independent of this new event is to confuse matters in the most serious way. The dependency is the reverse: This new event is new precisely in its historical development out of and reliance upon the validity of the one covenant of God with His peole. The new event or development is the beginning of the further aspect of God's relationship with His creation, whereby He began to provide in addition a way for Gentiles to be in the Way, God's own Way in which Israel has been walking or trying to walk from the beginning, and in which it still tries to walk.

The revelation in Jesus, then, was and is "conclusive" of neither more nor less than this radically new beginning for the Gentile church, which for the church was consequently the whole revelation of God and the whole of salvation. Whether it is an eschatological event, however, is a matter in part to be answered by the fact that the end has not come. It is related to that end, but it is not that end. In any case, the importance and validity of God's work in Jesus Christ cannot, with Hengel, be used to contradict God's unity with His people, for just that unity is the basis and foundation of His unity with His Son Jesus Christ and so His unity with the church.

Historically, the unity of the Father and the Son was worked out in other terms, those of God and His Word. The classic text for this development was the opening of the Fourth Gospel: "When all things began, the Word already was. The Word dwelt with God, and what God was, the Word was. The Word, then, was with God at the beginning, and through him all things came to be; no single thing was created without him." This is a picture derived from Jewish wisdom poetry: wisdom as God's way of work, in Creation and in history. God and His Word, God and His wisdom; both mean no other than God and His eternal plan or purpose. God's word is the presence of God in prophetic utterance or His activity in Creation: "For he spoke and it was done" (Ps. 33:9). God said "Let there be light" and there was light. Our English translations lose the immediacy of word and creation, for the Hebrew uses the identical letters to say "let there be light" and "there was light." God's word is not only creative, it is also history-shaping, calling Abraham out of Ur, sending Moses to lead his people out of Egypt and above all at Sinai.[11]

[11]George Foot Moore's *Judaism in the First Centuries of the Christian Era* (New York, 1971 [1927]), vol. I, pp. 414-19, is a helpful guide to the scriptural and early Jewish use of "the word of God."

And now, claims the author of the Fourth Gospel, "the Word became flesh."

"He came to his own, and his own did not receive him," said the author (v. 11). What are we to make of this? Were not Mary and Joseph "his own"? And Peter and Andrew and James and John? And the crowds who are reported to have heard him gladly? And the many priests and Pharisees who joined the young Jesus movement according to the author of Acts? Had not these who were "his own" received him, there could have been no talk of any others "who received him, who believed in his name" (v. 12). In fact some of "his own" did receive him, so the author must have had in mind the later development, when most of the Jewish people, under the leadership of the rabbis of Javneh and their successors, were beginning to consolidate and develop a revived response to the word of God as already heard from Sinai. The word heard in Jesus of Nazareth was coming in a voice by then so tinged with the Gentile accents of the new church that the rabbis felt it better to stay with what they knew Israel had already heard. Thus it was that "his own received him not," and just this fact set the young church more rapidly on its way among the Gentiles, so that among them, "to all who received him, who believed in his name, he gave power [i.e., a legitimate claim] to become [alongside of "his own," God's faithful people] children of God" (v. 12).

God's plan and purpose was hatched in history, a plan to bring Gentiles into the Way, to take one further step with His creation than He had so far made. A plan which was hatched in God's mind from the beginning, before Creation (or, as the classical creeds have it, "begotten of his Father before all worlds, begotten not made"), was now hatched in history: "the word was made flesh" (v. 14). The intimate relation of this Word with the Word to Israel must be observed. The word to Israel was that it sanctify the name of God, with the promise that this would bear fruit among the Gentiles. Now, in a new and unexpected way, the promise began to be realized. The new Gentile reality, the church, as it soon became, could never replace Israel, but it could by its very existence be a witness to the fruitfulness of Israel and of God's Word to Israel from of old. Now, as the earliest church saw it, there had come a man, in every way a human being like all others, or at least like all other Jews, who by God's prior purpose embodied Israel's light for the Gentiles (Lk. 2:32a) and so to be for the glory of his people Israel (v. 32b).

If Jesus were understood in any way that did not add glory to his people

Israel, then there would be grounds to wonder whether he could provide light for the Gentiles. Insofar as the church has not understood Jesus as contributing glory to his people Israel, to that extent he has not provided light to the Gentile church, but only darkness, or at best a distorted light.

It is in fact to the glory of Israel, if the church would but acknowledge it, that Jesus has become historically light for the Gentiles as God's Word to the Gentiles. He was and is a man, a Jew, not a second God, heaven forbid, not a deified man, but just a man. Only the LORD is God. But in the words of Jesus—"Come unto me!" and "I am with you unto the end of the ages"—many Gentiles have heard God's Word for the first time. What Jesus was and is we confess to be truly *God's* plan, His Word to us, a Word truly new yet which was God's plan from the beginning, "before the world was founded" (Eph. 1:4). God, the Spirit of Holiness, has caused His light to shine for us Gentiles in the face of Jesus Christ (2 Cor. 4:6) and by him drawn us to walk in His Way.

For us Gentiles in the Way, then, Jesus is not the LORD, but our Lord, the one Jew who has given us access to the God of the Jews. The categories of *hypostasis*, nature, substance and essence in which the fourth and fifth century church fathers "worked this out" (the "working out" had often more the appearance—perhaps the reality—of a power-struggle than that of a constructive conversation of those who walk together) are hardly the most appropriate or adequate, so think many of our day, for a matter as personal and historical as the events surrounding Jesus Christ. Nevertheless, in their own way those fathers wanted to maintain the genuine humanness of Jesus together with their conviction that the LORD, the God of Israel, was unqualifiedly involved in, committed to and responsible for what had happened concerning that human being. We too seek words to say that the LORD, the God of Israel, was fully involved in this new thing and therefore involved in our Gentile affairs, which He therewith made His own.

From the course of events of the first century, we judge Easter to be God's endorsement of a Gentile entrance into that relationship of love that He had with His people. Gentile intrusion into God's history with Jesus of Nazareth, however, took place first of all in the person and act of Pontius Pilate. Easter signaled God's willingness and ability to make use of that Gentile intrusion—as the followers of Jesus judged from the first and have continued to judge ever since—and to turn that negative and brutal Gentile intervention into a blessing for countless other Gentiles. A dead Jew hanging from a Gentile gallows is where it has been given to countless Gentiles, at least at moments, to see the heart of the God of Israel. If God has for His own reasons been more often silent than vocal, then it has been the cross of Jesus that has echoed that silence for countless Gentiles.

Whether with a silence that was the silence of God, however, or as a Word from the Father of mercies, that unspoken or at times uttered Word became flesh for us Gentiles in Jesus of Nazareth. God's eternal plan to lead all His creation into the Way of peace took a new step, concretely and historically, toward its total realization. Jesus, who has and continues to embody that plan, and so who is God's Word and Son, was given over to the Gentiles, so that Gentiles through him might worship and know the love of the LORD, the God of Israel. Through Jesus, the Son of God, we dare to join Israel and call on God as our Father too.

GOD OUR FATHER

The One whom we worship and dare to call our Father, the only God we know, is the LORD, the God of Israel, who by His Spirit through His Son has drawn us Gentiles into His Way. Our God is known by us, therefore, as first of all the God of Abraham, Isaac and Jacob, the God of the Jews, who watches over and provides for that which He has begun. He is the God who perseveres in preserving the Way and its goal of peace. And so He is the One who preserves Israel in the Way, as Father and Shepherd. Rabbinic texts along this line are numerous. An example cited by Solomon Schechter is characteristic:

> Indeed, the Holy One, blessed be he, says to Israel, you are my flock and I am the shepherd, make a hut for the shepherd that he come and provide for you; you are the vineyard and I am the watcher, make a tent for the watcher that he guard you; you are the children and I am the father, — it is a glory for the father when he is with his children and a glory for the children when they are with their father; make therefore a house for the father that he come and dwell with his children.[12]

[12]*Aspects of Rabbinic Theology* (New York, 1961), pp. 48f. (reference to *Exod.R.* 33:3).

We confess this same One as triune because that is how He is our God and how He has made us Gentiles to be walkers in the Way, alongside of His people. Because He has done this thing, we trust Him to be as He acts, really the God of Israel who has drawn us Gentiles by His Spirit into the Way through His Son. There have been those in the Way who have felt we should not even try to say anything about who or how God is "in Himself," but be content to speak only of how God is "for us." This distinction, however, appears to rest in large part upon a lingustic mistake. I do not know what it would be to know any person or anything "in itself." As for persons (and we shall have to return to consider the appropriateness of this category in the next step), if I know you "in your relationships," then I know *you*, unless you are a most deceptive person. If I know you as a person, that is *as persons know persons* (i.e., as our life and language work in this respect), then I may have surprises in store for me, but the possibility of novelty does not militate against my being able properly to claim that I know you. I can know you extremely well, indeed, yet always come to know you better, if, that is, you will allow this. It is a serious misunderstanding of the workings of our language, however, if I say that I can really only know your external behavior, the outside of you, so to speak, but that the real you is in principle unknowable. As Wittgenstein observed, we do not see a person writhing in obvious pain and yet say that his feelings are hidden from us. If, then, we have grounds for saying that we know God in His relationship to us (to history, to our world), then this is to know God as He is. God, we must believe, can be trusted to be Himself, especially when and if He relates Himself to us.

Having cleared up this linguistic mistake, we shall not want to continue making use of a distinction between God as He is related or relates Himself to us, perhaps a so-called "available God," and God as He is "in himself"—"the real God" (contra Gordon Kaufman).[13] And since our knowledge of God is of the sort according to which persons know persons, we may recall our readiness to admit the inadequacy of our knowledge of each other, as well as of our own selves. As persons know persons, there is ever the possibility of discovery, of a deeper understanding. In that sense, therefore, it will always be in order to say that God surpasses our understanding. Nevertheless, if we trust God in His relationship with us, then

[13]*God the Problem* (Cambridge, 1972), pp. 95ff., 148ff.

we are trusting that God has made *Himself* available. In which case, we shall want to say that we trust in Him who really is the God of Israel, the Father who is fully Himself in drawing us Gentiles by His Spirit and through His Son into His Way.

In this connection we can see the merit in the insistence of the theological tradition that there must be a doctrine of an "essential," not just an "economic" (i.e., in actions), Trinity. We intend to satisfy this demand — and yet provide an appropriate doxological expression of this — with our earlier formulation: By His Spirit and through Jesus Christ, the Jew of Nazareth, the God of Israel has made Himself to be our Father as well. Thus our confession of God as triune may be at the same time a prayer of thanksgiving. We acknowledge One God, who is Himself in the fullness of what He has done, is doing now and will do for Israel, and also for His Gentile church, and also for His whole creation.

As English-speaking Christians, we should not speak of God in three Persons. No capitalization can convert our present English word *person* into a responsible translation of the terms that were used to work out the early confessions of faith.[14] If *person* is to be used in our conversation concerning God, then we can only say that He is one person, one in the fullness of His personhood. It is almost inevitable that we shall use the word *person* in connection with God because, from the beginning and down through the history of Israel's and the church's ways along the Way, God has always and consistently been spoken of with the terms we use when speaking of our fellow human beings. The point is not that God is considered anthropomorphically. What the *morphe* (form) of *anthropos* (man) may be, other than a statue or picture, I do not know. Be that as it may (and we shall have to return to this question in our next step), what characterizes the tradition of Israel and so also the tradition of the church is the use of personal language, the vocabulary and expressions which we use of persons, when speaking of God.

Within the context of the doctrine of the Trinity, however, the issue on which we have touched makes all the more clear how misleading it is to translate the terms used by the old Fathers with our modern word *person* and say that God is in "three Persons." That can be nothing other than tritheism — an idea of three Gods,

---

[14]Barth's translation of *Hypostasis* — "way of being [Himself]" — remains, in my judgment, the most linguistically, historically and therefore theologically accurate.

however intimately related. No, what we want to say is that the only God of whom we know is the One God of Israel who, without in any way being other than Himself, is precisely the One who as Spirit draws us to Himself through Jesus of Nazareth.

Sometimes it has been said that the doctrine of the Trinity represents a succession in God's revelation: First God made Himself known to Israel—as Father; then He made Himself known in Jesus—as the Son; and finally He made Himself known in the church—as the Spirit. But that is only a modern and superficial version of an old idea long since voted down in our conversations. Just as it is false to all we know of God to say that He changed from being Father to becoming Son, and then changed to become the Spirit, so it is inadequate to think of Him as being Father as he was of old to Israel in any other way than as He is Father now for the Jews and also for the church. Likewise, He who as the Spirit draws us to Himself through the Son, is no other than the Creator and the One who made His covenant with Israel at Sinai. In all his actions—in His love and mercy as in His judgment and anger—He is ever Himself, ever the one God of Israel, whom we Gentiles know as the One who has drawn us by His Spirit to the Son and so to Himself.

Also to be avoided is the misunderstanding known as Modalism. The Spirit, for example, is no mere aspect, part or dimension of God. In gathering Gentiles into the Way as Spirit, God is fully Himself. So also as Son—in this opening of a new Way in which to set us walking, in laying out a path for Gentiles in the Jew Jesus of Nazareth—God is no mere aspect of Himself. In launching and nurturing this new beginning, God was and is He who from the foundations of the world intended the cooperation of His creatures in the completion of His creation.

Both the sequential misinterpretation of the doctrine of the Trinity (Sabellianism) and the three-aspects misunderstanding (Modalism) invite views of human history which clash with the historical realism of biblical narrative. Sabellianism invites us to see the transitoriness and therefore the ultimate insignificance of each preceding period. Modalism suggests the inauthenticity of each stage of history. Both would therefore lead us to question that the God who has called Gentiles into the Way is no other than the God of Israel. Each is therefore in its own way a variation on Marcionism and reveals how deeply rooted was the temptation of that rejected theory. The orthodox doctrine—that is, the one that prevailed in the fourth century of our conversation—alone invites us to see that the God adored by the church is precisely the God who *covenanted* Himself to His people Israel, the God of the Jews, and therefore the God for whom history matters.

At a later stage along the Way the point was reinforced by the teaching that *opera trinitatis ad extra sunt indivisa* — the works of the Trinity are indivisible — meaning all the works of God, Father, Son, Spirit. Anything done that we might at first think of as the work of the Spirit is at the same time in truth the work of Father and Son, and so with the works of the Son and the Father, *mutatis mutandis*. More simply if tautologically put, what God does is really done by God Himself.

More misleading has been talk of the *opera trinitatis ad intra*: the internal operations or relationships within the Trinity. Wonderful things have been said about the relationship of love and mutuality within the fullness of God in His three ways of being Himself. Nevertheless, it seems near to impossible to speak in this way without suggesting something close to tritheism. The Father hatching or begetting His Word and sending His Spirit are the "operations" in question here. But we can avoid the tinge of tritheism if we turn to another line of talk that has marked, in two similar ways, the conversations of both the church and Israel. Both are attempts to speak of the fullness or richness of God's reality. I refer to the patristic (specifically Cappadocian) distinction between the operations or agencies of God and God's nature or essence and the Jewish (specifically Kabbalistic) distinction betwen the *Sefiroth* (emanations) of God and the *En Sof* (the eternal essential reality of God).

Gregory of Nazianzus put it thus in a lovely passage from his Second Theological Oration:

> I was running to lay hold on God, and thus I went up into the Mount, and drew aside the curtain of the cloud, and entered away from matter and material things, and as far as I could I withdrew within myself. And then when I looked up, I scarce saw the back parts of God; although I was sheltered by the rock, the Word that was made flesh for us. And when I looked a little closer, not the first and unmingled nature, known to itself — to the Trinity, I mean; not that which abides within the first veil, and is hidden by the cherubim; but only that nature which at least reaches to us. And that is, as far as I can learn, the majesty, or, as holy David calls it, the glory which is manifested among the creatures, which it has produced and governs. For these are the back parts of God, which he leaves behind him, as tokens of himself, like the shadows and reflections of the sun in the water, which shows the sun to our weak eyes, because we cannot look at the sun himself, for by his unmixed light he is too strong for our powers of perception.[15]

God's own holy being, his "first nature" is hidden, and what we know of God is only God as he "reaches to us." Note that God's triune being is in the first category, "known only to itself." And this, it seems, we know only by "the tokens of himself," all that creatures can know of their Creator.

[15]*Library of Christian Classics*, vol. III, pp. 137f.

Gregory of Nyssa, in his essay "That We Should not Think of Saying There Are Three Gods," developed the distinction more carefully:

> We however, following the suggestions of Holy Scripture, have learned that His nature cannot be named and is ineffable. We say that every name, whether invented by human custom or handed down by the Scriptures is indicative of our conceptions of the divine nature, but does not signify what that nature is in itself. . . . The divine nature in itself is not signified by any of these terms. Rather is some attribute declared by what is said. . . . We perceive, then, the varied operations of the transcendent power, and fit our way of speaking of him to each of the operations known to us.[16]

The function of this distinction between God's ineffable "nature" and his "operations" is to hold together the absolute unity and integrity of God with the richness of God's life and activity, as these are praised in Scripture and in the life of the church. It is as if these men wanted to say that the unity of God is no bare unity, not a dead unity, but full and alive, and the diversity of God's fullness is in no sense a divisive or divided diversity, but the fullness and richness of just the one God.

Judaism's mystical tradition developed this idea in a far richer manner, especially in the writings of medieval Kabbalists. Gershom Scholem has magisterially brought together the work of these mystics in a number of studies, from which we draw only a few samples. The ten *Sefiroth*, according to Scholem, are "the potencies and modes of action of the living God. The Kabbalistic doctrine of the dynamic unity of God, as it appears in the Spanish Kabbalists, describes a theogonic process in which God emerges from his hiddenness and ineffable being, to stand before us as the Creator."[17] These potencies form the "unfolding of the divine unity."[18] The last of the ten is the *Shekhinah*.

> In Talmudic literature and non-Kabbalistic Rabbinic Judaism, the *Shekhinah*—literally in-dwelling—namely of God in the world—is taken to mean simply God Himself in His omnipresence and activity in the world and especially in Israel. . . . Nowhere in the older literature is a distinction made between God Himself and His *Shekhinah*. . . . Here the *Shekhinah* becomes an aspect of God, a quasi-independent feminine element within Him. . . . This mythical conception of the feminine principle of the *Shekhinah* as a providential guide of Creation achieved enormous popularity among the masses of the Jewish people, so showing that here the Kabbalists had uncovered one of the primordial religious impulses still latent in Israel.[19]

[16]Ibid., pp. 259f.

[17]*On the Kabbalah and Its Symbolism* (New York, 1969), p. 100.

[18]Ibid., p. 101.

[19]Ibid., pp. 104f.

One more passage from Scholem:

> In so far as God reveals Himself, He does so through the creative
> power of the Sefiroth. . . . But to the mystics it [i.e., the world of
> the *Sefiroth*] was divine life itself, insofar as it moves toward Crea-
> tion. . . . This life as such is not separate from, or subordinate to
> the Godhead, rather it is the revelation of the hidden root, concern-
> ing which . . . nothing can be said, and which the Kabbalists called
> *en-sof*, the infinite. But this hidden root and the divine emanations
> are one.[20]

Here too, the sense of God's fullness and richness was not thought to
qualify in any way the unity of God. These words, however, come from
the conversation of those other walkers in the Way—the Jews—and it is
not for us to say to them that they are saying just what we are. What we
may say to ourselves, however, is that we hear words which to us seem
similar enough to stimulate our own conversation and to encourage us to
think that we do indeed worship the LORD, the God whom they worship.
They further encourage us to think that we too are praising the fullness of
the unity of the one God, the Holy One of Israel.

The mystery of the Trinity is the mystery of a historical
event—the gathering of a Gentile church into the worship of
Israel's God. It is no surprise, then, that St. Augustine's attempt to
find reflections of God's triunity—*vestigiae trinitatis*—in the
natural world or in the make-up (as he conceived it) of the individual soul should end in self-confessed failure. He was looking
in the wrong place. His effort, however, is to be taken seriously, as
Karl Barth perceived, as a recognition of the problem of finding
words with which to speak of God. His search for *vestigiae trinitatis*
in nature sprang from the thought that the Creator as the supreme
artist had left signs of Himself in His creation.

As Augustine had no idea of the historical rootedness of the
Genesis Creation stories, so he had no awareness of the historical
rootedness of the doctrine of the Trinity. He did not see the Creation stories as an expression of the creative formation of Israel in
the Exodus and at Sinai, and he did not see the doctrine of the
Trinity as an expression of God's gathering to Himself of a Gentile
church. Overawed as he was by the fact that he as a sinner had
been called by God, he did not see the greater mystery that he, a
Gentile sinner, had been touched by the Holy One of *Israel*.

If the historical roots of both teachings are recognized, it should

[20]Ibid., p. 35.

be possible to see that there is one other model for the doctrine of the Trinity, one other way of speaking of God that can shed light on this doctrine. It would have to be that other creative act of this one God in which He was utterly Himself and so made Himself and His Way known to men: the gathering of His people Israel and His revelation from Sinai. The teaching, that God revealed His will from Sinai, has been as central for Judaism as the doctrine of the Trinity has been for the church and for the same reason: In each the wonder of revelation in His drawing of His worshipers to Himself is praised.

Sinai, however, is hardly a *vestigia trinitatis*. It is a historical event, as is that later event of the ingathering of Gentiles into the church of the God of Israel. The two have the consistency of the work of One Author. When we Gentiles look to the former of the two, Sinai, we see there as we see later the saving work of Him whom we worship with the language of triunity, for we worship Him also as our God.

Speaking of God:
The Nature and Attributes of God

INTRODUCTION TO THE PROBLEM

During our second step, we discussed our talk of God with special attention to the identity of Him of whom we speak. In the fourth, we analyzed the form of this talk which results from the fact that we are Gentiles who worship and therefore speak of Israel's God. With at least this much clarity about what we think we are doing when we speak of God, it is now in order to reflect on the validity of this talk and to face up to some problems of speaking of God which such reflection brings to the surface. The problems which we shall consider have come up in our conversation many times, but since they occur to us in their own way today, we must find a contemporary manner in which to deal with them.

We may begin by recognizing that, for all of us at some time and for some of us much of the time, there is something slightly preposterous in this last quarter of the twentieth century in speaking of God at all, let alone the God of the Jews. It is clear to most of us by now that what we call secularity is no mere passing phenomenon. Apparently increasing numbers of fellow human beings can and do seem to carry on without any serious reference to God at all in either the public or private realm, and this is at last as true of the Jewish people as it is of those whose ancestors were, but are themselves no longer, part of our conversation in the Way. Most of the citizens of Israel, for example, consider theirs a secular state and apparently many if not most Jews think of themselves not as the chosen people, but as the secular descendants of those who once so defined themselves. As for church membership, if it is not dwindling in absolute numbers, it constitutes an ever smaller proportion of the world's population. In the face of these facts, Christians and Jews who worship the God of Israel have become what one Israeli scholar has called "a partnership of losers."

That is a refreshingly open comment on our situation, but it is misleading, since it defines our situation from a perspective which begs the question. It looks upon our human enterprise and within that counts the size of the Jewish and Christian movements and finds them getting relatively smaller. It counts losers and winners, success and failure, on a scale that has been drawn up on a hidden premise. The hidden premise is just the point, however, for God is no part of this premise. Whether God, His plan or His creation is in any way a loser by the changing number of those who attempt to walk in His ways has not been settled. Our diminished actual or relative numbers would make us "a partnership of losers" only on the assumed premise of secularity.

The foregoing remarks illustrate how easy it is for us to make a mistake about how to move at this point. Indeed, a surrender to the premise of secularity is being urged by some theologians.[1] We are being asked to accept as our own a "contemporary scientific world view" because, so it is claimed, Christian faith "is at heart none other than the most adequate articulation of the basic faith of secularity," defined as "that fundamental attitude which affirms the ultimate significance and final worth of our lives, our thoughts, and actions, here and now, in nature and history."[2]

Before we lift a foot to take our next step, we had better make sure the other foot is on solid ground. Is there solid ground under us if we maintain the view that secularity, the spirit of the age, or the "contemporary scientific world view" warrants such confidence? And are we on solid ground if we suppose that our tradition or "Christian faith" affirms ultimate significance and final worth to our lives, thoughts and actions? It would seem not. It is no denigration of the achievements of the natural sciences and the use

---

[1] David Tracy seemed to be coming close to this in *Blessed Rage for Order* (1975), as was I in *The Secular Meaning of the Gospel* (1963).

[2] Tracy, op. cit., p. 8.

of the scientific method to hold that the extension of their approach to the scale of a world-view is hardly itself scientific. Indeed, just this extension, this pretension to science in matters which no responsible scientist would claim to be able to handle, is a root of the disease within modern culture. The abstracting, generalizing rationality that has worked such wonders in the history of modern science has, when applied to our larger social life, brought us such results as the murder of six million Jews and God knows how many others, not to speak of the horrors of Hiroshima. At best, the consequences of our modern world-view, which has ordered our present world as we find it, is hardly such as to inspire confidence.[3]

The conversation of those Gentiles who have been trying through many centuries to find and keep to God's Way, has surely sounded the themes of the significance and worth of human life. We have, it must be added in honesty, been clearest about that worth when we talked of the lives of Christians, for we have been singularly unclear about that worth when the lives in question happened to be those of Jews. But one looks in vain for voices in that conversation that were prepared to say that the significance of human life was ultimate or that the value was final. Perhaps the nearest to such a claim is that significance and worth centered in the one reality precisely excluded by the faith of secularity— God.

St. Bernard of Clairvaux, one of the more fascinating but not the most attractive of those who have walked before us, spoke more characteristically for the tradition in this matter, in his fifth sermon on the Dedication of a Church, which Calvin quoted approvingly (*Institutes*, III, ii, 25). Having reflected on the misery and evil of man, he concluded this first line of reflection: "Man has been reduced to nothing (Ps 72:22 *Vg.*). Man is nothing. Yet how can he whom God magnifies be utterly nothing? How can he be nothing upon whom God has set his heart?

Brothers, let us take heart again. Even if we are nothing in our own hearts, perhaps something of us may be hidden in the heart of God. Oh Father of Mercies, Oh Father of the miserable, How can you set your heart on us...For where your treasure is, your heart is also. But how are we your treasure if we are nothing? "All nations are as nothing before you, they will be accounted by you as nothing" (Isa. 40:17). So, indeed, before you, not within you; so in the judg-

[3]For an opposite judgment of those same consequences, see M. Diamond, "Miracles," *Religious Studies* 9 (1973): 307-24.

ment of your truth, but not in the intention of your faithfulness. So indeed you call those things which are not as though they were (Rom. 4:17). And they are not, therefore, because it is the things that are not that you call, and they are at the same time, because you call them. . . . We, I say, are, but in the heart of God. We are, but by his dignifying us, not by our own dignity.

There indeed is an affirmation of the significance and worth of human life that comes close to warranting the adjective ultimate, for it is found in that which is believed to be ultimate. This, however, is hardly the faith of secularity!

The secular character of the age poses in a new way for us an old question: to whom are we responsible in our relations with the rest of the world? Do we owe an answer first of all to the secular age, or do we owe our first answer to each other? I would suggest that we can be no more responsible to our age and the world than by being responsible to each other before God, and to God out of the concrete history in which we find ourselves. We shall offer our account, therefore, to each other and before God of what we mean in speaking of Him in whom we trust.

THE PRESENT FORM OF THE PROBLEM

Most of us are more or less acutely aware that our present situation is different not only from that of the men and women who first set out upon the Way, but also from that of those who followed on this walk for many centuries thereafter. Somewhere along the line — perhaps beginning with the Renaissance, more clearly with the rise of modern science, and brought to focus under the impact of the industrial and technological leap of the past century — a shift, frequently referred to as the rise of secularity, has taken place.

This shift is reflected in the judgment that miracles no longer happen. That conception of the change, however, is question-begging and really tells us only about a shift in our understanding of the miraculous. It is usually assumed today that miracles are divine interventions into the natural order of the world and that what the ancients took to be such interventions can better and more accurately be described in terms of the natural world. Apart from the value judgment, this is not be to denied. Most people do seem to use this modern definition of miracle, and no doubt we do manifest a preference for natural explanations. The thesis that miracles no longer occur is therefore analytically true: Miracles cannot occur when defined so as to be impossible.

The same difficulty arises with the common observation that God no longer appears to do any mighty works in the world. All the mighty works which now take place are, for better or worse, those of men or nature. Here again the claim begs the issue. Was not the Exodus under Moses the work of man, especially the man Moses and indirectly the man Pharoah? And was not Torah given to the Israelites by the mouth of Moses? Was it not David who took Jerusalem and Solomon who built the Temple? Was it not Cyrus who sent the exiles home to Jerusalem? Indeed was it not Jesus who forgave men their sins and Pilate who had him nailed to a cross? And did not Paul dare to say that "as by man came death, by man came also the resurrection from the dead"? The common view that God no longer works in history ignores such testimony and instead sets up the problem as a conflict between the natural and the supernatural; but the supernatural is thought of as being both of the same sort as the natural and also outside of it. Hence it is as if an act of God would be in all respects like an act of man or nature, yet at the same time be excluded from this category. Small wonder that such acts do not occur.

I should like to introduce a less self-contradictory approach to this issue by considering the contrasting responses of Dietrich Bonhoeffer and Richard Rubenstein to the assumed nonintervention of God as a "supernatural" power that works natural effects. Bonhoeffer, in his final letters from prison, was feeling his way to a fresh understanding—fresh as least for him—of the workings of God and man. His view was that there was taking place a change in their relationship, which he put in focus by speaking of man's "coming of age," our coming to adulthood and having to learn how to live and act on our own responsibility. Just this, as Bonhoeffer saw it, was what God had been leading us to do. It was almost as if, in Bonhoeffer's familial imagery, the parent were retiring intentionally or at least holding himself back, not offering the helping hand so needed by the young child so that the young adult would learn to get along on his or her own without parental help. It was no part of Bonhoeffer's imagery that the youth should then start pretending that its parent had never existed. His point was rather that we had our parent to thank all the more for a love that conferred freedom.

Rubenstein made a similar discovery, but his imagery is different.[4] For him the old way is presented by the spirit of Rabbi Johanan Ben Zacchai, who saw the handwriting on the walls of Jerusalem under siege, bowed to the inevitable, gave up resistance to the Roman army and began, with the academy in Javneh, the great development of rabbinic Judaism that taught submission and willingness to give up political claims. If restoration was to come to Israel, it must come by God's own doing.

Rubenstein's contrasting figure is that of the Zealots of Masada, who continued the fight for three years and finally died by their own hand rather than survive as Roman slaves. In contrast to the Zealots of Masada, rabbinic Judaism took a way that led to the Holocaust. The way of Masada leads to the Warsaw ghetto rebellion and Israel's War of Independence.[5] Masada was the work of men who recognized that if they were to survive, they would have to save themselves. The state of Israel exists because Jews resolved to take action themselves rather than wait for a restoration which God seemed never to provide. After Auschwitz, Rubenstein is convinced, no sense can be made of the God of Jewish tradition. If Rubenstein has no place for God as Bonhoeffer was trying to understand Him, he shares with Bonhoeffer a sense of the need for men to turn from dependence upon a God who does not rescue to human responsibility for their own future.

What Bonhoeffer was attempting and what Rubenstein has refused is a move clearly reflecting the thesis with which Calvin opened his *Institutes*: Our knowledge of God and our knowledge of ourselves are intimately related. If we find that we must change our views of ourselves, then with that will come changes in our understanding of God. If we are to speak of ourselves as being responsible for history, then we shall have to find a way to speak of God that corresponds. As we proceed to give an account of our understanding of God, we shall, at each step, have to correlate this with our account of ourselves.

Although what we say about God and what we say about

[4]*After Auschwitz* (Indianapolis, 1966).

[5]For a quite different interpretation of these alternatives, see J. Neusner, *First Century Judaism in Crisis* (Nashville, 1975), pp. 156f.

ourselves are related, they are nevertheless distinct. Rudolf Bult-mann's much quoted remark that, when we speak of God we are always at the same time speaking of ourselves, is correct only if this distinction is made clear. We do not speak of God by speaking of ourselves in a very loud voice, as Karl Barth remarked. When we speak of God, we are speaking of Him and of Him alone, however many implications this may have for what we shall then have to say of ourselves. Bultmann's thesis is made less ambiguous if we correct it to read: When we speak of God, our words imply certain things that we shall have to say of ourselves.

In reconsidering the relationship of our thoughts about God and ourselves, it will be helpful to set them in the context of our concept of Creation. When we speak of God, it is always as creatures speaking of our Creator. We know God always as the One who has created us and is therefore as different from us as the Creator would have to be from every one of His creatures. As creatures, we speak of One who stands in a unique relationship to us.

But how can this be? How can creatures speak of their Creator? There is and must be something fantastic in the very idea of creatures presuming to use their creaturely ability to talk, an art and activity developed for the purpose of living a creaturely existence, of their Creator. To what could we possibly liken Him, then? How could His thoughts be our thoughts? Is not such an undertaking to be judged at least presumptuous ad ultimately utile? How is this apparently vain thing possible?

The possibility of creatures speaking of their Creator has frequently been accounted for by the idea that God, a Being so other than us that we could not know Him, has accommodated Himself to our condition. Not by the power of our concepts or wisdom are we able to know God, it has been said, not by the arts and powers of human speech can we speak of God, but only by the love of God who, as it were, lowers Himself to our plane. He speaks to us in such a way that we can hear and understand Him as we would a fellow creature. Our creaturely words of praise can reach to His heart because He condescends to hear and understand us in our own creaturely terms.

This theory of divine accommodation or condescension is not without its problems, chief of which is that it reflects an inadequate understanding of Creation. The God who speaks to us or to whom we speak seems not to have created a world with which He can be in personal contact without this further act of accommodation. But if we were to say that the fundamental accommodation or condescension of God was in creating the world in the first place, then we will not need to speak of a further accommodation of God in order for Him to be in personal contact with His creation. It is no accident that the theory of divine accommodation was most influentially developed by Calvin, one thoroughly influenced by Augustine's idea that the created world had such a qualified reality that it could not sustain itself.

According to the biblical story of Creation, however, God saw what He had made and called it good. What He called good He had made by His Word. Creation began, according to the story, by God speaking. Grounded in this address, how could either God or the world need any further accommodation in order for God to continue to address His Creation? As for God's human creatures, they too were created by and for God's address. As the second Creation story of Genesis clearly emphasizes, Adam is made responsible and respondent by this address, a condition in no way changed by the so-called "fall." Just by being this creature of this Creator, we are free to call upon and to speak to and therefore of our Creator.

Seen in the light of the staggering idea of Creation, human talk of God is in no sense an odd or improper use of our creaturely language. It would be odd or strange only if we accepted as correct a point of view that already excluded the reality of God, that takes our language to be, not creaturely, but only human.

This is of course the premise underlying the rules of reference which philosophers have derived from the vast array of our use of language to identify any subject of discourse — except of course our Creator — and which not surprisingly leaves no room for reference to Him. God cannot be identified either by location in time and space or by a unique description independent of prior reference to Him.[6] On this premise and following these rules, talk of God cannot even get started.

[6]For philosophical analysis of referring expressions, see J. Searle, *Speech Acts* (Cambridge, 1969), especially pp. 26ff., 72ff. and 157ff.; P. F. Strawson, "On Referring," in *Mind* (1950); and P. Ziff, *Semantic Analysis* (Cornell, 1960). On the problem of God as a referring expression, see, e.g., I. Crombie, "The Possibility of Theological Statements," in B. Mitchell, ed., *Faith and Logic* (London, 1957), pp. 39ff.; V. Preller, *Divine Science and the Science of God* (Princeton, 1967), pp. 4ff.; T. Penelhum, *Religion and Rationality* (New York, 1971), pp. 145f., 155ff. The literature and the problem are discussed in J. Spillman, "The Problem of Theistic Identification" (unpublished dissertation, Temple University, 1978).

Those of us who walk in the Way must realize that we cannot refute such a position on its own premise. Our talk of God always presupposes the conversation of those in the Way, apart from which we would hardly say what we do. Those who are in the Way can make no other response to holders of this other premise than to admit that the Creator is part of our own premise, since we have made this conversation our own. On our own premise, we can only consistently say that our language, precisely as a creaturely activity, is a proper and adequate means for responding to and speaking of our Creator. That is one of the reasons why He has given us tongues and lips. We have the best of reasons for having developed the arts of understanding and dealing with creation in terms of itself, for as creatures we are called to a role within and on behalf of much of the rest of creation, or at least that part of it which we call the earth. As the Psalmist said, "The heavens are the Lord's heavens, but the earth he has given to the sons of men" (Ps. 115:16). But we have also the best of reasons for developing the art of speaking of our Creator, for the Creation is ours always as His gift. So the same psalm ends, "But we will bless the Lord from this time forth and for evermore. Praise the Lord!" (v. 18).

There are indeed problems in how we speak of God, but they are the result neither of attempting to put our creaturely language to a task for which it is not suited, nor of the inconsistency of such talk with the premise of secularity. The problems which we need to take seriously are those which have to do with the coherence of our talk of God with the Way He has given us to walk, that is, with our own premises. These problems of coherence can be considered by reflecting on how we speak of God's person and presence, His power and freedom and His love and suffering.

GOD AS NORMATIVE PERSON

Our conversation about God as we have moved along the Way has been marked by the use of the same verbs, adjectives and expressions which characterize our conversation about ourselves as persons. As we speak of human persons willing, intending, loving and the like, so we have spoken of God. We have spoken to God as we speak to a person, and we have spoken of God as we speak of each other (sometimes) as persons. We learned this way of speaking, of course, from Israel that walked before us, and we have followed, as have the people of God, the lead of Scripture in this matter. In the stories of Creation, man and woman were made "in the image and likeness of God" and Adam became a responsible person by being addressed and found out by God's address, "Adam, where are you?" Made in the image and likeness of God, we too can address each other and so be constituted persons in response to the call of the other. This is a frame of reference in which it makes sense to say that God spoke to Moses "face to face, as one man speaks to another" (Exod. 33:11).

We speak of God as of a person, not as *if* He were a person. We are no more "using the model" of a person when we speak of God than we use the model of a person to speak of each other. Nor are we using a personal analogy when we speak of God. Rather, we are following the lead of Scripture in speaking of God in a way that only makes sense if we admit that God is a person. This admission by no means requires us to say that God and we are the same. Our whole conversation in the Way makes clear that God and human beings are as different as Creator and creature. After all, even among ourselves we do not say that one person is the same as another, for one of the functions of our concept of person is to preserve the particularity of one so designated. When we address each other as persons, we imply the particularity, the unique identity of the other, expecting of the other the response and the responsibility that we do not expect from beings other than personal. Hardly less can be true when we speak of God. To say that God is a person is to imply that we respect His particularity and await from Him all and more than we can hope for from human persons.

The Scriptures, the Apostolic Writings, our own conversation and especially that of the Jews are all marked by a reticence of respect in speaking of God, for He is that one person who is above all and before all to be feared and loved. He is the one person whom we adore and worship, the one from whom we have our personhood by the gift of Creation. He made us in His image and it is therefore from Him that our personal reality is derived (cf. Eph. 3:14f.). God is not just *a* person; He is the normative person. Therefore it is appropriate that we be cautious of speaking of God as a person, lest we forget this priority in the one concept that links

God and human beings. God is that one unique Person by whom we measure what it is for us to be persons.

This reserve in speaking of God is one of respect, not logic. Bultmann's program of demythologizing rests on a logical reserve and invites us into an impossible undertaking. Mythological speaking, according to Bultmann, consists of speaking of the divine in terms of the finite, "of this world." If such speaking is to be rejected for more than cultural reasons, however, then the rejection appears to rest upon taking the classical *finitum non capax infinitum* as a logical rule rather than as a moral reminder. To this we must reply that, if we speak of God at all, we have no words to use but our own. There is no linguistic alternative to speaking of the Creator with creaturely words. In other words, there is no "non-mythological" way to speak of God. Human terms are all we have, so the only issue is which terms to use. We have of course many which are more abstract than those of personhood. Such abstract terms as *force, power,* the *Absolute,* and the *Infinite* have all been tried. These words are no less human for being abstract, no less "of this world."

When we speak of God as a person, we open ourselves to the charge of projecting our self-understanding upon reality. I think we should have the courage to admit that we *are* reading into reality our own awareness of ourselves as persons, for this must be the consequence of our conviction that we are called to do just this by the personal reality who has made us in His image. Our only response to the charge of projection is our conviction that we have in the gift of our created personhood precisely that which makes it proper for us to speak of God as a person. The concept of person, we are saying, is our fundamental bridge term which crosses, by the grace of Creation and revelation, by the grace of our having been made persons in the likeness of the God who is normatively personal, the gulf between the Creator and those of His creatures who have been called by Him to cooperate in completing His work of Creation.

From this point there follow two consequences which must be considered. If God is a person, then His relationship to the world must be and should be conceived to be personal. He would have to be related to His creation as a person is related to the work of his or her hands and to us as a person is or ought to be related to human persons. It would then be wrong to speak of God being related to the world as a self is related to its body. The idea of a relationship between the self and the body, let us say between myself and my body, depends on the validity of the Cartesian dualistic conception of my person being a compound of self and body. On that analysis, "self" and "body" are the primary concepts, denoting the fundamental individual entities, whereas "person" is a secondary and composite entity. This dualistic and secondary conception of "person" leads to the strange conclusion that I am not an individual and that it is actually false to say that a person is responsible for his or her own actions. Presumably the self (whatever that is supposed to be) is the individual and the responsible agent, the body being merely a tool which the self employs.

The conflict between the Cartesian analysis and the workings of our language, not to speak of common sense, has led to another and more satisfying analysis, the thesis of which is that "the concept of person is logically prior to that of an individual consciousness."[7] On this understanding, "person" is the fundamental concept. A person is an individual. John Smith is an individual. Consciousness, even self-consciousness, like embodiedness, is a secondary characteristic of being a person. Self is then seen to refer to nothing other than a person, as when I say that I do not think much of myself or wonder why someone else doesn't put more of themselves into their work.

It follows from this newer and, to my mind, better analysis that the only relationship that there could be between a self and its body would have to be logical. That is, wherever we can locate a person by locating his or her body in time and space, there we are also entitled to say is a person who can speak of his or her self. And wherever a person can speak of his or her self, there we know, logically (no empirical investigation will be needed), is to be found a body. What could not be said is that the self is related to its body (any more than a body to its self) *personally*. Consequently, if God is a person, his relationship to His creation must be personal and therefore not at all the relationship (note that the word *relationship* is here being used in a logical sense) of a soul and a body.

The decision to say that God is a person has another consequence that is more difficult to resolve. In every case other than that of God, the persons we know and relate to are human persons, and an essential feature of their personhood is that they have bodies. Body is as much an aspect of the primary concept "person" as is self. Human persons are embodied selves or enselved bodies.

[7]P. F. Strawson, *Individuals* (London, 1959), p. 103.

Such is the logic of our normal language, as we have argued, and such is also the understanding of persons which we find in the Scriptures. It takes more than a body to make a person but it never takes less. On this view of the concept of person, the idea of a disembodied person is incoherent, and this incoherence is reflected in the fact that the Jewish and Christian hope for a new existence after death—that is, a new personal existence, since only that could matter—takes the form of a hope for the resurrection of the body.

Persons have—or are also—bodies. This holds true for all created persons. We are, however, using *person* as our fundamental bridge term, claiming that God is also, properly speaking, a person, although always of course the normative person. It follows that God must have a body. It is consistent with this logical conclusion that the Scriptures speak freely of God's finger, hand and arm, His voice and mouth, His eye and face. God is said to have talked to Moses "face to face," although at another place Moses is said to have been allowed to see only God's back. Isaiah claimed to have seen the Lord sitting on a throne in the Temple. The scriptural conception of God as a person does not seem to be that of a disembodied person. It is rather that of one who has what logically goes with being, living and acting as a person: a body. Only, God as embodied person is, with the rarest exceptions, unseen.

In the Scriptures, God is never said to be invisible. He is occasionally said to hide Himself or to hide His face (Ps. 10), and it is said that to see God face to face must result in death (Moses on Sinai, Isaiah in the Temple)—a threat which would make no sense if God were in principle invisible. With but the rarest exceptions God is in fact not seen. There is, however, no suggestion that it is logically impossible to see God, only that in fact God does not show Himself or allow Himself to be seen. The term used in the Apostolic Writings (there is no term at all for it in the Scriptures) is therefore best translated "unseen" rather than "invisible." It is not as though God is unseen because there is nothing—no body—to see. Rather, God is unseen because He chooses to hide Himself. His hiding is not a denial of His personhood and so not of His embodied personhood.

This line of reflection appears to run counter to a great deal of what has been said in our conversation up until now. In the Christian tradition from the beginning, and in much of the Jewish tradition prior to Maimonides and in all of it since then, God has been said to be without a body. Every scriptural reference to His face or hand or eye has been almost universally held to be figurative, only properly understood if taken metaphorically. Divine appearances are taken to be visions, accommodations to our human limitations. Indeed, to say that God has or is a body has been judged blasphemous and philosophically impossible. It has been held to threaten the divine unity and in every way to deny God's perfection. Behind this tradition, however, stands a conception of unity and perfection drawn from neither the Scriptures nor from reflection on the concept of person. It rests upon a conception of the body as being imperfect because it can be acted upon. The body has been thought of as a prison of the soul or the tool of the intellect. It would seem that those who have carried on this conversation for so long have thought that there was something more valuable than that which we name with the word *person* and a higher unity than that of a person. We propose a change in how we speak of God primarily because we know no higher unity than that of a person and find the unity of a person to be most fitting as an account of God's unity.

Some important contributions to this agreement which we have had in mind in arguing the contrary are Maimonides, *Guide of the Perplexed*, trans. by S. Pines (Chicago, 1963), *passim*; Thomas Aquinas, *Summa Theologica*, I, Q.3; and Calvin, *Institutes*, I, xi, xii. Of these the most weighty is Maimonides, but whether we are really in conflict is not certain. Leo Strauss's introduction to the cited translation contains the following summary of Maimonides's teaching:

> But this evil [idolatry] can be completely eradicated only if everyone is brought to know that God has no visible shape whatever or that He is incorporeal. Only if God is incorporeal is it absurd to make images of God and to worship such images. Only under this condition can it become manifest to everyone that the only image of God is man, living and thinking man, and that man acts as the image of God only through worshiping the invisible or hidden God alone. (p. xxii)

Reflection on the contemporary form of "this evil" and the recognition that living, thinking, acting, worshiping human beings — persons — are the image of God lead me to think that we are proposing only what appears to be the opposite of Maimonides's concern. The difference between us may come down to the different philosophical backgrounds which have shaped our thinking.

A support for the denial of God's corporeality can be provided by taking the apostolic assertion (John 4:24) that "God is Spirit" as if this were a definition of God's nature rather than of His function, activity or purpose.[8] If "spirit" is thought of as a state or kind of being in contrast to body or physical nature, then God is thought to be without body. The rest of the classical definition will follow: God will then be also without parts or passions. Whatever else may be said of such a God, *person* will hardly be appropriate. A God without feelings, without hands to wring or eyes to weep, who cannot rejoice over the repentance of a single sinner, cannot be personal in any sense of the word. Such a God—more appropriately "It" than "He"—cannot suffer with Its "children" when others of Its "children" ignore Its will and bring all sorts of horrors into Its creation—and we do indeed have Auschwitz in mind here. Such a God can only be a steady-state condition of "everything there is" as it develops or unfolds its process, for the process is here presented in impersonal terms.

Our conversation's characteristic of referring to God with terms implying a personal referent forces us to choose between alternatives, none of which is without problems. Whether we think of God as disembodied, with the classical tradition, or of having the world for His body, or of being embodied in a way that is hidden, we shall end with difficulties, and the choice comes down to which difficulties will least hinder our walking in the Way. If we conceive of God as disembodied, then we are forced to abandon the thought of God as a person, since the logic of the concept "person" rules out the coherence of the idea of a disembodied person. If we say that God is the unique case of a person without body, we are left with the question how the concept "person" can still function here. With the concept "person" in question, God will be more easily conceived as a metaphysical principle, such as a First Cause or a Principle of Creativity. Fortunately for our conversation, we have gone on speaking of God as a person and most of us have not followed the lead of those who have insisted that God is without a body. So-called popular piety has held to a personal God and so always thought of Him as embodied. Popular piety has in this matter shown a truer sense of matters than the theological sophisticates. The classical theologians and philosophers of both church and synagogue, it must be remembered, were not aware of the logic of the concept "person" and so it never entered into their speculations. Once we do become aware of it, however, we are

[8]See G. W. H. Lampe, *God As Spirit* (Oxford, 1977).

forced to reconsider the wisdom of the choice of our tradition to speak of God as disembodied.

Since the idea of a disembodied person is incoherent, the obvious alternative would appear to be to think of the world as God's body. If God has the world or some aspect of it as His body, then He can coherently be called a person. Unfortunately, He could not then be the creator of the world in any sense which we have hitherto had of creation. If the world is God's creation, then God's body is a creature and God as person becomes both Creator and creature. And if the world is God's creation, then it is created not by the person God, but only by God's self or soul. The concept of person is then shattered and becomes a secondary idea constructed out of the supposedly primary concepts "body" and "self." This alternative would therefore appear to be more incoherent than the first. It has, moreover, a disastrous consequence for the concept of God's personal relationship with the world for, whatever the relationship between self and body may be, it can hardly be called personal.

In defense of this alternative it has been claimed that "what I think and feel has its most direct effect on my own brain cells and central nervous system, and thence on the rest of the organism in which I as a self am incarnate."[9] Is it clear what it means to say that my thinking has a direct effect on my brain cells? Surely I do my thinking with my brain cells, so perhaps the activity of those cells has the effect that I call thinking. The claim is entangled in a mind-brain puzzle by no means simply resolved. But we need to recall that, when it comes to the relationship of love, the usual subject of the verb is a person. I can say that I love my body, meaning that as an embodied self I rather like the way in which I am embodied, but it would be odd to say that my self loves my body. Moreover, if with this alternative God as a self loves the world as His body, then we are once more back to the image of classical Aristotelian theology in which God as the unmoved Mover contemplates Himself (or Itself) with utter self-satisfaction and only moves anything else by the sole force of attraction. There is no place here for the sort of relationship to the *other* which is so essential to the concept of love, whether human or divine. Love re-

---

[9] S. Ogden, *The Reality of God* (New York, 1966), p. 58. One helpful therapy for such a case is provided by L. Wittgenstein's *Philosophical Investigations* (Oxford, 1953), e.g., pars. 406-22. Cf. also N. Malcolm, *Problems of Mind* (New York, 1971).

quires a relationship which is interpersonal. On this alternative, the only interpersonal relationship that God could possibly have would have to be with some personal being outside of and distinct from His embodied self and therefore outside of the world. But since the world in this argument is "everything there is other than God," God could have no personal relationship with anything at all. Clearly this is no solution to our problem.

The third alternative is that which we are proposing, since we do not see any others. We propose to say that God is a person and therefore an embodied person. God has a body, His own body, the body of the Creator, but a body which is ordinarily not seen by us. The visibility of God's body depends on His will. It is not by definition invisible. God is as a matter of experience unseen—except when He chooses to show Himself. The advantage of this alternative is that it secures the coherence of our personal conception of God, but it does so at the price of possible incoherence in the concept of body, for God's body is normally unseen, does not prevent God from being present in more than one place at a time, and indeed seems to be unrestricted as to motion and location. To put it another way, once we say that God is an embodied person, we find that we can say nothing clearly about His body. We have thus won a coherent concept of God's personhood at the price of an incoherent concept of His embodiment. The price seems worth the gain, however, for representation of God's embodiment is explicitly forbidden in the Decalogue.

A. J. Heschel's study, *The Prophets*,[10] especially chapters 12-15 (or the first four chapters of the second volume), warrants careful attention in the matter before us, particularly for its nuanced discussion of anthropomorphism. "To speak about God as if He were a person does not necessarily mean to personify Him, to stamp Him in the image of a person," Heschel said (II, p. 53). "The essential error is not in *how* man depicts God, but in depicting Him at all" (II, p. 52). To our conclusion that we can say nothing about God's body, Heschel's argument adds that we ought not even try to do so. Heschel's study, however, adds solid support to our contention that the personal is the decisive link between the God of Israel and His human creatures.

Whichever way we move, we are confronted with the fact that there is some incoherence in our attempts to speak of God. If we

[10]New York, 1962 (in two volumes, 1975).

opt for the concept of person as fundamental, we are left with other problems for which we have no solution. Nevertheless, assuming that we do not give up speaking of God altogether, the third alternative seems preferable and its difficulties are no worse than those of the first two alternatives. The other choices have their own difficulties, and we judge them to be more damaging to the walk in which we are engaged, for only when we have settled for God as a person can we have grounds for being concerned about the consequences for our personal relationship with Him of the manner of our walking in the Way.

Our conclusion needs to be qualified by recalling the voices raised so often in our conversation along the Way reminding us that God is inconceivable, that we can never define or describe God adequately with any of our thoughts or ideas. When people have said this, they have intended more to make a positive than a negative point. They were making an assertion of faith in saying that God is inconceivable, not a complaint that nothing can be said about God at all. There is of course a negative side: To say that God is inconceivable is to acknowledge our limitations as creatures. It is an act of intellectual humility. The thrust of the assertion, however, is primarily positive and, if it were not, I doubt it would have occurred so frequently in our conversation. Positively, the assertion is a confession that our knowledge of our Creator is a gift, that we know Him only because He has given Himself to be known by us. The assertion that God is inconceivable is therefore primarily an act of thanksgiving.

Recalling these voices, we may review our conclusion about God's body. Our concern, it should be remembered, was not to maintain God's embodiment, but to acknowledge His personhood. We spoke of God's body in order to avoid saying that He is disembodied and for the sake of holding fast to the central affirmation which seems essential to our response to the word that our Creator has made us in His image and likeness as persons. If our concept of person in its creaturely application entails the concept of body, then, with due reserve and an appropriate sense of humor, we need not fear speaking of God's body insofar as speaking of His personhood leads us to do so. After all, even with the concept of person we are only doing the best we can as creatures to conceive of our inconceivable Creator.

GOD'S PRESENCE

The implications of the concept of God's personhood can be opened up by considering what we should say about God's presence and, therefore, what we should say about His absence. "Plato thinks of God *in the image of an idea*," said Abraham Heschel, "the prophets think of God *in the image of personal presence*. To the prophets, God was not a Being of whose existence they were convinced in the way in which a person is convinced of the truth of an idea. He was a being Who is supremely real and staggeringly present."[11] In our consideration of God's personhood, we were led to speak of His body by the logic of the concept "person." The difficulty we then acknowledged in saying anything about God's body should not let us lose sight of the fact that the strange notion of God's body is subservient to the major matter of God's personhood. We do not hear in our past conversation that God's body is unseen. Rather we hear that God is unseen. We should therefore note in Heschel's words just cited that *personal* presence is the central scriptural image of God. The presence which concerns us is that of a person, not just that of a body.

If we talk of presence, then we must also be able to talk of absence. Again, the absence in question will be that of a person. The relationship of the absence to the presence of a person is not simply that of negation. In the context of interpersonal relationships in which each person matters greatly to the other, our sense of the absence of the other can be as acute as our sense of their presence. The other is not simply not there. We are, or can be, acutely aware of the other precisely as being absent. Because God is a person, our concern is with this sort of presence and absence.

The conversation of those who have walked before us has generally focused on God's presence, for it was often said that God was present at all times to all places—that He was omnipresent. That conception of presence, however, is in danger of becoming impersonal. Perhaps it would be better to say that God can be wherever He chooses to be.

Aquinas proposed an interesting interpretation of the idea of God's omnipresence: "He fills every place by the very fact that He gives being to

[11]A. Heschel, *The Prophets*, vol. II, p. 55.

the things that fill all places."[12] Evidently Aquinas was assuming an Augustinian idea of creation, according to which God did not give independent existence to His creatures, but only a dependent, conditional existence, the condition being that He continue to sustain the world in existence at every moment. If, however, God has created the world without such a condition, as we would prefer to say, if His love is such as to confer freedom, especially the freedom to exist, then God's being in the relationship to creation as a person is to all he or she has made would satisfy Aquinas's concept of God "filling every place." Aquinas is clear that God is not everywhere the way a body might be in all places. On our own premises, then, and using our language in its usual sense, we would not be contradicting Aquinas if we were to say that God is not everywhere, not omnipresent.

There have been times when one or another of us in the Way has been aware of God's presence. On the other hand, it seems perfectly possible for God to be present and yet for us not to be aware of it, as was the case with Jacob at Bethel (Gen. 28:16). Since God is ordinarily unseen, present or not, we have no agreed criteria for determining His presence. Perhaps it may depend upon what we are looking for. If we can recall that we are in a Way provided by Him, that we walk in His Way, however stumblingly, then we may come to see the simplest aspects of our life and the world around us as signs of God's presence. Indeed, we may see His presence in the grimmest aspects of life, for surely we must think that God was present when His beloved son Jesus suffered on the cross. If God was not there, where would He have been? Whether Jesus was aware of God's presence is not easy to tell. His cry of dereliction was the opening line of Psalm 22, and it is not even clear whether the Psalmist thought in writing it that God was present for him. Perhaps we can say that he, and Jesus after him, thought that God was at least near enough to hear his cry of dereliction.

If we can believe with one of the apostolic authors that God was at least that near to the cross (Hebr. 5:7), then we have grounds to believe that God was at least that near to His people in their anguish in the Holocaust, as well as in many other sufferings in their past. Whether they were aware of His presence we do not know. Whether they thought He heard their cry we cannot answer. No doubt many thought He was absent or deaf. That, however, raises another matter than that of God's presence or absence. The issue raised by such doubts is that of God's power and freedom.

[12]*Summa Theologica*, I, I, qu. 8, art. 2.

GOD'S POWER AND FREEDOM

What can confuse our reflection on the presence and absence of God is the way we have conceived His power and freedom. It is, as far as I can see, of the utmost importance that we talk about these two matters together. Let us state bluntly the problem which concerns us in our conversation today. It seems to many of us in the Way that God does not have the power that some of our forewalkers claimed that He had, or at least that He does not use today the power which it is thought He used of old. Likewise, it seems to many of us in this conversation that God no longer has the freedom to do what we think He still must will. So marked is this sense of God's lack of power and freedom that some of us not so long back were exploring the thought that God is no longer the living God of history, or (more cautiously) that it no longer made any sense to talk of God at all.[13] These strange thoughts appear to be unnecessary, however, when we reconsider the problem in the light of our present reflections on the personhood of God.

The problem that has bothered many of us for some time now is that God, whom we believe to be loving, seems to have done so little so often to help those whom we believe He loves in situations where His help, indeed any help, was desperately needed. The conclusions to which we are tempted are that God either has no power, that He is not free to help us, that His love is so unlike personal love as to make its affirmation meaningless, or that there is no God to help. Against this apparently powerless God, we are prone to contrast the God of the Bible, who seems to have acted in history, to have rescued His people and to have intervened powerfully in history to carry out His purposes. Has God changed, we have wondered. Is He still there to do anything at all?

Those who appeal to the God of the Bible have in mind perhaps Psalm 135 or 136 — which recite the story of God's mighty deeds in delivering Israel from bondage — but not Psalm 10:1 ("Why stand so far off, Lord, hiding thyself in time of need?"), and certainly not Jeremiah 14:8 ("O hope of Israel, their savior in time of trouble, must thou be a stranger in the land, a stranger pitching his tent for a night? Must thou be like a man suddenly overcome, like a man

---

[13]A thorough discussion of the problem, its background and reasons given for these and related "solutions" will be found in Part I of Langdon Gilkey, *Naming the Whirlwind* (Indianapolis and New York, 1969).

powerless to save himself?"). Our so-called "modern" problem seems to have been around a long time! The "God of the Bible" appears to be no other than the God we find to be so often inactive and silent today.

If God is the normative person, then of course we shall want to say that He can indeed change, as a person can change. Immutability and impassibilty are simply not characteristics of persons. If there were a person who could not change or suffer, we would surely pity such a one for being deprived of the best we know of ourselves. How then can we possibly wish to ascribe to God characteristics which we would never attribute to a friend? Surely God's freedom, His personal freedom to change and to suffer, must be at least as great as our own.

These things may be said without appealing to a supposed change of human consciousness over the past few centuries or to a partial reading of the Bible to support the contention that once God acted in history and now no longer does. God's activity in the world has always been susceptible to other interpretations, and the events of our recent history are in turn open to the interpretation that God is very much a factor in the way things are developing. There is, moreover, a crucial reason for speaking of the power of God to refrain from interfering in history and of His freedom to leave us free to find our own way to walk in His Way.

We are convinced that in the events surrounding Jesus of Nazareth nothing less than the heart of God was opened to us Gentile Christians, so that we may rightly define that Jew as the historical, personal shape of God's own word for us Gentiles, a word not in conflict with His other words and His purpose for His whole creation. As the Word of God, the figure of Jesus confronts us with himself, a human being, who saw himself as God's co-worker, or was so presented in the traditions which came to make up the Apostolic Writings (Jn. 9:4). As God's co-worker, Jesus is presented as having the obligation and the right to forgive men their sins (Mk. 2:5ff and parallels) and to call others to do so as well (Mt. 6:12). He is presented as one in and through whom God's mighty acts took place (Lk. 11:20), and whose own actions required the cooperation of those about him (Mt. 13:58). Above all, we have understood the crucifixion to be God's greatest act; yet where is God to be seen in this act? He was as apparently absent as from the death camps and ovens of the Holocaust. There a human being took evil, hatred and dumb brutality into himself and suffered, and there, we have always said, is to be seen God's own heart; there, we have always said, is where redemption is revealed. But we have not always thought this through with sufficient care.

Anselm of Canterbury's *Cur Deus Homo* is the classic interpretation of the cross as a great transaction carried out over our heads, as it were, all accomplished then and there, once and for all. Man had broken God's law and violated the divine honor, and so man had to pay the price. Since only God could do this, it was necessary that there be a God-man who, as God, could do what man could not and, as man, could accomplish what man had to do. The price having been paid, the debt is cancelled. The matter can be more attractively presented, as in Calvin's theology. There the relationship between Christ and the rest of humanity is more firmly established.[14] The one on the cross became, by the decision of God, the effective representative of all of humanity. But, even at its best, the idea of a great transaction carried out over our heads cannot be denied. And it is just such a trans-historical, trans-personal transaction that is difficult to reconcile with our conviction that we are set by God as persons into His Way in history.

If, as an alternative, we take the cross as the revelation of how God works and what He wills for us, then it may be seen as the eternal sign over the Way that stretches from then until now and into the future—the sign of God's redemptive intent for His creation. We are to act, to live, to be engaged in serving God and whoever is next to us, taking full responsibility for our walking, and by so doing we may discover that God's redemptive goal will have come a step closer to us. We should not expect God to appear in this, as He did not appear on Golgotha. Only after the fact, only looking back, we may want to say with Jacob, "Truly the LORD is in this place; and I did not know it" (Gen. 28:16). And we did not know it because we lacked the audacity to see God precisely in the suffering and the failure of the cross. God steps back to leave us free to work His will, if we will, and suffers with us in all our failures. Therein lies the power and majesty of His infinite freedom, that He is free in the fullest power of personal love to hold back, to sit still and to suffer in agony as His children move so slowly to exercise in a personal and loving way the freedom which He has willed for them to have and exercise.

[14]Paul van Buren, *Christ in Our Place* (Edinburgh, 1957).

Let us take the matter at the hardest point that has yet been presented: Was God involved in the blind, perverse slaughter of a third of His people? Could we in all humility and fear find a way to say that He was and how He was that would fit with what little else we know of this strange Other who has willed the free otherness of His creatures? I think we can say a little and even see it as an act of His love. His act of love, let us be clear, was not that indecent, unspeakable program of "the final solution" to God's election. His act was to suffer in solidarity with His people. Where else would He have been at such a time? Dare we say why He chose to act in this way? Here we must dare to speak for our Creator—a laughable audacity—or remain sullenly silent. Perhaps He was trying to awaken His creatures to their irresponsibility. Perhaps He was trying, by simply suffering with His people, to awaken His church to a new understanding of love and respect for them. The cost seems out of all proportion to the possible gain, so silence may be the wiser choice. One can add, however, that minimal as has been our Gentile Christian response, at least something new has been started by the events of the middle of this century. Seen in this way, God may be detected as being most present precisely when we have thought Him to have been most absent. Or to make the point in its sharpest, but for the church, most central way: God's presence was and is most total in the utterly nondivine, utterly human person of one who could say, "Why do you call me good? No one is good but God alone" (Mk. 10:18). God was most thoroughly Himself in the moment in which this man cried out, "My God, my God, why have you forsaken me?" The God whom we know revealed in this man is present precisely in the history and the events which He has willed that we construct on our own. He is present just where He wills us to be most present. If God is a person, then His presence would have to be of just this sort. We can only say that God is the truth about Jesus if we can first grant that Jesus is for us the truth about God.

This perspective is, I believe, the same as that to which Dietrich Bonhoeffer had come at the end of his life: It is God's will that we live *before Him* as though He were not. To live in full responsibility in the world is precisely to live as God wills us to live whether at the moment He be present or absent.

GOD'S LOVE AND SUFFERING

God so loved the world that He gave. What He gave has to be unfolded. He so loved the world that He gave it its own free existence, its genuine sonship. He gave His world the freedom of otherness, but since He gave freedom to this other, since this was a gift of love, then the freedom was to have been that of sons and daughters, the freedom of personhood and so of responsibility.

Only His peculiar people, Israel, seemed to have an inkling of what this involved—a life of thanksgiving that turned in love to the neighbor. So in order that this might be for Gentiles as well, God gave His Son, the embodiment of His purpose and love in one faithful Jewish son. As by man came death (by and through our own lives and actions, we human beings create most of our own problems) so, for countless Gentiles, by man might come also the resurrection from the dead (since God embodied His love in a Jew for us Gentiles, we are to work out our salvation through our own lives and actions). There, in our human history, God is at work to carry out His purposes.

That the Creator should so love His creatures as to make His own heart's desire depend upon their longing to fulfill His plan bespeaks a love that surpasses understanding. That the Creator can choose to make us creatures His co-workers means that He, in His freedom, has chosen to make Himself our co-worker. And that can only mean that His love shows Him to be a lover who suffers. He suffers in His own right over our failure, our unwillingness to be responsible and our failure to recognize that, when we are most fully taking responsibility, we are only cooperating with Him who is most fully present and active when we are fully present and active. And He suffers in a co-suffering, a sympathy, a suffering along with us, as we suffer in a world which is still so far from the freedom that God has in mind for us as our destiny.

If this sounds different from what has usually been said in the conversation of those who have walked before us, then let us recall that they too have said again and again that God revealed His heart in the cross of Jesus. If we take that seriously, then we must surely see that to suffer is not foreign to God and that, in the moments in history when affairs seem to be most in the hands of human beings and when they seem to be most on their own, precisely then is God most present and most fully disclosed.

If this sounds paradoxical, it is because of a confusion in our thinking. We have said in a variety of ways, over the centuries, that the truth about Jesus is God, sometimes by saying that Jesus is God. But that cannot be the right way to see this matter; Jesus himself insisted he was not God, that he was God's son or servant, in the sense in which Judaism at its best has always known the meaning of sonship. What we Gentiles who worship the God of the Jews must say, grounded in the very fact that we worship the God of the Jews, is that Jesus is the way which God has used to bring us to Himself. So we have been speaking directly from our own historical experience when we have insisted that Jesus the man appeared on the human scene for the sake of what God was about to accomplish through him. And we are right to insist that the God so made known to us is the true God, the One God of Israel.

It is better, then, if we say that Jesus is the truth about God, that the serving, suffering, utterly free person whom we take Jesus to be is what we understand God to be. We know no God but the one whom we have seen in the face of that suffering man. It is therefore not out of order, if extremely hard to say, that God must have been present in the ovens of the deathcamps and in the mass graves of Eastern Europe. Where else could He have been than there precisely where His beloved sons and daughters were being tortured and slaughtered? The God of the philosophers may have withdrawn. The God of Golgotha—who is no other than the God of Abraham, Isaac and Jacob—would have had to be there. Some may have been aware of Him there. Most, perhaps, were not. So it has always been. But to say He was not there because He did not act—independently, as it were, apart from human action, removing from us the responsibility for righting the wrong we had brought about—assumes that God should have done what He could not have done without ceasing to be the God of love and freedom who has in His love conferred responsibility and free creative power on His creatures.

STEP SIX

Light for the Way:
The Bible and the Church

INTRODUCTION

With each new day and step along the Way, we set out with a book
in our hands that tells us of our beginning. The opening words of
that book are "In the beginning. . . ." In all our beginnings, that
book in our hands has been light for our feet to help us get started.
That book is the Bible.

It is to be noted that the light we receive comes from a *carried*
book. It is neither a book once read and left behind, nor a book in
splendid isolation, set in a glass case for us to admire. It has always
been for us in each generation, through all the turns and twists of
the Way we have come, a book very much in our hands. We have
never had it otherwise than with the smudges of our fingers on its
pages, just as we have never read it with other than our travel-
strained and dust-filled eyes.

Historians may tell us how there came to be the presumed original manuscripts of this book we carry in our hands. They can tell
us about the different communities which produced the various
documents that came in time to be put together to form that collection of documents of which we hold a recently printed and more
or less recently translated version in our hand. The more we learn
of those communities, however, the more we must be impressed by
the fact of the great difference between them and their situation,
and ourselves and ours. We are certainly not the children of Israel

gathered in the Sinai wilderness, nor post-Exilic Jews going up to Jerusalem for the great festivals. We are also not the Syrian community to which the Gospel of Mark was addressed, nor the Corinthian community to which several of Paul's letters were addressed.

The book we are carrying differs from those older texts not only by being a translation, but by having been carried all this way for all this time, providing light for other feet that walked before us and are now at rest. The book we carry is no more a part of that ancient world than we are, for we do not want light from the ancient world to light our way in these last years of the twentieth century. We want light in the present. This is precisely what the book which we carry provides and has been providing for us all along. The book which offers actual light on our actual way is the one we carry.

So it is this carried book which we try to understand and let play the major role in our conversation, as it always seems to have done. In a highly qualified way, this carried book is the same as its presumed original. Although not a shred remains of a single original document that lay behind this book which we carry, historical scholarship in the form of textual criticism can establish with a high degree of probability, approaching historical certainty, that presently published and available Hebrew and Greek editions of those books are accurate reproductions of the lost originals. Of no less importance, historical scholarship in the form of redaction criticism can go a long way in helping us to understand the communities—the social, economic and cultural conditions—which provided the context in which those original documents were produced. But historical scholarship can only *help* us to understand these books, for we shall not have reached the understanding we seek until we have found a way to receive light upon our present path for the steps which we are about to take. For such an understanding, we need to know the steps we have already taken and what light our predecessors received—or thought they received—from this book. In short, we have to realize that we have this book in our hands not directly from its original authors or even from the communities for which and in the context of which they were first written, but from those who immediately preceded us in the Way, and through the whole long line of those who have walked before them. This carried book—the one we actually read and keep bringing into our own conversation—is the one from which we hope to receive light for each step along the Way.

THE SCRIPTURE, THE APOSTOLIC WRITINGS
AND TRADITION

The book which we carry with us contains, first of all, the Scriptures — the collection of books written in Hebrew (with a bit of Aramaic) which make up the Bible of the Jews. Although many of these writings come originally from ancient Israel, most were composed and the whole was put together, arranged and edited by the Jews after the exile of the sixth century B.C.E. and especially during the Second Temple period. The first and largest block of pages which make up the book we carry we owe, therefore, to the Jews. The rest of the pages, of which we have yet to speak, refer to this earlier and larger block simply as "the Scriptures."

Because the first and largest part of our book is the Jewish Scriptures, and because the rest of the book in turn leans so heavily on these Scriptures, it has come about, as we have mentioned in another connection, that we Gentile Christians have learned and come to use Jewish concepts whenever we have wanted to talk about the things which matter to us most. Further, we have reached our various understandings of God, His purposes and of this world as His creation through our conversations about the events which lie behind and gave rise to the Jewish Scriptures, as those Scriptures present them. Finally, it is from these Scriptures that we first discerned a Way in God's world, a Way given by God and first walked by His people Israel. Here is indeed the Scripture of the beginnings of all that we have and are as Christians.

The Jews have a name for the Hebrew Scriptures: *Tanakh*, an acrostic from the opening consonants of *Torah* (see below), *Neviim* (Prophets) and *Khetuvim* (Writings). Of these, the most complex is the concept "Torah." The best way into an understanding of the meaning of Torah is to translate it as "instruction," meaning of course God's instruction, God's word of wisdom, God's guidance. It also carries the sense of "tradition," the wisdom of God which has been handed down. The scope of Torah is no less complex than its sense. It can, at its narrowest, mean the first five books of Scripture, the books traditionally ascribed to Moses. At its broadest, it can include all the wisdom and instruction of the whole tradition and also any words of wisdom which a rabbi or indeed a fellow Jew might offer to an inquirer. To ask for a word of Torah within

Judaism can mean to ask for any word that is a help or light for walking in the Way of Israel. With respect to the Scriptures, Torah can refer to the whole of it, but more specifically it refers to the Pentateuch, the first five books.

Traditionally, these are the five books of Moses — the instruction from Sinai, the revelation whereby God shared and shares with His people His Way for them. Torah is God's gift whereby He has made His creatures His co-workers in His purpose of achieving the holiness of His whole creation. In that work, Israel, the people who received and accepted Torah, were constituted "a kingdom of priests and a holy nation" (Exod. 19:6), the "point of contact" between man and God. Torah is therefore the crown of all that follows in Scripture, as the rest of Scripture serves Torah. It is appropriate, then, that the scroll of Torah is sheathed in a priestly-royal robe and capped with a crown in developed Jewish liturgical use.

The second part of Tanakh is the prophets, but this includes Joshua and Judges, the books of Samuel and of Kings, as well as what Christians call "the major prophets" (but not Daniel), and the twelve books of the so-called minor prophets, from Hosea to Malachi. The third part, the Writings, contain the rest, including (unlike the order of our modern translations) Ruth and Daniel.

Such are the Scriptures carried in the Jewish and Christian hands of these two different communities of walkers. But how differently they have been read! For each of these walking communities has carried not only the Scriptures, but also other books which have guided them in reading Scripture — the lens through which the light of Scripture has fallen on their paths. For the Jews, the great commentary, elaboration and guide for walking in the light of Scripture has been the Mishnah and its commentary, the Gemara, which together make up the Talmud. For the Gentile church, it has been the Apostolic Writings, and the patristic and conciliar interpretations thereof.

In addition to and usually bound together with the Scriptures in one volume, we also carry the Apostolic Writings (usually called the New Testament). Although originally attributed to individual apostles, modern scholarship would not support the tradition that the original apostles were their actual authors. The traditions which lie behind their composition, however, were almost certainly those of communities built up by the apostles and other early disciples. We may say, then, that the book comes with the blessing and authority of the apostles as the Pentateuch comes with the blessing and authority of Moses.

Although Paul was not one of the original apostles, his letters make up an important block and were from the first counted as part of the Apostolic Writings. The warrant for Paul's apostleship was the same as that of the other apostles: he was a commissioned witness of the risen Jesus and so was accepted as a compeer by the rest of the apostles. Because Paul's are the earliest documents of the young Jesus movement, and even more because of his understanding of his special commission as the apostle to the Gentiles, his letters help us to understand the whole collection of Apostolic Writings as coming out of a movement within the Jewish people which was open to Gentiles in a manner untypical of other movements and which was on its way to become an overwhelmingly Gentile enterprise. Indeed, in his last, longest and most carefully developed letter, he alone of all the authors of the Apostolic Writings seemed to have sensed the dangers in this transformation which he did so much to bring about. His uneasiness about the possible consequence that a Gentile church might turn against the Jewish people gives particular interest to his thoughts for us at this time.

The Apostolic Writings, however, begin with the four Gospels, and these have always had within the church at least something of the priority which Torah (understood as the first books of the Scriptures) has had for the Jews. For most of its history, the church has taken the Gospels to be the story of the revelatory event of which the other writings were commentary and elucidation. Only recently have we come to realize not only that the Gospels are later in composition than Paul's letters, if not the other writings, but that they too are reflection upon, commentary on and adaptation of the tradition of the early Jesus movement to the conditions and circumstances of the communities for which they were written. As a body of literature, the Gospels no less than the epistles are historical sources for the life and teaching of the early church far more than for the life and teaching of Jesus. Nevertheless, the fact that they preserve at least what the early communities of the Jesus movement understood or remembered to have been the life and teaching of Jesus clearly accounts for the relative priority they have always had in the mind and the liturgical practice of the church.

The Scriptures of the Jews, and the Scriptures plus the Apostolic

Writings of the church, however, are books that have been carried now for many centuries. Their role for us can only be understood adequately as carried books. We must therefore recognize that, to speak of the Scriptures of Judaism apart from the Talmud, and to speak of the Bible of Christians apart from the patristic interpretation, will hardly help us to see the role that these carried books have played. Indeed, we must see that, in both communities, a great formative period began in the later first century that continued some four hundred years. By the end of the period in which the Talmud was formed and the patristic/conciliar development took place, Judaism and Christianity took on a shape neither obvious nor inevitable when viewed from what we can see of their beginning in the first century. The Jews glorified Moses and the revelation from Sinai, but in fact the oral Torah preached by the Pharisees and developed by the rabbis gave Judaism its decisive character. The Christians glorified the apostles and the revelation in Jesus; in fact the doctrinal tradition developed by Gentile, Greek-speaking bishops and theologians gave the church its crucial shape. Of course the rabbis never thought of themselves as doing other than expounding the Torah of Moses. And the church fathers and conciliar bishops were sure that they were only expounding and drawing out the clear implications of the Gospels. Nevertheless, it is clear that both communities were engaged in a creative undertaking that shaped their understandings of Torah and Gospel. Neither community, however, was engaged in a course contradictory to its beginnings. The written Torah demanded an oral Torah, itself to be committed to Halachah (rulings, guidelines for walking). The written Gospel demanded an oral tradition, itself to be committed to doctrine. The only question to be raised is whether either of these developments ought properly to be closed or considered final.

Before continuing, it should be pointed out that we could present this double development of Judaism and Christianity slightly differently. The alternative starting point would be the assertion that neither of the two existed at the time the Apostolic Writings were being composed. Both Judaism and Christianity are exact contemporaries, end-products of developments both of which began in the first and were completed by the end of the fourth century. It could then be maintained that both were the fruit of interpretations, *midrashim*, of the same Scriptures, the legacy of Israel. In the middle of the second century, in writing what from our point of view was presumptuously called a "dialogue" with Trypho (a rather hypothetical Jew) — today we would call it a monologue vis-à-vis a symbol — Justin Martyr devoted almost all of his essay to an interpretation of the Scriptures. Precious little is cited from the Apostolic Writings. Justin's gospel simply *was* this interpretation. Judaism and Christianity could therefore quite properly be called the products of two quite different interpretations of Israel's Scriptures, two differing views of what it was to be the heir of God's relationship to Israel. Each took the oral tradition (for the Jews, the Mishnah and the Gemara, for the Christians the Apostolic Writings and the patristic exposition) to be the only proper interpretations of Tanakh, the Scriptures to which both appealed. Both of them lacked our historical perspective which could have led them to see that they were both doing something quite creative, but also something which had no grounds for any claim to finality.

The Bible demands interpretation. It begs that we hear what is there to be heard and then dare to say our own words of response in our own times. It asks that we hear its words in their original situation so as to find words which address our own situation. It demands that it be heard as the word of God, not just to those for whom it was written, but to us today.

This pressure of the Bible for interpretation arises both from what is said in the Bible and also from how it has been said. What is said — that is, what has been heard by those who have carried this book from the beginning of the Way to our own point on the road — is the Word of the LORD, the Holy One of Israel, Blessed be He, the living God who accompanies His people and His church on their various ways, and the One who loves not only them but also His world, His whole creation, for the sake of which these ways are walked. Had we of the Gentile church heard only the voice of a God who once was, or even of a static God who never changed, who was not responsive to how things have gone with His creation over these past nineteen centuries, then it might be adequate to listen only to the words of the book. But it has not been so, either for the Jewish people, the people of God, or for us Gentiles, the church of God. We have surely been asked to find ourselves present before Sinai (the Jews) and present before the cross (the church), but we have been told also to keep walking, and by One who goes with us until the end. So although the book draws us back into its beginnings, it also addresses our present and speaks words of encouragement into our future. It speaks to us contemporary words and so asks for our ever renewed contemporary reading and hearing.

The Bible also begs for interpretation in *how* it comes to us and speaks to us. It comes to us as itself a multilevel series of interpretations and reinterpretations. Each new historical growth of this corpus which we call the Bible was a reinterpretation of the tradition as it had been received to that time, as though the marching orders which had been given needed amendment and elaboration as the Way led through swamps, or up steep slopes, or through heavily wooded places. Only thus could the original command turn out to be concrete orders for progression along an actual Way. Nor should this surprise us, for how else could it be if our Creator really gave instruction to His creatures? Surely He would know that they were creatures in time, that instruction for the Way through the desert would have to be amended for the time when they became settled and nation-builders, and that again the instruction would need modification in national defeat and the conditions of exile. Ezra's and our canon of Torah (on this see J. Sanders, *Torah and Canon*) and our corpus of Tanakh were the results.

This being the case with Tanakh, how could it not have been that the further conditions of Diaspora under the Roman Empire, then the increasingly difficult circumstances of survival in the hostile atmosphere of Christendom, called for the fresh instruction found in the Talmud? And it must surely be the case that God's people need today to be imaginative and receptive to further instruction in the radically new situation under which their faithful walking must now be done after the shattering experience of Europe from 1933 to 1945, and their new responsibility to walk once more in the land of Israel since the 1880's. The need has been made all the more pressing since 1948 by the renewed responsibility for nation-building and the strange new condition of once again walking partly in Israel and partly (and by choice) in the Diaspora. For such new and baffling conditions, the Jews must be driven to hear a new word, a fresh interpretation of instructions for how to walk the particular stretch of the Way that is set before them now. This, however, we must leave to them.

New interpretations produced Tanakh because Israel was confronted again and again with new situations. For the church, however, its very beginning was no other than the result of new and utterly unexpected events, and its Apostolic Writings are the results of just such reinterpretations of the received instructions as would account for these latest events. Nothing in the received instructions could have prepared them for a crucified messiah, nothing gave them grounds to be prepared for that one's resurrection and nothing in their past braced them for the shocking event of an inundation by Gentile converts. But, like the reinterpreters of the Scriptures, the apostolic reinterpreters retold the tradition in such a way as to present it all as one instruction, one story leading up to and including these last chapters as their culmination—to date.

We must add that last qualification, "to date," for staggering and unexpected events have occurred since the Apostolic Writings. Not least of these is the historical fact that the early church of Jews and Gentiles soon became an overwhelmingly Gentile enterprise. This happened, moreover, during a period in which the Jews experienced a period of consolidation and flowering to match any in their history. Other events also occurred, to which we can only allude at this point, such as the continuing minimal results of a mission to the Jews and a yet more fruitless mission to the Muslim world, and thus the concentration of the church in the world of Europe.

The "world of Europe," of course, has expanded in time to include geographical areas which Europeans conquered and settled (e.g., the Americas, Australia, New Zealand) or held for a while, leaving some traces of influence. The rise of indigenous forms of Christianity in the latter is a relatively recent fact and one by no means digested by "European" Christians.

Each of these events demands of the church that it so reinterpret its own instructions for walking so as to account for the resulting new situation. How could it be otherwise when we have believed that our walk was in response to the word of a living God, the Creator whose loving will it was that we really set out on this walk through history for the sake of his larger plan for His whole creation?

This then is the book we carry. It includes the book of the Jews plus the Apostolic Writings, as the instructions of the living God, the One who loves and suffers with us as we move ahead in what is first of all His Way for His whole creation and consequently our own Way through time and history. When we see how tradition was formed by events to make up Scripture and Apostolic Writings, and how these have needed continuing reinterpretation in order to be a living instruction for our present walk, one must wonder over that hardening of lines back four centuries ago that split the church between those who thought that tradition was on a par with the Scriptures and those who thought that there could be a "pure" Scripture untouched by the traditions of men. No, we have never carried in our hands a book that was other than itself a piece of our human history, just as that carrying and that history has never been other than that which took place at the call and under the judgment of the LORD, the Holy One of Israel.

THE CONTENT OF THE BOOK: THE SCRIPTURES

We should not take for granted, any more than that we are walking together, that the book in our hands is the same book that has been carried and handed over to us by those who have walked before us. Why is it just this book and not some other that we carry? The alternatives are endless. And why do we still carry it? Karl Barth's answer to this question should not be dismissed: It is precisely from the reading of this book that those before us and we too have heard the voice of the One God as we Gentiles are able to apprehend Him, as the One God of Israel who, as His own self-expressing act, ever true to Himself, has reached out and drawn us to Himself, through His Son the Jew, Jesus of Nazareth. Where else could we even begin to expect to hear the voice of *that* God? True as this is, we need to express it in words slightly but importantly different from those which Barth used. The answer to our questions—why this book, and why do we still carry it—can only be found in the answer to the following question: What is this book about, what is its content? To this question, however, there is no simple answer.

It has been said that the content of this book is a story, and indeed it is. Yet there is much in these pages that does not tell a story. There is poetry of love, distress, victory and defeat; there are sayings and proverbs; there are detailed regulations of cult and government. It has been said that it is the book of the mighty acts of God, and indeed it is. Yet the mighty acts of God are so largely unfolded as the acts of men and nations that, as we have said, the principal protagonist is more accurately defined as Israel. There are reports of those historical events which are praised as the mighty acts of God, but there is much more.

This book has been said to contain the sum of revealed truths concerning God and man, but those truths, such as they are, come always embedded in historical documents concerning historical events. The enunciation of broad universal truths seems not to have been the intent of the authors and editors of these documents.

No wonder then that from an early time the meaning of this book was felt to lie on many different levels, so that it needed to be read and understood not simply as it stands, but also allegorically, or anagogically (discovering a hidden, mystical sense), or that even the method of a numerology, that found the meaning in the numerical value of the Hebrew letters, was tried.

Each of these proposals has had its adherents and may have them still. Each is an attempt to explain how we have taken this book. Each is an attempt to explain what we have made of it (understand it to be) and what we make out of it (our interpretive apprehension of it). Indeed, there is no other course we can follow. The reason we seem unable to arrive at any one simple answer to what this book is and how it should be understood is that it is not and has never been a "pure" text abstracted from our interest in it. What we are trying to understand is just this book-in-our-hands, the book of our beginning, distinguished by the fact that we carry it and not another. It is conceivable on some level of abstraction that we might one day find that we were no longer carrying this book, that we were carrying none at all or some other book, or perhaps this book but only along with others. By the same process of abstraction it is conceivable that we might some day find that we were no longer walking in the Way. Then our conversation would be of quite another sort. As it is and until that time, we are confronted in this book with no abstraction, no text-in-itself, but with a concrete, tangible book, the one of which we are forever making something. What we make of it is itself an important part of our conversation as we walk in the Way.

As a contribution to this conversation, then, we offer the following proposal for discussion: The content of this book, generally, is the story of the beginning of God's Way with His beloved creation into which we have been called to walk. It is therefore the story of the beginning of our Way. God is the subject matter of this book always as the Giver of the Way, as its ever new beginning, and as its not-yet-realized end. Since it is the story of our Way—both as the

Jews and as we Gentile Christians are walking it—its protagonists
are those who set out on this journey, beginning with Abraham.
Israel and his descendants are the protagonists of the Scriptures,
Jesus of Nazareth and his disciples of the Apostolic Writings. That
is to say, flesh and blood Israel holds the center of the stage, for
this is the story of a Way through time and place and, as such, its
dramatis personae are historical people. First come the patriarchs
and matriarchs, then Moses and the people, then judges, kings and
prophets and lastly that prophet of the End-Time who was more
than a prophet among prophets for his Gentile church. Surrounding these major figures come the others, the families, friends and
foes, the faithful and the unfaithful, the full reality of the
historical people Israel and then that later historical community
that sprang from Israel and took seed in Gentile soil.

Israel is the protagonist, and Israel means "wrestler with man
and God." Israel is presented as a God-driven, God-striving people
because it was possessed by God. Not obsessed, but possessed,
taken as God's peculiar possession for a plan which we must believe
is still unfolding because not yet completed. The plan is for that
whole creation which is spoken of in the opening chapter of Genesis
and whose renewal is longed for so dramatically in the final
chapters of Revelation. Israel's possession by God, and so the way
whose ever new beginnings are told of in this book, and so this book
which we carry, and so the Way in which we walk now with this
book, all have this world as their context and purpose. Israel's
struggle to walk in such a Way, to walk before and with God as if
He were not there, is the content of the book. No wonder then that
we still carry only this book.

The Scriptures comprise the book of the Jews and, as such, the
book of the church. This book tells how God's people were set into
and then set out to walk in God's Way, what they said and did, and
what happened to them. In it may be found their songs of joy and
their laments, sayings and proverbs that grew up among them,
denunciations made and consolations offered by one or another of
them, their narrations of their journey and their reflections upon it
all. They told and retold, interpreted and reinterpreted their story
as they moved on to new stages along the Way into which they were
called. If we Gentile Christians can keep firmly in mind that this is
the story of the beginnings of their way *on which they are still moving,* then because we too carry this book there may be occasions on

which we can share some of our conversation with the Jews and, more importantly, take some of their conversation into ours. Indeed, if we do not keep our ears open, we shall miss things which we ought to hear, for they have been longer in the Way than we have, much longer.

THE CONTENT OF THE BOOK: THE APOSTOLIC WRITINGS AND AFTER

The Scriptures tell a story which can account for the fact that the Jews carry this book, but it does not account for the fact that *we* carry it. The explanation can be found in what we have appended to the Scriptures and presumed to bind with them into one volume: the Apostolic Writings. When bound up with the Scriptures, the Apostolic Writings become what the Scriptures are for Judaism: the book of our own beginnings, the book of our identity. The Apostolic Writings tell the story of a new thing, a series of events which its authors at first thought was a new thing for Israel, but which turned out in historical fact to be, rather, a new thing for Gentiles.

As is the case with the Scriptures, the Apostolic Writings both are and are not about God. The protagonist of the Gospels is Jesus of Nazareth; he is presented as a personification of God's Israel, living over in himself the history of his people, realizing in himself their identity. This is, we should add, what every Jew was called to be. Every Jew, according to Judaism, was and is to understand himself as called out of Egypt, present at Sinai, chosen by God and accepting his election. Jesus, then, is presented in the Gospels as the fully faithful Jew, which is perhaps a more historically responsible way of saying what the church has usually said: Jesus was the fulfillment of Israel's history.

With Jesus—the protagonist of the Apostolic Writings—stand the disciples, the apostles, following him and then carrying on the work he began. Increasingly in the writings which focus on the situation after Easter—the Acts and the Epistles—the apostles and disciples and their successors, the community of the "believers," indeed the church, becomes the protagonist. Israel is there in the background, an increasingly negative background. The new community is not Israel. It is the church.

Once, at the very end of his letter to the Galatians (6:16), Paul pronounced a blessing on "the Israel of God." The reference is not clear; it could be the church. The expression occurs nowhere else in his letters and certainly not in his lengthy discussion of the relations of the church to Israel in his last letter. Apart from this one uncertain point, the church is always just that, the church of God. Nowhere in the Apostolic Writings is the church called the "new Israel."

If one allows that the focus of the Gospels on Jesus is still a focus on Israel, then the Apostolic Writings as a whole have a shifting center. The spotlight, so to speak, swings from Israel to the church. This means that the Apostolic Writings, within the context of the total Bible of the church, bear testimony to the fact that a genuine fork in the road was occasioned by the response of the church of the next few generations. That fork in the road resulted in the church going its own way, convinced though we are that it was God who called us into this deviation from the Way of Israel, whereas Israel continued in the Way in which it had been called to walk. By the end of the fourth century the different paths were laid out, although the divergence was clear already by the end of the first century.

There is, however, a further feature of this development that did not follow of necessity upon the fact of the fork. The increasingly Gentile church and the Jewish people went their several ways, not as God's elect called to walk in God's Way each in its own manner, not as though the obedience or faithfulness of the other might have been for each a matter of the gravest concern for the furthering of God's purpose with His creation, not as though each in its own way had a vital role to play in the history of God's creation on the way to its redemption. On the contrary, they went their several ways in a spirit of increasing hostility, each convinced that God's election could only take the form that they knew themselves. They reviled each other in the bitterest of terms. They called down upon each other the curse of the One God they both worshiped. Blood was shed on both sides. It is a sordid story which must shame those who know it as their own.

The cause of this hostility was the conviction, on both sides, that there could be only one Way of God *and* that it could only be walked in one way. Each community saw itself as being in the Way that had begun with Abraham and was made much clearer and more explicit at Sinai and in the further history of Israel. Neither was prepared to admit that God's purpose might allow more than one way for His creatures to walk according to His will, that His will for differing communities might be that they walk in His way differently, according to their particular situations and His special intentions for them. Israel, the Jews, could only see this new movement as heretical, insofar as it was a Jewish movement, and then as apostasy and paganism as it moved to become more and more a Gentile movement, especially as it began to insist, without any warrant, that the way of Torah was wrong for Jews. The church could only see the Jews as having rejected the new fork in the road, the direction which they felt compelled to follow. Since they too recognized only one way to walk in God's Way, they could only see the Jews as having abandoned the Way altogether. They saw themselves then as the continuing people of God who had now replaced the Jews as the Israel of God.

The early signs of this development are evident in the Apostolic Writings. It is therefore incumbent upon us to realize that they were written in the time in which this antagonism was growing rapidly and that this book which we carry was soon going to be used as the basis for a theology of hate. The gospel of love and salvation was soon to be used to preach hatred and damnation of the Jews and to teach the church of succeeding generations to despise the Jewish people and all things Jewish. Whatever else we may have to say of this book which we have carried and still carry, we cannot forget to say that it has been used for centuries to teach contempt for the Jewish people.

It need not be so read and used. It was written under the shadow and in part as an expression of this contempt for the Jews. But by the fact of the domination which the church came to exercise in Europe beginning in the fourth century C.E., the Jews paid for this hatred with well-documented suffering at Christian hands. In the light of this grim history, we have now to discuss among ourselves whether we are obliged to go on reading and telling the story of our beginning in the Way as it has been told in the past. We have at the top of our agenda, I suggest, the need to find our own way of telling that story, such that the seeds of hatred evident from the early days of the parting of the ways can be dug out, identified and repudiated, to be replaced by other seeds more worthy of the Sower whom we and the Jews together worship, and more worthy of that

human sower of Nazareth, that Jew whose coming led to the fact
that we Gentiles too can freely worship the God of Israel.

The search for a fresh way in which to tell the story that is the content
of this book, so as to explain why we carry it, is made far more necessary
by the recognition that the Apostolic Writings come clothed in hostility
toward the Jewish people than from the recognition that they come
clothed in mythological language. If its mythological language is a fact,
so is the hostility to the Jews. But the price paid for its mythological form
is merely that it clashes somewhat with our naive commitments to our
own age and its picture of the world, a picture not without its problems.
The price may be that those most committed to modernity, who have no
sense of humor about our modern culture's view of what it thinks to be
reality, will find the story incredible. The result is that fewer of the Gentiles will come to walk in the Way along with us. It could be, of course,
that our staggering gait and our meandering in circles, appearing to have
lost the way ourselves, send far more away than the mythological aspect
of our conversation. But for the sake of the comparison, let us say that the
mythological aspect of the story is a problem for many, leading us to
search for new ways to tell the story. The price for the hostility toward the
Jews, however, has been actual human lives. Jews have been humiliated,
plundered, tortured and killed because of this aspect of the story. No
sneers of the secularist can possibly match in seriousness the actual death
of real people as weighty reasons for a fresh account of the content of this
book which we carry. Now that we have seen the result of our teaching of
contempt, carried out by pagans no longer under the control of the
church but able to use our own words against any who objected, the
slaughter of a third of all the Jews in the world, and with the church on
the whole unable or unwilling to raise a voice in opposition, we must surely account anew for the fact that we are still carrying this book which was
used for so long in such a way as to provide a supporting context for that
horrendous deed. Without at this point going into detail, we offer here
an outline of such an account.

The book which we carry contains an incredible story which we
nonetheless believe. It is the story of a love beyond all imagining.
The lover is the LORD, whose love is such that He wanted there to
be another, an other, His creation. He therefore backed away from
His totality and fullness, shrinking into Himself, as it were, in order
to make place for this other. (Astronomers have their own version
of this event, or of as much of it as their criteria for facts and
evidence will allow them to tell.) In this other, He set the conscious
other, the other made in His likeness. (Paleontologists and

archeologists may tell us how long this took; the story in our book only sums up the final results.) That men and women are made in the image of God must say something about God as well as about us. It must mean that God is at least a person, one who can share Himself with other persons. This love that shares itself, that wills the other to be and to be freely, that confers freedom, this is the beginning of the story.

Then, in order to share this love fully and to allow His creatures to share love with Himself, He made Himself known to Abraham and then more fully to Abraham's descendants. He may well have made Himself known to others, but our story tells only of this way in which He made Himself known.

My concern here is with what the story is, not with whether or how it is unique. It is psychologically healthy—i.e., in accordance with the *logos* or logic of *psyche*, personhood—to seek to know who I am. It is psychologically unhealthy—destructive of other persons and therefore of my own personhood—to seek to know who I am uniquely, who I am that others are not. It is a feature of the story in our book that God and God alone is unique. We creatures just are, which is really quite wonderful enough.

God made Himself known by calling a people to Himself to bear His intention through history, on into the time when He could complete His creation by bringing it to the goal of His loving intention, its own holiness. Much of the story, then, concerns the people of Israel and the history of their walking in the Way in which God had instructed them.

Then came something new. At a time of great difficulty for Israel under the occupation of the Roman Army, there grew up and came on the scene of history a particular Jew who exemplified Israel's special relationship with God with such an immediacy that he drew to himself a following of other Jews who sensed in him some new step in the history of God's dealing with His creation. This small group seemed a potential source of unrest to the occupying authorities so they executed its leader, as they did leaders of other movements that expressed Israel's unwillingness to fit unobtrusively into the Roman view of things. And then, to the amazement of his closest followers, Jesus appeared to them after his death in such a way as to convince them that he was alive. This was, so they were convinced, God's confirmation that their hesitant judgment concerning this man was right: God *was* inaugurating with him something new in His dealings with the world.

The interpretation which that first community gave to these events was one shaped entirely by the Jewish context in which they occurred. They took these events to be the beginning of the End, the breaking in of the New Age, the time, according to the hope of many Jews of the time, in which God was to bring His creation to its completion, into full holiness. So they called to their fellow Jews to join with them in living in the new way appropriate to the last moments of history-as-we-have-known-it, a new way based on the interpretation of the Way as they understood Jesus to have taught it. To their chagrin they found that not many of their fellow Jews would accept their new midrash or their ideas of what was happening. On the other hand, and even more shocking to them, their ideas were eagerly heard and accepted by more and more Gentiles. The new events were turning out to be even newer than they had first imagined.

Then came the revolt and the Jewish war for independence from Rome. The Jews of the new Way, and of course their Gentile fellows, felt that they had no part in the revolt, for their eyes were fixed on a more cosmic transformation which they were sure was about to take place. The fact that they did not align themselves with the rest of the Jews in this war, and the disastrous end of the war with the sack of Jerusalem and the destruction of the Temple, contributed to a total break with the other Jews and increasing hostility between the people of the Way, called Israel, and the people of the new Way, now being called the Christians—the church. There, *in medias res*, as all this was going on, at this point in God's dealings with His creation, the Apostolic Writings, our second book, came to be written. The conviction of the communities which produced it was that God had initiated them into the Way that would lead into the new age of God's completion of His creation, and that those in the Way were already free to live the coming life of a renewed world in anticipation of its arrival. They were convinced that the decisive signs of the transformation had already come and that the powers of the new age were already available to those who threw themselves into this new Way. The end of the old age and the beginning of the new had been inaugurated by God in the life, death and resurrection of Jesus. He was, therefore, the new Adam, the first born of the new creation which his followers awaited from God with high expectation. There, unfinished, the story stops. This book which we carry takes the story of God's dealings with His creation up to that point. It need hardly be said that, by the testimony of the book itself, this cannot be the end of the story. If the word of the Apostolic Writings is to be believed, this cannot be the last word on the subject which is its own content.

HANDLING THE BOOK: TRADITION

The book which we carry is, in its first and longest part, a book that is also carried by the Jews. How do they handle this book that they carry? They *engage in Torah*. The verb *to engage* catches their dual emphasis on study and practice. It is not enough to study Torah, though that is essential; one must also do it. One should not simply set out to do it; one must know it, ponder it and meditate upon it. The result should be a Torah-saturated person who, in all one is and does, is a living response to Torah.

The engagement with Torah has meant primarily an engagement with the Talmud, the formative interpretation of Torah. Engagement with Talmud in turn gives rise to a living conversation with great interpreters of the past, thus leading to a living interpretation in the life of the Jewish people. To engage in Torah is thus to set oneself in the long line of those who have engaged in Torah from the beginning. It is to set one's feet into the way of walking which has been that of Israel from its beginnings.

Historical criticism of the Scriptures has posed no great difficulties for the Jews, due to this open-ended tradition of engaging in Torah. The modern view that the Scriptures are a cluster of varying traditions welded together by later editors or redactors fits well into the Jewish practice of living with Scripture. Any presumed final redactor, whose additions, compilations or reworkings of earlier material might be identified critically as the work of "R," as distinct from earlier sources designated by other letters, simply makes of "R" a later interpreter, the presumed last of a line within Tanakh, but then followed by the later rabbinic interpreters of the Mishnah and the Gemara. Franz Rosenzweig spoke out of a genuinely Jewish tradition, in responding to the findings of historical criticism of the Scriptures, when he said that for Jews "R" simply means *rabbinu*, our rabbi. Since the revelation is of a living God, it calls for a living response and so a living interpretation, always a matter of the feet and hands as well as of the head and heart.

There is a sobriety in Jewish interpretation of Scripture. There is also humor. What can only be called a certain light-heartedness appears again and again in rabbinic midrash, as though the rabbis knew that they were only making a creaturely response to the revelation of the Creator, and so saying things which simply must not be taken literally. It has been said that angels can fly because they take themselves lightly. So the Jewish interpreter of Scripture can often take himself lightly and fly to fresh new understandings of God's instruction for His people in their present circumstances. And indeed, if Scripture testifies to a God who is living still and accompanying His people on their way through history toward the days of creation's fulfillment, such a fresh listening and fresh interpretation of the beginning of the Way are just what is needed and what should be expected. If the Scriptures are in any sense the Word of the living God, then they call for a living interpretation.

The book which we carry, however, is one that is in our own Gentile Christian hands. Because the book in our hands, unlike that in the hands of the Jews, contains not only Tanakh but also the Apostolic Writings, not only the translation of the Hebrew Scriptures which our editions usually label "the Old Testament," but also what they generally call "the New Testament," we have thought it of prime importance heretofore to answer the question of how these two collections of writings are related to each other. It is of the utmost importance today, however, that we understand that the question has been badly put.

The relationship between the Scriptures and the Apostolic Writings is first of all that which exists between the book which the Jews carry and the one which the church carries. It is therefore unavoidably a question of the relationship between the Jewish people and the Gentile church. Any attempt to answer the question on simply literary grounds, or even on historical grounds that did not include the history of the relations between the Jewish people and the church, will not do justice to the actual books whose history it has been to be in the hands of the Jewish people and the Gentile church. The history of that relationship is an unavoidable part of the problem.

The beginnings of the problem can be seen clearly in looking at one of the early writings of Christian authorship written after those which are found in our Apostolic Writings—Justin Martyr's *Dialogue with Trypho*, to which we have already referred. This document, which sometimes strays from dialogue to diatribe, is set as a "discussion" between Justin, a Christian, and Trypho, a Jew. It is Justin, however, who does all of the talking. Moreover, his talk is mostly about the Scriptures. For Justin, in this early stage of the history of the church, "the Gospel" was primarily the Christian midrash or interpretation of Scripture which distinguished the church from the developing form of Judaism under the leadership of the Tannaim. At that time, the Tannaim were beginning to consolidate and commit to writing the midrash coming down from the Pharisees; by the end of the second century this had become the Mishnah. But Justin was a champion of another way of reading the Scriptures, an interpretation which saw them pointing to and preparing the way for the coming of Jesus as the word of God, a messiah who suffered and died, who was raised by God and who was to come soon to usher in the age of redemption.

Justin's argument with Trypho, then, did not consist in setting Apostolic Writings against the Scriptures but, rather, in setting the church's reading of Scripture against that of Trypho. What he did in effect — indeed explicitly — was to claim those Scriptures for the church in such a way as to deny them to the Jews. The Scriptures were for him the Scriptures as he interpreted them, which of course is what they have always been for anyone for whom they were "the Scriptures." The result was that the Jewish people who resisted this interpretation were denied not only any right to their own interpretation of the Scriptures, they were also denied their right to the Scriptures as theirs (ch. 29) and thus denied their identity as the people who wrote, preserved and were themselves the protagonists of the Scriptures. To Trypho's astonished question, "Are you then Israel?" (ch. 123), Justin's answer was "Yes!" The church's interpretation of Scripture evident in Justin entails a view of the church as having totally displaced the Jewish people as Israel, as the people of God.[1]

The original denial to the Jews of the right to their own interpretation of their own book, and so the denial to them of the right to their own sacred literature, led to denial of the Jews' basic civil rights, once the church was able to influence and then write the

---

[1] The tragic history of the consequences of this early development has been described, first in James Parkes's Oxford doctoral dissertation, *The Conflict of the Church and the Synagogue* (published in 1934 and presently available in paperback), and later in further studies by Dr. Parkes and many others.

laws of the Empire. From there, the steps led inexorably—as documented by Parkes, Hay, Isaac, Katz and others—to a denial of the right to live among us (expulsions from England, Spain, etc.) and Hitler's denial of the right to live at all.

The relationship of the Apostolic Writings to the Scriptures is of a *novum* to that in the context of which it is seen as new. It is then a question of how one can define what is new in terms of that which is, by contrast, old. Our traditional answer has been to say that the old prepares the way for the new. The new is not really all that new, for it was always there by anticipation in the old. The new only makes clearer or more explicit what the old already contained. This has been the logic underlying the way, already clearly enunciated by Justin but also evident in many passages of the Apostolic Writings, in which we have spoken of this matter during most of our conversation in the past. When we realize that the question concerns not simply the relationship between two collections of documents, however, but also the relationship between two collections of human beings—between the Jewish people and the church—we must hesitate. For, when we become aware of this more basic frame of reference, we are confronted by the fact that the Jewish people still lives, that its own interpretation of its own Scriptures continues to this day and is heir to as rich a history of interpretation as our own. This history undermines any theory of displacement as it challenges the conclusion that the Scriptures find their only adequate interpretation in the Apostolic Writings.

Our traditional answer, moreover, does not even do justice to the sense of the radically new, the unexpected, the genuine novelty which so marks the Apostolic Writings themselves. They do more than merely make explicit that which was implicit. Here, they seem to shout at us, is a new beginning, a radically new step, indeed a final step after which there would be no time for any more. History has undercut that note of finality in the unavoidably temporal sense which those Writings intended, but the thesis of a new beginning can be preserved if we say that, with the events concerning Jesus of Nazareth, something new was launched in God's creation, something more novel than the fulfillment of what was all really there already to be learned from the Scriptures. A new day had arrived in which a renewal of the people of God was to be accompanied by a new gathering of Gentiles into the Way of God and His purposes for His creation.

Inevitably, the apostolic authors defined this new day almost exclusively in the conceptual patterns of the Jewish people, for they were Jews writing to largely Jewish audiences. The Gospel of Mark, for example, as Howard Kee has recently argued,[2] was addressed to a community which we could call a predominantly Jewish sect. The whole of the new is there presented in the framework of one or more strands of Jewish eschatology.

There is, however, more than one way to define the events concerning Jesus of Nazareth as a new stage in the history of the Jewish people. They can be seen as the culmination and completion, the final chapter of the story, as in Mark, or as the final denouement of all that which preceded it (Justin). In the light of the fact that we have carried these books for all these centuries and that the larger part of them have also been carried by the Jewish people, there is another possibility: These events can also be seen as the radically new beginning of a further stage in God's dealings with His creation. They can be seen as neither replacing nor annulling what went before, nor making explicit what had already been said in signs and figures. In contrast to all such ahistorical views, they can be seen as a genuinely new event, a new beginning, a *further* step, which adds to what we think we know of God's dealings with His creation up to that point.

The logic of my argument should be clear. That which is a realization or fulfillment of what has come before is less novel, certainly less historically novel, than a wholly fresh departure, a change from what has gone before. What resulted from the events concerning Jesus of Nazareth was a new beginning in this world of time and space. What began was a way for the Gentiles to walk in God's Way, and that really was new. Forgiveness of sins was an old reality for Israel; it became a radically new fact for Gentiles. Atonement: one with the God of Israel! When had the Gentiles known that? God drawing near to Gentile sinners! Unheard of in all of pagan mythology and, indeed, not really anticipated in Israel's understanding of its tradition. The truly new had come:

Remember then your former condition: you, Gentiles. . . .
You were at that time separated from Christ, strangers to the community of Israel, outside God's covenants and the promise that goes with them. Your world was a world without

---

[2]*Community of the New Age* (Philadelphia, 1977).

hope and without God. But now in union with Christ Jesus
you who once were far off have been brought near through
the shedding of Christ's blood. (Eph. 2:11-13)

That was indeed a new thing. Indeed, the writer thought that
something more had happened which we now know to have been
only a short-lived reality within the Jesus movement, but not the
historical fact of the relationship between what that movement was
to become and the Jewish people. Christ, he went on, "is our peace.
Gentiles and Jews, he has made the two one, and in his own body of
flesh and blood has broken down the enmity which stood like a
dividing wall between them" (v. 14). No, that is not what happened. What did happen, however, was new enough.

What happened was so novel that one can well see why those
Jewish authors of our Apostolic Writings, living as they were in the
context of Jewish eschatological expectations, were sure that the
events which had initiated their movement revealed and were
already part of the transformation of all things. Howard Kee, in his
recent study of Mark, summed up the self-understanding of "the
community of the New Age" by saying that they saw themselves as
sharing "in the powers of the New Age at work through Jesus."[3]
They expected a catastrophic calamity to follow upon the end of
the war of the Jews with Rome (Mk. 13:7, 14, 19, 24-26), at least
within their own generation (13:30). These events were for them
totally reorienting. So overwhelming did this new beginning seem
that all that came before seemed to be passing away. It was one
thing for them to have said that, it is quite another matter for us to
say it today, nineteen centuries later. For Israel, God's covenant
with His own people has clearly not passed away. The Apostolic
Writings, then, cannot be for us a new which replaces an old. Indeed, the further course of life in the Way, as it has been walked by
the Jewish people and by the Gentile church, must refute Justin's
denial of the Scriptures to the Jews. It is true that we Gentiles read
it in our own way, but we must also allow that it is still read by
those whose claim to it is prior to and the foundation of our own.
In the light of this further history, we cannot pretend that the end
has come or even be sure it is near at hand.

The Scriptures recount the first stage on God's Way toward the
redemption of His creation. The Apostolic Writings tell of a radi-

[3]Ibid., p. 92.

cally new addition to what has been told before. For the Jewish people, the Talmud—their own oral tradition of interpretation of Scripture—marks a further development along the Way, even if the oral tradition is usually considered older than the written tradition. Taken together, they mark only beginnings. Neither can they any longer be taken as God's last word before the end. They have turned out, rather, to be the first word. The story, which opens with the Scriptures and continues in the Apostolic Writings and the Talmud, is not over. We find ourselves now somewhere in the middle of it. The task of interpretation and reinterpretation in the light of reorienting events remains open.

If the course of these past nineteen centuries compels us to leave unanswered the question of whether the word which we hear in the book we carry is the last word, there can be no question that it has always been the first word in our conversation, the one which we listen to afresh with each new step we take along the Way into which we have been called. When we consider (in the next steps) this matter of the last word, we shall certainly turn again to this first word in order to get our bearings. For if we find later events than those to which this book bears witness demanding our attention and pressing on us the claim to reorient our thinking and living and our walking, then we shall want to consider with care whether the Scriptures and the Apostolic Writings do not provide criteria by which such events may be identified. Not every event in the history of the world from the time of Abraham to the first century was seen by the authors, redactors and compilers of the book which we carry as demanding a fresh interpretation of their received traditions. This same book may therefore give us light when we discuss among ourselves whether certain recent events call us to interpret the tradition afresh in order to see how we should continue our walk into the future.

USEFUL LIGHT

We have carried this book all this way primarily because it has provided light for our feet and upon our path. From it we have heard again and again our call into the Way in which we walk and instruction in how we should walk. From it we have this reminder to encourage us in the Way and to cheer us as we continue. It has been the voice that tells us that we walk not alone, but in the unseen company of Him who has called us, so that we may proceed with hope in God's future. As instruction, as good news, as call and assurance, it is a book we have found indispensable for our journey. Without it, we would surely wander further from the Way than we do even with its help.

That is why we use it in so many different ways: We read it individually; we sit down by the side of the Way and reflect upon it. And this, in turn, feeds our conversation. This book reminds us who we are, why we are here and where we are going. So we share what we read there in our conversation as we walk. We call to each other's attention now this aspect, now that, of what we have read, or what we have seen for the first time, although we have read it many times before. And so, of course, when we pause on our walk to open our hearts and minds to God and to offer Him our thanks and our adoration, this is the book we read aloud together, and this is the book that our appointed leaders open to offer us in their own words what they and we have to hear from this book.

The activity which we call preaching is the paradigm of all our use of this book. In preaching, one of our number, duly assigned and prepared for this task, takes the words written in this book and attempts to interpret them in the light of the events of our own time, and to let the events of our own walking both shape and be shaped by the words of this book. It is a model of our conversation, which certainly has no other focus than our present walk, and yet which cannot go on except as part of a walk long since begun, the beginnings of and directions for which are to be found in this book which we carry. Preaching is therefore always the exposition of the Bible addressed entirely to our immediate bit of the Way on which we walk. Its goal is to show that that past is really the past of our present moment, and that our present follows from that past.

Preaching can take place now because it has happened before. We can take this book into our conversation because it has been so taken before. That is, it has simply been our experience in the Way that this book has been able to hold a prime place for itself in our conversation, and it has been able to open for many a preacher and hearer the words of its authors and so the voice of Him who has called us into the Way. Because it has made itself heard again and again during our long journey, giving fresh instruction, new encouragement and rekindled hope, so we can open it again in the confidence that it will hold its own in our present conversation and in that which will take place after we have died.

The Scriptures have proved to be light for the Way for Israel and for the Jewish people. The Scriptures and our Apostolic Writings have been light for the Way for the church. They shine out ahead upon a Way that we know must in some sense lead to a Way for the world. Carrying this book, then, we are not quite in Abram's situation of journeying not knowing where he should go. But then, a light is no road map, so our situation is not all that different from Abram's either.

The Functions of the Book:
The Authority of the Bible

INTRODUCTION

Traditionally, we have referred to the book which we carry as "the Word of God." We have generally agreed that this book constitutes the test of our conversation and the norm for our understanding. Some of us have also felt that this book should serve to guide not only where and how we should walk, but also the formation of our company and the sort and rank of our leaders. That is, the Bible has generally been taken as a norm for teaching and preaching and, by some, as a norm for the structure and organization of the church. The subject of conversation which this tradition raises is the role or function of this book in our continuing conversation, and so the role that this book plays in our walking. In more traditional words, our topic is the authority of the Bible.

If calling the Bible "the Word of God" seems to imply that this book serves as God's speaking tube, then there would appear to be something wrong with the tube, for it is notoriously the case that it has been and can be read in ways so different that it might be considered not one but many. The different understandings of Scripture which Jews and Gentile Christians have had should warn us against any simple indentification of the book and the mind of God. Moreover, within the Gentile church, Lutherans, Methodists and Roman Catholics, for example, have read the Apostolic Writings in importantly different ways. What needs reflection and discussion, then, is what happens—what has happened, what conceivably can happen now and could perhaps happen again tomorrow—when we turn to this book which we carry. As David Kelsey has put it, the question is not so much what God is saying to us in this book as what God is doing among us with our reading of this book.[1]

The question of what happens in the church's reading of this book could be expressed in a number of ways, but the actual weight which this book possesses in our conversation can be shown by considering what it has enabled us to do in the past and can conceivably enable us to do now and in the future. Because it has served us in the past, we trust that it will be of like service to us in the future. That service is one of reminding us who God is, and also who God is not; who we are, and so who we are not; what has happened thus far on the Way, and what has not happened. Because this book has served us in these crucial matters, it is proper that we serve it with the respect and attention which we have given it. It is therefore right that we call this book the Word of God, so long as we recall what we have said about who God is. If we thought of God as some utterly total All, in comparison with which we are a Nothing, then to call the Bible the Word of God would be to invest it with some total, unquestioned and unquestionable authority. But, in fact, that is not the God of Israel. The God of Israel is the Creator, who has willed an other, His creation, into full and unqualified existence, and has above all willed an other, humanity, into co-responsible, co-creative walking. He does not speak words of an omnipotent monarch to us, because He has engaged us in a cooperative relationship with Him, in a covenant. Being the Person that God is, He speaks to us as persons, which we are by His act of free love. We hear His word, therefore, as personal conversation and give it a prime place in our own conversation. That is how we have to understand the role of the Bible as the Word of God. To put the matter in another way, we shall best understand the authority of this book which we carry by attending seriously to the limits of its authority. It is in the light of the service which the Bible does not perform for us that we can appreciate the inestimable service which it can and does perform for us.

[1] *The Uses of Scripture in Recent Theology* (Philadelphia, 1975).

RECALLING WHO GOD IS

The first service which this book which we carry has performed for us in the past and which, therefore, we may hope that it will continue to perform for us in the future, is to recall to us who God is. At the present stage of our walking, we need this recollection. We seem in these days to find it most difficult to recall who God is and, therefore, that God is. We are, however, not at all clear as to why we find this so difficult. We offer a variety of arguments, all of them suspiciously thin in their warrants, in support of our difficulty, which suggests that we have in fact no more difficulty now than men and women have ever had.

The fundamental reason why God has become such a problem for us is that we tend to dehistoricize Him and detemporalize Him in the name of a certain conception of His eternity. By His eternity we mean, with all the best of intentions, to regard Him as Lord of time—that He is outside of and unaffected by time. He therefore cannot change His mind and there can be no question of His forgetting or remembering, for, with Augustine, we rule all temporal categories out of order as applied to God. Because we take "time" to be a category of creation, we assume that it does not apply to God.

Time may properly be considered a category of the condition of creation. However, now that God has become Creator, He has creation on His hands, so to speak, and He can only be related to and work with creation under the conditions of time. Thus, it would seem proper to speak of God remembering and so, at least theoretically, of being able to forget. In which case, it must be true that God too has a history since Creation, that He too, not just His creation, moves together with it through history and in time, able to change His mode of working with His creatures (Heb. 1:1-2). Is not this the God of whom we are reminded today by the book which we carry? I speak not of the book as it was carried by Augustine, or by the Schoolmen, but the book which we are carrying today. Aware as we are today of our own historical conditionedness, our own historicity, why should we not speak openly of the historicity of God?

The Bible recalls to us the God who has ever dealt with His creatures in historical, temporal fashion, not as an Absolute outside of history and time. He is recalled to us as One who created in sequence and in time (Gen. 1:1-2:2; 2:4-9, 18-22), as One who repented of what He had made (Gen. 6:6-7), who grieved that His creatures had made the worst of the freedom in which He had created them, but who finally promised He would never retreat from that fantastic commitment which He had made by creating them (Gen. 8:21-22; 9:11), sealing his promise with the rainbow (Gen. 8:12-17). He is recalled to us as the one who in time called Abram (Gen. 12:1-3), and later called him Abraham (Gen. 17:5), who called Isaac and Jacob, who called Moses and his people. And again in, not apart from, the fullness of time (Gal. 4:4), He called His servant Jesus to reveal His call to us Gentiles and to promise that He will be with us too in our Way through history. He sends us ahead each day to live with Him in time and for the sake of the future history of His creation. From Creation to Redemption, He is this temporal, historical one. That is the service of the Bible: It recalls for us who God is. Because it has so served us in the past, we read it in hope, not just that we shall discover some new aspect of what was said back then, but that in the process of reading and reflecting on it we shall be led to see and say a new thing.

The One the Bible recalls for us is the One who called His people Israel into His Way, and then called His church into its own way of walking in His Way. He called His Israel and His church both for the sake of His whole creation. Since the beginning of His temporality, He has revealed Himself again and again, leading us to ever new understandings of Him. With the next step, we shall propose that He has been showing us in His recent history that He has decided to raise the level of responsibility that He requires of us and so has given to us as His partners and friends more and more of the task of working for the completion of His creation.

God, Creator and Revealer, is also Redeemer. That is to say, He intends the completion of His creation. He intends its fulfillment. But as the fully, abundantly temporal One, He intends this as a historical, temporal fulfillment, and He evidently intends that He shall bring this about through us. "God has told you what is good; and what is it that the LORD asks of you? Only to act justly, to love loyally, and to walk wisely before your God" (Micah 6:8). His call is to start that walking, wisely and humbly, lest with all the power that He has placed in our hands, we forget that we are responsible to Him for what we make of His creation.

RECALLING WHO GOD IS NOT

The Bible has served us in the past, and so we trust it to serve us now and in the future, by reminding us who God is not. By reminding us that He is the One who has called us into the way, to be responsible not only to Him but also with Him, it awakens us to the fact that God is not alone in the enterprise of His creation. He created us to be cooperators, to stand on our own feet and care for His creation, doing His work which He has called us to do. Adam was to care for the garden, Abram was to get up and go to a new land, Moses was to lead his people out of Egypt, David was to fight and win Jerusalem, Nehemiah was to rebuild the walls of the city. Yes, and Jesus was to heal the sick and forgive men their sins and so were his disciples. It is remarkable to trace through those events which we call "the mighty acts of God" and see who were the evident actors. To a surprising extent, the actors were human beings. With the closing verses of Torah (Deut. 34:10-12), we are reminded of this: "There has never yet arisen in Israel a prophet like Moses, whom the LORD knew face to face: remember all the signs and portents which the LORD sent *him* to show in Egypt to Pharaoh and all his servants and the whole land; remember the strong hand *of Moses* and the terrible deeds which *he* did in the sight of all Israel." God is not a God who does it all for His creatures.

It seems to many of us today that in times past most of those in the Way thought that they did God honor by conceiving of Him as One who alone bore the responsibility and had the power to affect the course of history and even of each individual occurence in the world. When we read Augustine or Aquinas, Calvin or Luther, on the subject of Providence—that is, on their views of where, when and how God rules over His creation—we come away with terms such as omniscience, omnipresence and of course omnipotence. Whatever happens, they seem to us to have been saying, it happens always and without fail according to the will or at least the permission of God. So concerned were many of our predecessors in the Way with the dangers of pride or arrogance that they refused to allow men and women the right, not to speak of the duty, to act on their own, responsible for the outcome. When we look into this book in our hands today, however, we do not so hear of God. Far more we hear of a God like that of which William James spoke when he said: "Suppose the world's author put the case to you before creation, saying: 'I am going to make a world not certain to be saved, a world the perfection of which shall be conditional merely, the condition being that each several agent does its "level best." I offer you the chance of taking part in such a world. Its safety, you see, is unwarranted. It is a real adventure, with real dangers, yet it may win through. It is a scheme of cooperative work, genuinely to be done. Will you join the procession?'"[2] James hoped that we would, for he was convinced that this was just the sort of world in which we live. It is, I suggest, also the world of the God of whom we hear today when we listen to the Bible.

So today, as a result—but only in part—of a better historical understanding of Judaism in the first century, we hear, for example, so differently from them, the passage which our forewalkers fought over as the so-called "gift of the keys": "I will give you the keys of the kingdom of heaven; what you forbid on earth shall be forbidden in heaven, and what you allow on earth shall be allowed in heaven" (Mt. 16:19). Binding and loosing (or forbidding and allowing) were Pharisaic terms for stricter and more relaxed interpretations of commandments, and originally the saying probably had this Pharisaic sense. But "the gift of the keys" is in any case the revelation that what we had thought was God's decision was now given to us human beings to decide! It shall be in fact and in reality as we decide and carry out here in God's creation. We cannot "take it to the Lord in prayer," because the LORD has delivered the decision into our hands.

Dietrich Bonhoeffer seems to have been one of the first—Franz Rosenzweig had been twenty years ahead of him—to clarify this different way in which we read this book. I do not believe there is any way to establish that this is what the Bible *really* says. It has *really* said many things to many people. When we read this book— and this has always been true—we read it with our own eyes, our own questions, coming to it with our own experience. As one coming from our post-modern world, Bonhoeffer heard there of the God who called us to live in the world as though we had to do it on our own without support from Him. Gone, God is calling, is the God of the Gaps, the divine crutch. God is not, He seems to be telling us, the One who will provide for every contingency. On the contrary, we are called to provide for ourselves, that is, for one another and for the world in which we live.

God the Absolute, omniscient, omnipresent and omnipotent is

[2]*Pragmatism* (Cleveland and New York, 1955), p. 187.

not the One we read of in our Bible today. Of such a Being who is not yet Creator, a God before "the beginning," our Bible tells us nothing: "Where were you when I laid the foundations of the earth?" (Job 38:4). Perhaps in this matter we have changed, coming to see ourselves as bearing more responsibility for history and our world. It could also be said that God has changed. In light of what we have proposed concerning the temporality and historicity of God, however, it would be more consistent to say that of course we have both changed, as should be expected of historical beings. History has not stood still. Having led us with guiding hands, even with a pillar of smoke and a pillar of fire through a long wilderness, God has apparently decided that it is time we assumed the obligations of adulthood. So Bonhoeffer thought, and we agree. This, it would seem, is part of the commitment that God made in creating the world: Sooner or later He would have to draw back and let it try to stumble along on its own, without His support. If that is how it is, then God will not be a dictator, or even a sovereign king. He wills to love us as a father, not as an emperor. If God is indeed that sort of Creator, then He is not the all-sufficient power by which alone His creation endures. Such a power is precluded by the love whereby He chose there to be a genuine other, a creation over-against Him, endowed by Him with independent existence.

Even the most cursory review of the course of this past century suggests strongly that we are not doing at all well with our newly accepted or recognized responsibility. We are passing through a painful stage in the development of the human enterprise and, during all this agony, God has surely not been the distant Absolute, untouched by our inability to handle the responsibility that He has placed in our hands. If the figure of parenting is in order, then this must surely be an agonizing period in God's life. His children remain very much children, quite inadequate as the adults that they may be chronologically and as the grown children that He has asked them to become. No, we need not worry much about Augustine's horror of human pride; we have so little to be proud of. We should instead strain every nerve and find the right word to encourage ourselves and our fellow human beings to strive once again to take responsibility for God's creation.

Never more clearly than in our century has God made it clear to us that He is not the All-Doer which we think of the ancients as having believed Him to be. One clear sign of this, so difficult to digest is the birth of the state of Israel. For centuries His people had said to themselves (and we surely didn't disagree with them about *this*) that the restoration of the Land, the return of His people to the land which He had destined as theirs, and above all the restoration of Jewish autonomy in the Land, was something which only He could accomplish when He sent His messiah. In fact, it was not so. In fact the state of Israel was not born out of divine intervention, so far as the eye can see. When the British declared their mandate over Palestine at an end, within less than twenty-four hours the land was surrounded and invaded by the regular armies of no less than five countries, all bent on the destruction of the Jewish people. In that context, the Jews declared themselves a sovereign state. But what good is a declaration of independence? In fact they then were required to prove that they were actually not dependent, not so much as on a faith that God would rescue them. Israeli men and women fought and died to hold every possible square inch of the Land that they could. The state of Israel was born out of that battle, and its first national frontiers were such as could be held against invading armies from each and every neighbor.

Where was God during that battle? Indeed, where was He during the Holocaust? Was He not right there, suffering as only a parent suffers when he finds that His love compels him to carry through with that which he has begun? No, the Creator remains who He committed himself to be by His act of Creation. He will not, He cannot, be untrue to Himself in His first great act of love and step in to treat His children again as if they could never learn anything. Whether we *can* learn remains to be seen. What is sure is that God is not now, whatever He has been thought to have been in the past, the All-Doer.

RECALLING WHO WE ARE

The book that we carry serves us not only by recalling who God is and is not, but also by reminding us of who we are: We are those called out from among the nations (Gentiles, *Goyim*) to belong to Jesus Christ. The result of this calling is the church. In that church there were at first only Jews, then Jews and Gentiles and, finally, almost only Gentiles. Although it seemed at the time Paul wrote to have been almost of the essence of the church that it be made up of Jews and Gentiles, it would appear to have developed that the presence of Jews in the church (or from the point of view of Judaism, apostate Jews) is an unnecessary but welcome "extra." Only one Jew is essential to the church, and that is the Jew Jesus. He is the one Jew to the hem of whose garment we cling (Zech. 8:23; cf. Mt. 14:36). He alone is the one who conducts us into the way of the God of Israel. If a few Jews leave their people to be with us in the church, we can thank God for this extra reminder that we Gentiles are called in the church to walk in our own given way in the Way of none other than the God of the Jews.

The Apostolic Writings, coming from the period when the church was taking shape by growing away from the Jewish people, reflect the un-finished character of that separation and contain evidence of the resulting intergroup strife. Although generally the church is seen by their authors to be distinct from Israel, there are passages in which the church is called "the people" in the sense in which the Scriptures speak of the people of Israel (Tit. 2:14; 1 Pet. 2:9f; Rev. 21:3). This way of speaking reflects the ahistorical debate of the first century about who was the "true" Israel. Since we now see that both rabbinic Judaism and Catholic Christianity are later developments arising from two different interpreta-tions of Israel's tradition, we can no longer carry on that debate. Historically speaking, the Jewish people were the continuation of Israel and they remain so today. The church was something new in God's plan for His creation.

The book we carry reminds us that we are Gentiles with a par-ticular calling—to belong to Christ, to be "in" him, to be one with him, to be the disciples of Jesus, in short, to follow him. We are called, therefore, to an activity and an existence in time and history, as is God's Israel. In this historical Way which we are to walk, we are not alone. We walk, as Israel walks, as God's beloved, and with our head, the one Jew Jesus, always with us. Whatever is to come in God's future, we are called to walk together here and now, a "here and now" that has stretched on far longer than any of the authors of the Apostolic Writings dreamed of. We walk in the light of revelation on the way toward redemption, but we walk always with real feet on the real ground, as creatures. The book that we carry reminds us of our creatureliness not only in the sense of our mortality or limitations, but also in our responsibility to God the Creator for the rest of creation. We are to yearn, to pray for redemption, the completion of Creation. We are to pray for the coming of the Kingdom. In this we join Israel in its great commissioned work. Now we Gentiles are called to join our voices to that of the Jews. We are to entreat the Kingdom. In the introduction to Part III of *The Star of Redemption*, Franz Rosenzweig developed the thesis that, by this prayer, the believers in congregation are, by God's will, forcing God's hand. Their prayer is not vain chatter. In the prayer for the kingdom, the community brings closer the final redemption of creation. Our prayer, after all, is not optional. It is commanded. It is intrinsic to walking in the Way. It is that to which we have been called.

RECALLING WHO WE ARE NOT

The book which we carry also reminds us of who we are not. It does this by telling of the others, those who are not of our company, those who do not walk with us. It reminds us that there are those who were called before us, apart from whose calling ours would be inconceivable. It further reminds us that we are not all but only some of the world and have no reason to suppose that we were ever meant to include the whole world. Further, this book makes it clear that we are not those actual people of, by and for whom either the Scriptures or the Apostolic Writings were written, edited and collected. We have much in common with them, but we shall misunderstand this communion if we do not also see that we are different, distinguished from them by the fact of a long intervening history. By reminding us of all these others who we are not, the Bible helps us to recall who we are.

The largest part of the Bible, namely, the Scriptures, does not speak of us at all. Its subject matter is Israel, those who were called before us and who continue to this day to know themselves as having been rescued from Egypt and called and committed at Sinai. We are reminded, then, that we are not the first to be called. We are reminded by the Apostolic Writings that our election comes out of and is framed in a specific relationship to that of the Jews. We are called not to be Jews, but to be the historically continuing body of the one Jew, Jesus Christ. Empowered by the Spirit which worked in him and now works also in us, we are to bear witness before the world that we have been sent by the one who sent Jesus, by the one God of Israel. In the name of Israel's God, we are called to be His Gentiles sent to make Him known to other Gentiles. We do this as those called to be, in our own way, also heirs of God's promises to His people, signs of the hope that those promises are meant for the whole of God's creation. But we can never understand and so practice this responsibly if we forget that we hope in Him who from the beginning was Israel's Lord and Lover, and who can be trusted and hoped in because He remains Israel's Lord and Lover.

If we are reminded that we Christians are not Jews, but Gentiles called out of the world, we are also reminded by this book that we are not all the world. We cannot read this particular book without becoming aware that we live in a world in which most people do not read this book. The Christians of all the churches form but a small part of the world's population and, since the latter is growing faster than the former, we are becoming an ever smaller part. The history of Christian attempts to convert Hindus and Buddhists has a rather modest record, whereas the record among Muslims has been almost nonexistent. When one adds to this the millions who are now swept up by a quasireligious Marxist vision, it is clear that, though we are Gentiles who worship the God of Israel, we are not anywhere near a majority of the Gentiles.

In the light of these facts, it is well to recall that it is written in our book that many were called—not all—and that we were ordered to go and make disciples from among all the Gentiles. If we understand that calling as a service to, but by no means identical with, God's redemptive purposes, then we shall be able to let this book remind us of our minority status. As rabbinic Judaism realized, there are those among the Gentiles who have a place in the world to come. Election as God's Israel did not draw the line around those who received God's love or would receive His salvation. This we can learn from Israel's Scripture and ours, as we can learn it also by considering how the Jews to this day read and understand those Scriptures.

Finally, this book reminds us that we did not write any part of it and that we live in a markedly different situation from that of those by and for whom it was written. It does so by the mere fact of being written in Hebrew and Greek. It has of course been translated into many languages, but if the translations have been well done, they will show that the patterns of life and thought are those of men and women who lived long ago, and understanding their words is always a matter of understanding words written by and for people whose world was, in all respects affected by time, a different one from that in which we find ourselves today.

Paul could write to the church in Corinth, concerning a passage written centuries earlier in the Scriptures, that "these things . . . were recorded for our benefit" (1 Cor. 10:11). The Apostolic Writings consistently expressed the conviction that the Scriptures were to be read and heard as immediately addressed to their readers in the first century. Yet just this conviction shows how different is our situation from that of those authors, for our conception of history and of what it is to be a creature of God's time and space — nowhere more powerfully expressed than in the development of redaction criticism — calls us to a more complex relationship to those ancient texts. Our way to find "benefit" in those texts can only be a way through time. We can understand them only as coming out of particular historical situations and reflecting their contexts. They carry weight in our conversation today only insofar as we can understand ourselves to be within a historical continuum of which those texts are a part. In other words, precisely as we let those texts be themselves in their own time and context, and also believe that the One of whom they speak, the God of Israel, is continuing His work in history to our own day, can we take those words with utmost seriousness. Taking them with utmost seriousness entails, with this understanding, taking them in their historical relativity. They can only lay claim on us now if we allow the history in which the text was written, our own history today and all the path of history between, to lay a like claim upon us. We allow *both* claims insofar as we allow the claim of the Creator of just this world, the Creator of history, and so the God who has made Himself to be One fully involved with history, to count. Just this distance from the text is what the text of the book we carry teaches us.

If it is charged that on more than one occasion we have said something other than the biblical authors, our reply is that the Bible itself invites us to speak our own words, insofar as our situation differs from that of its authors. Insofar as our situation remains the same — e.g., as creatures, as men and women called into the Way, as servants of the God of Israel — we have every reason to test what we say by the biblical witness. Faithfulness to the text, however, cannot take a form which requires that we abandon the history of the further course of the Way for a gnostic timelessness. The book that we carry demands that we take our own stage of the journey as seriously as that traveled by the biblical authors, so that we may be led to converse and walk as responsibly before God on our stretch of the road as they did on theirs. This is the proper test of whether we are "in accord with the Scriptures."

RECALLING WHAT HAS HAPPENED

We are reminded by the book which we carry that we find ourselves, or are invited to find ourselves, within a drama that opened with Creation, began to make sense with revelation and is headed toward redemption. Creation defines the terms of our condition. Revelation defines the possibilities of understanding who we are and in what context. Redemption remains an unclear goal because it has not yet come, so we speak of it only in poetic imagery. The world does not know of Creation because it is unaware of revelation. It is unaware even of the revelation that Creation itself contains because it does not know itself as a creature. Israel knows of it, because it was born in revelation, and therefore it knows also of Creation. By Israel's revelation into which we Gentiles have now been drawn, the church knows of Creation too. But neither the church nor Israel knows of redemption except as promise, as hope. We both know that our Redeemer lives. We both know that He has made Himself known. But we both know that the redemption of God's unfulfilled, incomplete creation has not happened (Rom. 8:19-22). We Gentiles are sure of our adoption as sons, but for this too the apostle Paul reminded us (Rom. 8:23), we still wait and, if he knew this nineteen centuries ago, how much more sure may we be today that we are still waiting.

Nevertheless, we know what has happened. We know that a codicil has been written to God's covenant with His people for the sake of His creation. Our names are inscribed on that codicil. It is not a new will which could replace the original. God is not faithless. His covenant with His people stands. But there is now a codicil which adds to the Way for His people, a possibility for Gentiles to walk in their own manner in His Way.

What has happened is, therefore, a new thing. One can only read with wonder—and a sense of humor—how those in this new way were convinced that nothing had changed, that their being in the Way was perfectly clear in the original revelation. This was as clear to them as that the commandment to allow the ox treading the threshing floor to eat what was at his feet (Deut. 25:4) entailed that the apostles should be supported by their congregations (1 Cor. 9:7-12). Of course there is an entailment, of a certain sort. Does not He who hovered over His creation ever yet hover in love? Would He not care for His poor verbose apostles as He did for His poor dumb oxen? Paul's logic is not bad. But, nonetheless, a new word to the Gentiles is hardly the same as instruction in the Way that was to be walked also with respect to wheat and oxen. Paul's word must not hide from us the fact that something radically new, not to be simply read off from the past, by no means a logical entailment, has happened.

This fact of something new, a codicil as distinct from a will, reminds us that this book presents us with history. It is bound to and reflects places and dates with every page. Redaction criticism only underscores the point. Every page of the Bible reflects and is a product of history, even those written by men utterly weary of history, such as the beginning of Ecclesiastes. It presents us history and therefore it comes to us unfinished. It tells a story only up to a certain point. In the Apostolic Writings, we have a story remembered from early in the first century, told from roughly the middle of the century on, and stopping unfinished toward the close of that century at the latest. Surely by the reckoning of the authors of the Apostolic Writings themselves, the history that followed must matter. They had high expectations. The day was far gone, the moment was at hand. Be ready! How they would have wanted to live another fifty years to see how it would turn out.

The canon, however, has been closed. With all due respect to those who made that decision, whoever they may have been (and that is hardly clear—it seems to have happened without any official action other than the recognition of the fact), the result has been to distort our conversation ever since. The closing of the canon is not itself the problem, for it emphasizes that the Apostolic Writings, like the Scriptures, are history-up-to-a-point. The middle of the second Commonwealth is an arbitrary point in Israel's history; the end of the first century is an equally arbitrary point in the early development of the history of the church. So much was to happen in the following centuries. So much more has happened in more recent centuries. Had we not closed our eyes to this continuation of the story, there would have been less distortion of our conversation as a result of closing the canon. The closing of the canon only closes an important chapter in the *continuing* story of God's history with His people and His church, and of their history with Him.

The book which we carry tells us what has happened—an unfolding, unfinished history of God's people and God's church which has been for us the clue to understanding God, ourselves and this world. Not in any simple way, but nevertheless in an utterly unavoidable way, this history *is* revelation; we may not rest content with saying that it *was* revelation. If that history, suddenly cut short, is our clue to understanding God, ourselves and the world, then what has happened since the canon's last books may tell us more. The history as it has continued calls us to attend to it as well for the revelation of the God of Israel.

RECALLING WHAT HAS NOT HAPPENED

By recalling for us what has happened, the book which we carry also reminds us of what has not happened. The Bible, among other things, tells a story and, as it does so, it points ahead to a conclusion for which its authors were waiting eagerly. The events which they expected had not occurred by the time the last of its pages were written. The very definiteness of the book, its specific content, forces us to note that there is much that is not in this book. This is true not just in the sense that the Bible is no encyclopedia, but even more in that its pages were all written by a certain time. Since then a long history, almost nineteen centuries of it, has come. Of that history, naturally, they could tell us nothing.

The biblical authors longed and prayed for a Day, the Day of the Lord, when suffering and injustice, war and catastrophe would be no more. No more typical an expression of this is to be found than that in the book of the prophet Isaiah (2:2-4; also in Micah 4:1-3):

> In days to come
> the mountain of the LORD's house
> shall be set over all other mountains,
> lifted high above the hills.

> All the nations [*Goyim*] shall come streaming to it,
> and many peoples shall come and say,
> 'Come, let us climb up on to the mountain of the LORD,
>> to the house of the God of Jacob,
>> that he may teach us his ways
>> and we may walk in his paths.'
> For instruction [*Torah*] issues from Zion,
>> and out of Jerusalem comes the word of the LORD;
>> he will be judge between nations, [*Goyim*]
> arbiter among many peoples.
> They shall beat their swords into mattocks
>> and their spears into pruning-knives;
> nation [*Goy*] shall not lift sword against nation [*Goy*]
> nor ever again be trained for war.

Approximately 2700 years later, there is to be observed a sign at "the Good Fence"—the open border-crossing into Lebanon at the northernmost tip of Israel—which contains that last verse. It has been so long, and still it has not happened.

The Apostolic Writings are even more marked by a conviction of the communities for which they were written that the Day was at hand (Rom. 13:12), that the great cataclysmic restoration of creation would take place within their own generation (Mk. 13:30; Mt. 24:34; Lk. 21:32). But it is today as it was toward the end of the first century. It seems, as one author of the Apostolic Writings put it, that scoffers can still ask, "Where now is the promise of his coming? Our fathers have been laid to their rest, but still everything continues exactly as it has always been since the world began" (2 Pet. 3:4). (*Fathers* referred to the patriarchs or, more broadly, the great men of Israel's tradition.) The *parousia*, the appearing, the coming on clouds of glory, the advent of the Kingdom announced by Jesus, has not happened.

I would not want to say that there is no truth whatsoever in the various ways with which we have in our past conversation attempted to deal with the fact that the expected end did not come. We have spiritualized that concrete hope, and also internalized and individualized it. Nevertheless, an honest reading of the Apostolic Writings shows that, although what they expected may have included all or some of this, it centered on an event that would be historical, possibly even cosmic, and that *their* hope, as they defined it, has not been fulfilled. We must either say that they hoped for the wrong thing, or admit that what they hoped for cannot be, or else confess it as that for which we *still* hope — because it has not yet happened.

We should notice a further expectation of the Apostolic writers which has not been fulfilled: The church did not remain a community of Jews and Gentiles. As early as the time of Paul's letters, it must have seemed that it could never be otherwise, although this view was colored by the conviction that the end of this age, which we might translate as the end of history, was not far away. But, as we come to later documents from other authors, we hear increasingly of the Jews as "them," in contrast to the church as "us." This distinction grew out of an argument among Jews about the right meaning of Jewishness, but by the beginning of the second century Jewishness had become an evil. Ignatius of Antioch could write, "If we go on observing Judaism, we admit that we never received grace" (Ad. Magn. 8:1). And again, "It is monstrous to talk Jesus Christ and to live like a Jew" (ibid., 10:3). The claim of the author of the letter to the Ephesians, that Christ "has made the two one, and...has broken down the enmity which stood like a dividing wall between them" (2:14) was falsified by the church within several generations.

There is one passage in the letter to the Hebrews (8:13) which may reflect another expectation that was not to be realized: "By speaking of a new covenant he pronounced the first one old; and anything that is growing old and aging will shortly disappear." If it was expected that Judaism would "disappear," then this unknown author's prediction was certainly contradicted by history. Out of the ashes of the Temple came the phoenix of the rabbis of Javneh who gave birth to one of the greatest and most enduring renaissances of Judaism.

The book we carry reminds us of what has not happened because we cannot help but recall, as we read it, all that is not in it, that long chain of events which stretches from the late first to the late twentieth century. Contrary to the expectation of the Apostolic Writers, history did not stop. If, however, we can share with them the faith that history, or at the least Israel's history and that of God's church, is the history of God's presence and life with His people and His church, then we are led by this conviction to conclude that God's history with His people and His church has not come to an end. If God did not die with the close of the canon, what else can we say?

Our response to the closing of the canon needs to be reconsidered. It will not be enough to say that the canon is closed in fact but not in principle, or, if we say that, it will not be sufficient to think only of the possibility of some archaeological expedition turning up one of Paul's lost letters, or another Gospel book, or the hypothetical Q document. We are concerned, rather, with the issue of further revelation of the living God since the close of the first century. The closed canon should always open our conversation, but it should never cut it off. What has been closed in fact and not in principle is the opening stage of the conversation of Gentiles on the Way. The conversation itself goes on, and not just among ourselves; we are speaking not simply of our Way, but of Him whose Way we believe it continues to be.

If the Bible has served and continues to serve the function of opening our conversation, the issue, to which the book itself leads us when we read it now in the late twentieth century, is whether the book can lead us to see God's hand and hear His word also in places other than in that book and in the distant past of which it tells. It can be argued that there have been times and places in which new circumstances have almost forced God's people to revise their understanding of God's dealing with them. What else could we call that but new revelation? The long-standing judgment of Judaism that prophecy ceased with Ezra would seem to require qualification. The oral tradition as embodied in the Talmud itself raises a question about the Jewish decision to close the canon of Scripture. And, as we have seen, events in our own time are forcing Judaism to rethink their understanding of God and His relationship to His people. In our conversation in the Gentile church, we are only beginning to find words with which to say something of this sort. The idea that the God who made himself known in Jesus Christ is still making Himself known is familiar. Many have said that. That revelation is and continues to be an ever new possibility along the Way which we walk is a possibility that calls for fresh discussion at this stage of our journey. The Scriptures and our own Apostolic Writings themselves force us to take this possibility more seriously and more radically than we have in the past. The question to which we must turn, then, is whether the book which we carry can really open this sort of conversation for us, our conversation with each other and with the Giver of our Way concerning the events of our own day. What we must now discuss is whether we can be led by the Bible-as-revelation to see the revelation of our own times. Precisely this, as I see it, is the present form of the question, whether the Bible will be for us the word of God.

The Course of the Way:
History as Revelation

INTRODUCTION

Who or what is to determine the further course of the Way on which we find ourselves? If the answer is or ought to be God, then how do we know His intent for us? The answer which we have traditionally given in our conversation has been that we learn God's directions by means of revelation. But what do we mean by this term? How is revelation to be identified? What are its criteria? We have said often enough that Jesus Christ is the revelation of God for His Gentile church. We have also said that the Bible is—or can become again and again—God's revelation. But does God also instruct us in other ways? Can there be further revelation, further instruction, given as it were since the writings which made up the book which we carry? Is it only by rereading this book that we learn what our next step ought to be, the direction of the road ahead, or can we learn from the Bible to attend to more than is in it? How we understand and settle this matter depends on what we understand by the term *revelation*. We touched on this matter in a preliminary way in our second step. Now we should consider it more fully. I shall begin by presenting briefly the elements of revelation, next clarifying the pattern into which these elements fall, then presenting evidence for the reemergence of this pattern in our own time and conclude with some suggestions about the consequences of these recent happenings for our further conversation about God and ourselves.

THE ELEMENTS OF REVELATION

The word *revelation* means disclosure, an appearing, literally an unveiling. Such a dictionary-definition, however, will not take us far unless we realize that for our past conversation, generally, the disclosure of revelation has been conceived as an occurrence which takes place between persons, specifically between the Creator and certain of His human creatures. Since we are analyzing a personal transaction, we shall do well to avoid generalization on the one hand and inappropriate precision on the other. As is so often the case with our analyses of personal transactions, we can only speak of the matter itself indirectly. Love, to take the classical analogy, is not so simply defined, or dies under our microscope if it is simply defined. We describe love more appropriately by saying what goes on, what the effects are, what is consistent and inconsistent with love. Love can best be portrayed by telling a story. In some such fashion we must proceed here for, like love, revelation is something which takes place between persons. Indeed, Franz Rosenzweig defined revelation as God's declaration of love addressed to man which transforms the isolated self into the responding soul.[1]

Revelation begins with God, or so it has always been judged after the fact. It is an act of the Creator toward His creatures. Yet the realm in which it takes place is entirely that of the creaturely. God the person causes something to happen with respect to His personal creatures, men and women, yet the only aspect of this which we can see and discuss is what happens to those women and men who are, as we say after the fact, the recipients of revelation. In the event called revelation, something happens to certain human beings.

Those to whom revelation happens, as the Christian tradition has portrayed them, have always been men and women who are already in or are thereby set upon the Way, the path or course through history, beginning with Abraham, leading to Sinai and through the wilderness under Moses, in which both the Jewish people and the Christian church have, in their rather different views of it, understood themselves to be walking. If there has been or can be revelation to others, those in the Way cannot testify to it. Other things may or may not happen; this, the church has been convinced, has happened. Revelation, as Christians have spoken of it,

---

[1] *The Star of Redemption*, pp. 159ff.

has happened always to those in the Way. This is how the church has agreed to use the word.

Not every happening to those in the Way has been called revelation. Revelation takes the form, generally, of leading, of instruction in the Way. Judaism has testified to this by seeing revelation in its totality as Torah and by the importance it has given to Halachah. Revelation is God's instruction, and the joyous response of man is to walk according to this leading. This character of revelation is exemplified in Israel's stories of God's calling of Abraham and Moses.

The story of revelation, as the story of the Scriptures could be called, began with God's call of Abram to leave his land and people and go to a place which God would show him. Thus began the Way. Abram was told only to go, to start moving, to walk. His destination was not given. The outcome of his journey was left open. All he was told to do was to start. The effect of this instruction was immediate in the case of Abram; he was pointed in a direction, oriented as we say, but the reason for and the implications of this orientation of the one man Abram only becomes clear as the story unfolds. Abram was oriented in order to become Abraham and so to orient his descendants. We shall be missing essential elements of the concept of revelation if we ignore this wider social effect. Revelation is not simply the orientation or instruction of the individual to whom the divine voice speaks. Revelation consists always in the orientation or reorientation of one person that leads eventually to the direction given to the community which follows in the path so designated, the Way so defined. The judgment that there has been revelation is one made by the community that comes after. Apart from them, we have only the special experience of some individual.

The communal element of revelation is made even clearer in that *locus classicus* for our subject, the disclosure of the divine Name to Moses in the wilderness, as told in Exodus 3 and 4. Here the communal element both precedes and follows the disclosure of the Name, for the context is God's concern for the condition of the people, their plight in Egypt and His purpose to have Moses lead them into the Land of promise. God's disclosure of His purpose to Moses takes the form of instruction as to what Moses is to do and what the people are to do, how they are to proceed in God's Way out of their present situation into the next stage of their journey.

Moses is given a new direction so as to set the people in a new direction, and the revelation of the Name has its importance because of this context.

The implicit content of the revelation of the Name to Moses, therefore, is the revelation of Torah from Mt. Sinai. Torah defines God's purpose for Israel, pointing out the Way, in the walking of which they are to be what He would have in His creation: a holy nation, a people serving Him for the sake of His plan for His creation. This is a recurring theme of the prophetic literature. Israel received light in order to be a light for the Gentiles and so to be the reoriented people for the sake of that reorientation of all creation that we call redemption.

THE PATTERN OF REVELATION

Our preliminary sketch of the elements of revelation already shows that they form a pattern. The story of Abram's call must of course prove exceptional, since that is the beginning of the very story which leads us to speak of revelation. In all other cases, revelation occurs in the context of the life and history of the people on the Way. It comes to the people who are bearers of a tradition. The longer the people have moved along the Way through history, the stronger is their sense of their tradition and the clearer is the pattern of revelation. The revelation to Moses builds on the tradition of revelation to the patriarchs: The God who speaks with Moses is "the God of your fathers, the God of Abraham, the God of Isaac and the God of Jacob" (Ex. 3:6). Revelation begins against the background of a tradition of revelation.

The first aspect of the pattern holds even for the case of a story of revelation to the Midianite prophet Balaam (Num. 22f.), for the story is obviously told as a piece of Israel's history. What God had to say through Balaam, not to speak of Balaam's ass, rests entirely on the tradition of Israel, its rescue from Egypt and its movement toward the Land of promise. Even when a Gentile is the chosen agent of revelation, revelation is rooted in the tradition of revelation, back until the beginnings of its history with the call of Abram.

The pattern of revelation begins with tradition. Then comes one or another historical event or development which becomes the occasion for the reorientation of a prophet, typically, which leads in turn to the eventual reorientation of the people, or, as we can also say, the reinterpretation of the tradition. This second bit of the pattern becomes clear when Israel's traditions begin to be established, as in the time of the monarchy and later. In such an early stage as that presented in the story of Moses in the wilderness or at Sinai, the historical context is important, but it is less obviously the occasion of that reorientation of the prophet that leads to what we have come to call revelation. The situation of the Hebrews in Egypt, historical and political, however, is basic to the conversation between God and Moses. Indeed, without that situation, there would be little point to the story as it stands. And again at Sinai the situation of Israel newly formed into a people by the Exodus event and the pressing problems of their common life runs through every element of Torah. Torah is nothing other than instruction for proceeding ahead on the Way in all its historical reality.

The more firmly tradition became established, the more clearly the impact of historical events in Israel's social and political history emerged as the occasion of revelation. Revelation has to do with what is going on in Israel's history, not only in the sense that it speaks to that history, but also in the sense that the history itself is seen to be revelatory. Time and again it is said that what we call revelation is addressed to Israel's history. The stories in Exodus have already been mentioned, and we can add the "still small voice" that spoke to Elijah, since that voice ordered him to return home and start a revolution (1 Kgs. 19:15-17). Amos, Hosea, Isaiah and Jeremiah all understood the voice of the Lord to be addressing Israel (or Judah) in its social and political life, and they took threats to Israel's life to be warnings from the Lord.

Can we conclude from these stories that history was seen to be revelatory? That is too general a claim. Evidently not every event in or aspect of Israel's history was taken to be a sign from God. When an event or development was so taken — as in the threat of Assyrian invasion, the defeat by Babylon or Cyrus's decree allowing the exiles to return — there was always a prophet who was himself struck by one or another of these historical events in such a way that he interpreted God's purpose in a manner that was new and sometimes shocking for his compatriots. Under the impact of certain events, particular individuals felt compelled to reinterpret the traditon in a manner which clashed with the received understanding. A word of the prophet Amos can stand for the others: "For you alone have

I cared among all the nations of the world. . . . " That was the received tradition. ". . . Therefore will I punish you for all your iniquities" (3:2). That was the unexpected reinterpretation, made in the light of economic injustice in Israel and the threat of Assyria from the north.

Further examples of this pattern are provided by the stories of three major moments of renewal: under Joshua at Schechem, under Josiah and the discovery of the Temple scroll and under Ezra after the Exile. In each story, the people accept a new interpretation of their Torah tradition which reflects the changed historical circumstances that led to the demand for reform. Indeed, the Scriptures as we now have them are the result of successive reinterpretations of Israel's tradition made in the light of developments in Israel's historical circumstances and accepted by the faithful community as the expression of God's further intent for their Way through history. In the course of their long history, from Abraham down to Ezra's reform, this tradition-bearing people was confronted again and again with events which challenged that tradition and led one or more of its number to reinterpret it in such a way as to account for the latest event. Nowhere is this more evident than in the canon of Torah which Ezra brought back to Jerusalem from Babylon: Torah closes with Moses and the people not yet in the Land. The condition of Exile was thereby set into the core of the tradition in such a way that recent events could be seen to be compatible with Israel's ancient story.[2]

The pattern of revelation which we have drawn from the Scriptures is strikingly evident in a later collection of material written by Jews — the Apostolic Writings. To a remarkable extent, the Gospel, the "Good News" of the Jesus movement which became the church, was nothing other than a new interpretation of Israel's tradition. Its various authors were united in at least this: They thought that everything they were saying was "according to the Scriptures." All of Israel's tradition, its promises and prophecies, was interpreted in such a way as to lead up to the event of Jesus of Nazareth, including his death and resurrection. This, those first century Jews were convinced, was what their tradition had been about all along and it had been given to them finally to see it aright.

The decisive events which effected this reorientation leading to

[2]See James A. Sanders, *Torah and Canon* (Philadelphia, 1975).

this new interpretation of the tradition were the crucifixion and the resurrection of Jesus. That is not to say that there had been nothing new in the preaching of Jesus. The expected beginning of the reign of God, however this is to be conceived, lent at least a note of urgency to his message. Yet his interpretation of the tradition, insofar as it can be determined, lay generally well within the scope of first century Palestinian Judaism. For a genuinely new interpretation of the whole tradition, we must turn to the preaching of the post-Easter movement.

That God had "raised up" or "exalted" Jesus, as the speeches attributed to Peter in Acts put it, confirmed for the first disciples that Jesus was, precisely as the crucified one, Israel's messiah. The unveiling, the revelation of who Jesus was and of his significance, therefore, was the content of Easter faith. In the light of Easter, the unthinkable, the utterly unexpected and profoundly negative event of Jesus' crucifixion by the Roman authorities came to be seen positively as God's act of love for the world. As heirs and beneficiaries of Ezra's reform and its implementation by the Scribes and the Pharisees, the disciples searched their tradition with new eyes, seeking to reinterpret it so as to be able to see that it had been leading up to this latest event all along. For them, as for their ancestors, Israel's tradition was never a finished piece of the past. Tradition, *paradosis*, was literally "handed over" into the present. Thus the recent events were incorporated into the story as its climax.

The life, death and exaltation of Jesus were the first events which led to that new interpretation of Israel's tradition which was to turn the Jesus movement into the Christian church. But they were not the last; one further event—the deluge of Gentiles that began to flood the movement—was to have a similar reorienting effect. This event or development was evidently as unexpected and almost as unsettling as the crucifixion itself. It was resisted strongly by some in the movement and almost led to a split during the first generation, yet it had a decisive role in shaping the church. If Paul's experience on the way to Damascus is understood as a calling to take up the mission to the Gentiles,[3] his case shows the effect of this new fact of Gentile receptivity to the apostolic preaching. Paul came to understand his mission to preach to the Gentiles as a constituent

---

[3]See K. Stendahl, *Paul Among Jews and Gentiles* (Philadelphia, 1976), pp. 7-23.

part of the new thing which God had begun in Jesus Christ.

The entry of the Gentiles into the new movement, seen as a revelation of God's purpose in history, thereby became the key for reinterpreting the tradition of Israel in such a way as to show that this latest development was already God's intent from the very beginning of revelatory history. Beginning with Abraham, the story was now read as one leading to this Gentile mission. The pattern of reinterpretation under pressure of events which proved themselves to be reorienting in Israel's history—we should now say, Jewish history—continued.

THE REEMERGENCE OF THE PATTERN

The reinterpretation of Israel's tradition which constitutes such a large part of the Apostolic Writings was, in the eyes of the young church, the correct interpretation. It was the truth, they were convinced. As a result, they denied the validity of the understanding of Scripture held by those who did not share with them the reorienting effect of the events concerning Jesus of Nazareth and the Gentile mission. Specifically, the church denied any validity to Judaism, which under the leadership of the Tannaim (whose work continued at the academy of Javneh after the destruction of Jerusalem) was beginning the consolidation and codification of its own interpretation of the tradition, the Mishnah, and entering into a period of renaissance perhaps unparalleled in its history. Although the church was becoming, during this period, an almost totally Gentile enterprise, it saw itself as the true and therefore only continuation of Israel's line. Further Jewish history was therefore ignored, except to the limited extent that fitted into the church's self-understanding. The great flowering of Jewish piety and life under rabbinic leadership was not seen. Increasingly over the centuries, the Jews became in the view of the church only the remnants of the ancient people of God who had failed to respond to the revelation in Christ, who, that is, had not been reoriented by those events of the first century and so had lost their standing as God's beloved people. Thus, the theory that the church had displaced the Jewish people as the people of God and the heirs of God's promises came into existence. That theory, already clearly enunciated in Justin Martyr's *Dialogue with Trypho*, continued without major change for the following eighteen centuries. During all that time, the pattern of revelation which shaped the Scriptures, created the Apostolic Writings and formed the basis of Christian doctrine lay dormant. From time to time new events may have had reorienting effects on one small group or another, but this never led to a reorientation of the larger church and so to a new interpretation of the tradition.

In view of the stability of the church's interpretation of the tradition of Israel over so long a period, the change that has begun to take place in the last third of the twentieth century is astounding. A mere suggestion of what was coming could perhaps be detected in a minority position at the Amsterdam Assembly of the World Council of Churches in 1948, and the document *Nostra Aetate* of the Second Vatican Council in 1965 at least opened the possibilitiy of a fresh consideration of Israel's tradition. Since 1968, however, there has been building a series of statements by ecclesiastical authorities of ever-increasing clarity and penetration which have been moving in the direction of a frank contradiction of our interpretation of the past eighteen centuries. A published collection of such statements up through 1975 runs to over 150 pages.[4]

Illustrative of the change taking place was the decision of the Pastoral Council of the Catholic Church in the Netherlands in 1970 (cited on p. 56). That reversal was based on the recommendations of the council's Committee on Relations between Jews and Christians which included: "The Jewish people must be seen as the people with whom God concluded His covenant *for all time*."[5] The council also voted to encourage the study of the Scriptures together with Jews and declared "the Church has the duty to reflect on the entire history of the Jewish people before *and after* Christ and on *their* self-understanding."[6]

In 1973 the French Bishops' Committee for Relations with Jews said: "We cannot consider the Jewish religion as we would any other now existing in the world. . . . Even though in Jesus Christ the covenant was renewed for *Christendom*, the Jewish people must not be looked at by Christians . . . as the relic of a venerable and finished past but as a reality alive through the ages. . . . This vitality of the Jewish people . . .poses questions to us Christians which touch on the heart of our faith."[7]

[4]*Documents* (see note 10 on p. 42).

[5]*Documents*, p. 53. (Emphasis added here and in the following citations.)

[6]*Documents*, pp. 54f.

[7]*Documents*, pp. 60f.

In its 1967 report the Faith and Order Commission of the World Council of Churches also took note of the seriousness of the issue. Recognizing that those who held to the old view of the Jews and those who had shifted to an affirmative view needed to deal with this difference, they said: "The conversation among us has only just begun and we realize that in this question the entire self-understanding of the Church is at stake."[8] More recently, the United States National Council of Bishops, in a statement of 1975, underscored the seriousness of the theological consequences of the change taking place: "The brief suggestions [on Catholic-Jewish relations] of the Council [of Vatican II] have been taken up by some theologians, but their implications for theological renewal have not yet been fully explored."[9] Indeed, they spoke of "a task incumbent on theologians, as yet hardly begun, to explore the continuing relationship of the Jewish people with God. . . ."[10]

Although the Catholic statements in this collection have on the whole gone further in the new reinterpretation and probed it deeper than those of Protestant churches, one of the most suggestive proposals is to be found in the statement adopted by the Synod of the Reformed Church in the Netherlands in 1970: "Jesus Christ has a fundamentally different function for the nations and for Israel. The Jews are called back by him to the God who bound himself to them from their beginning. But the Gentiles are not called back to their origins by Jesus Christ; rather, they are called to something which is radically new in their history."[11]

There can be no doubt that this whole body of statements from which we have cited but a few examples constitutes a radical reversal of long-held teaching and presents a new interpretation of the church's tradition at a crucial point. In place of the theory of displacement we now hear of "the continuing relationship of the Jewish people with God." A qualification unheard of in the received tradition appears when we hear that "in Jesus Christ the covenant was renewed for Christendom." And where have we heard before that "Jesus Christ has a fundamentally different function for the Gentiles and for Israel," namely that he called the Gentiles to something "radically new in their history"? And if we now hear that he called his fellow Jews "back to the God who had bound himself to them from the beginning," we are by now well enough instructed in the history of the first three centuries of the Common

[8]*Documents*, pp. 79f.

[9]*Documents*, p. 32.

[10]*Documents*, p. 33.

[11]*Documents*, p. 98.

Era to know that, indeed, the Jewish people heeded God's call, not as sounded by Jesus but filtered through a Gentile church. They heard it and responded to it as it came to them from the rabbis of Javneh and their successors who produced the Mishnah.

The ecclesiastical statements which we have heard make clear that the reinterpretation of the tradition which they both call for and already express has been impelled by particular historical events and, indeed, events in the recent history of the Jewish people. The Holocaust and the establishment of the state of Israel are named explicitly in some of them and clearly implied by the rest as having exerted a reorienting effect on the authors of these statements. The ghastly reality of Hitler's mass shootings and death factories, which wiped out one third of all the Jews in the world, followed by the political reality of the state of Israel, won by courage and guns against apparently insuperable numerical and material odds, are what have worked this change. The driving force behind this shift in the church's understanding of its tradition was neither some aspect of the intellectual history to which theologians have been giving so much attention, nor Kant and the Enlightenment, nor Marxism, nor secularism (important as all these have been). Rather, the pattern of revelation which shaped the Scriptures and the church's beginning has once again reasserted itself. Events in Jewish history, perhaps the most staggering and unexpected events in its history since the church split off from the Jewish people, have worked a reorientation in the mind of many responsible Christians which has led to that new interpretation of the tradition of which we have spoken. If there follows eventually a reorientation of the community of the church, then it will be appropriate to speak of these events as revelatory.

Before developing this last point, I want to add one more observation on the effect of events in Jewish history upon the church. If one reviews these Christian statements concerning the Jewish people, one may notice a difference between those which preceded and those which followed the Six Day War of 1967. Despite many questions properly raised at the time and since about "the silence of the churches" at the threat of a second Holocaust, something may indeed have been happening to the churches in those days. Israel's stunning victory over armies massed along all her borders dealt a heavy blow to the Christian stereotype of the passive, suffering Jew. The silence of the churches, then, may have marked a deeper change and one with greater consequences than any sudden rally to Israel's support.

THE ISSUE OF NEW REVELATION

The emergence of the revelatory pattern which shaped the Scriptures, the Apostolic Writings and so the theology of the church is a historical fact of our most recent history. I have done no more than call attention to and describe this fact. No hortatory note has been sounded and none is necessary. I have not said that these events in recent Jewish history ought to or must have a reorienting effect on the mind of the church. I have only pointed out what has in fact been taking place among responsible ecclesiastical authorities. I have only called attention to the evidence for the claim that the old pattern of events in Jewish history reorienting the church in its understanding of God's way with His creation, to which we have traditionally given the name revelation, has reemerged in our own time.

It is instructive to contrast this fundamental change in a matter central to the church's self-understanding with the Reformation of the sixteenth century. The difference is striking. No new events in Jewish history triggered Luther's discovery or rediscovery of justification by grace alone, to be apprehended solely in faith. None of the reformers conceived of their movement as a change of direction, a reorientation. Rather, in the spirit of renaissance humanism, they understood themselves to be returning to the sources, rediscovering what had been the true revelation all along. They saw themselves as reforming a corrupted church, not as recipients of new instruction turning them in a new direction. They saw themselves as returning to the original path of the early church. What we have been discussing, however, is in no sense a return to origins but a matter of new directions being shown us by events of our own times. Finally, it must be granted that the Reformation split the church. Every voice that has taken up the new orientation of our time, whether Protestant or Catholic, has on the contrary seen this new direction as one that can work only for the reunification of the church. Unlike the Reformation return, as it was thought, to the purity of the early church, both the Catholic church and the major Protestant churches are beginning to contradict their historic teaching concerning the Jewish people and to reconsider those reorienting events which led to the theory of displacement. The issue that appears to be confronting the church is that of a possible new revelation.

Any claim that there has appeared a new revelation must be handled with the utmost care. Both the church and the Jewish people have had their fingers burned with such claims before. Because both the Jewish people and the church have believed that they walked under the instruction and leading of a living God, they have had to be sensitive to the possibility of new leadings. New revelation, therefore, has always had to be reckoned at least a possibility. The record, however, has not been encouraging and points to a course of caution if not skepticism.

For the Jews, two examples can be mentioned. The great Rabbi Akiba was convinced, and not alone, that Bar Kokhba was God's messiah, with the consequence that he sided with the Bar Kokhba revolt against the Romans and paid for this action with his life. His experience was hardly an encouragement to look for new messiahs. More painful by far was the messianic movement centered on the seventeenth-century figure Sabbatai Zevi, for whom Nathan of Gaza served the roles of both a John the Baptist and a Paul, discovering the messianic identity of Sabbatai Zevi and becoming the principal interpreter of the events which followed, including the claimed messiah's apostasy to Islam. In the light of such examples of claims to new directions from God in his dealings with his people, or new revelations of God's will, one can appreciate the wisdom of a conservative skepticism among Jews when there is talk of a new revelation within Judaism. Yet, in spite of this, the power of the Holocaust has been such as to lead as sober a thinker as Emil Fackenheim to speak of "a commanding Voice from Auschwitz," thereby taking up the language of a new revelation.[12]

The church's experience with claims to new revelation has scarcely been more encouraging. From its early steps along the Way, it was plagued with esoteric groups and self-proclaimed prophets, of which Montanus and his followers were but one example. In the face of such movements, the conservative tendency of the monarchial episcopate and the closing of the canon made eminently good sense. Whatever we may think of the harshness with which the later Albigensians were suppressed and the fate which met Savonarola, there remained a certain wisdom in resisting claims to new revelations. Luther spoke for the conservative tradition in attacking Thomas Münzer, whom he accused of believing that he

[12]*God's Presence in History* (New York, 1970).

had "swallowed the Holy Spirit, feathers and all."[13] New revelations in any respect at variance with the received tradition have always and only been deemed heresy.

Charges of heresy are less easily mounted, however, when what is new comes from councils of bishops and church synods, as is the case today. Moreover, in the case confronting and changing the church's mind in our days, the credentials of revelation are noticeably in order. The criteria which can be derived from that which has been accepted as revelation in our past are all being met in the present case. Historical events, not ideas or theories, are at the root of the matter; these events are primarily those of the history of the Jewish people, although of course they are public events and in that sense common to all. Further, these events of primarily Jewish history, the Holocaust and the state of Israel, have in point of fact effected a reorientation of the church at least sufficient to launch a major reinterpretation of our traditional understanding of the Jews and therefore of ourselves, and so at a point that touches every aspect of our tradition and theology. What has been happening is no theological fad, no "new theology" developed by a few professional theologians. The work of individual scholars, such as Moore, Parkes and Rosenzweig, have of course helped to prepare the way and have provided at least some historical knowledge and priceless conceptual tools for thinking out how the church is now going to move ahead on this unmapped stretch of the Way. But the change slowly coming over the church is occurring not as a movement of scholars, not as a new academic "twist," but as a profound reorientation emerging in statements of councils and synods. What else are we to say of all this if not that it is a new revelation?

If the emergence of the pattern of revelation in our time at the very least opens up the possibility of speaking of these new events as revelatory, the question of exactly what is being revealed will have to be faced. What is it that we are being shown now, that we have not seen or have not seen so clearly before? Let me begin with what seems to me to be clearest and then proceed to what is less obvious.

What is clearly revealed to the mind of the church in the events of modern Jewish history is obviously the continued existence of God's people. The people of God's covenant are still here, still very much alive, and the faithful among them are still devoted to the

---

[13]R. Bainton, *Here I Stand* (New York, 1950), p. 261

life of that covenant. This surely implies that God continues to concern Himself with the history of His people. Whatever He is doing with us Gentiles in the Way can in no sense contradict or detract from what He is doing with His people. Any thoughts that we may have about the significance of history, the future of human life and the course of this planet will have to take this revelation seriously. If the history of God's people continues, then we must assume that this history, and therefore the whole of human history as its inescapable context, matters to God. This insight is not absolutely new, but it has never been forced upon us so sharply as by these new events.

That way of putting the matter, however, is rather abstract. What is at stake becomes clearer if we notice a common element in both of the events which have forced themselves upon our attention: Both events raise to the highest degree the issue of human responsibility. The first does so in a negative way, the second in a positive way.

The Holocaust negatively raises the issue of human responsibility for history by throwing a floodlight on a failure of human responsibility. What happened could have been prevented, humanly prevented, and it was not. That may be evidence that God will not intervene to do what He expects us to do for ourselves—and for Him. Earlier in this century Protestant theologians exposed us to a theology of "the mighty acts of God," without sufficient attention to the fact that the acts in question were all in the distant past.[14] Such a theology helped to make it increasingly difficult to speak of the living God in the present tense. Had we been listening more to the Jews, we might have paid more attention to Torah and so noticed how it ends. Mighty acts and signs had been done in Egypt all right, but they are not quite so simply denoted God's acts as this strand of Protestant theology led us to think. On the contrary, the last book of Torah concludes with Israel's verdict concerning Moses which bears repeating:

> There has never yet risen in Israel a prophet like Moses, whom the Lord knew face to face: remember all the signs and portents which the Lord sent him to show in Egypt to Pharaoh and all his servants and the whole land; remember

[14]E.g., G. E. Wright and R. H. Fuller, *The Book of the Acts of God* (Garden City, N.Y., 1957).

the strong hand of Moses and the terrible deeds which he did in the sight of all Israel. (Deut. 34:10-12)

It has been pointed out that the major literature of Judaism produced during the Holocaust was not focused on the problem of theodicy, the question of what God was doing to justify Himself in that event. The major literature was Halachic: questions concerning how Jews ought to act when faced with some of the agonizing choices with which they were confronted by the prospect of mass murder.[15]

The Holocaust does indeed have something new to say to us in the church. It asks about our responsibility for what took place and so about our responsibility for the future. It tells us what Dietrich Bonhoeffer discovered in the midst of the horror, that it is God Himself who is forcing us to live in His world as if it were our own world, which indeed by the gift of Creation it is. It is God Himself who is forcing us to live in this world as if the God of our theological tradition, the one classically defined in Latin, e.g., as *actus purus*, were not there (*etsi deus non daretur*)[16] to do for us what He expects us to do for ourselves and for His creation. Had more Christians come to this realization earlier, perhaps millions murdered by Hitler might have been saved. The new in the revelation from Auschwitz, then, is that God requires that we take unqualified responsibility before Him for His history with us.

If the Holocaust is a negative revelation of God's requirement of human responsibility, the founding of the state of Israel says the same thing in a positive form. Israel was founded not by divine intervention from heaven or the sending of the messiah, but by Jewish guns and Jewish effort against seemingly insuperable numerical and material odds. Had the early pioneers, the fugitives from the Holocaust or the supporters of the project from the Diaspora waited upon a so-called act of God instead of daring to be the act of God, they would in all likelihood be waiting still, those who were still alive. This event which has begun to reorient the church, this event of the founding of Israel and Jewish return to the Land, was one of humanly assumed responsibility for history, yes, for God's history with His people and their history with Him.

For Judaism, especially its most orthodox members, this development seemed in 1948 a dangerous departure from their tradition

---

[15]Cf. I. J. Rosenbaum, *The Holocaust and Halakhah* (New York, 1976).

[16]D. Bonhoeffer, *Widerstand und Ergebung* (Munich, 1959), p. 241.

and one to be resisted. Slowly, almost all Jews have come to accept the rightness of this Jewish effort to move the history of God with His people a step closer to the realization of God's promises. God's promises, we could say, have become increasingly seen to be promises of what shall be, but not promises of what God alone will do to bring about that which He has promised. Israel too has its responsibility for the fulfillment of the promises, as well as in all other aspects of its history with God.

This may not be an altogether new word to Israel. Perhaps it is only clearer now, or that now we think we see that God had willed this all along. Such a view could be supported by Irving Greenberg's interpretation of the teaching of Rabbi Johanan Ben Zakkai, the founder of the academy at Javneh and, in one sense, the founder of rabbinic Judaism. Since some may know of Johanan only through the quite different interpretation of Richard Rubenstein as the counselor of passive submission, be it to Gentile authority or the will of God, Greenberg's estimation is worth giving at length. Johanan's response to the destruction of the Temple and the fall of Jerusalem in 70 C.E., he writes,

> became the dominant post-Destruction form of Judaism. This type of response continues the tradition but reinterprets the nature of God and God's relationship to Israel and develops new channels for the expression of the tradition. The crucial development is the shift from the revealed intervening God of the biblical period to the relatively withdrawn Deity of the exilic period. God is close now as *presence*, as *Shekhinah*, not as the automatic intervenor who brings victory to the deserving.
>
> A number of talmudic comments that have become staple cliches over the centuries of exilic existence leap into fresh life in the context of the response to the Destruction. The talmudic statement that prophecy ceased after the Destruction is not merely descriptive, it is normative. Prophecy ceases because God no longer intervenes overtly in the old mode. The old mode is credible in the context of the dominance of the Exodus model, not after a catastrophe. Similarly, the story of the disagreement between Rabbi Eliezer and his colleagues becomes a brilliant theological response to the tragedy. Eliezer wishes to confirm the validity of his legal ruling by divine intervention, and miracles and a heavenly voice uphold him. But the majority rebuffs these intercessions on the claim that 'it is not in the Heavens!'—the Torah is not in the divine domain anymore.
>
> This is an incredible riposte, coming from a group which interprets every letter in the Torah and sees even the curlicues, jots, and tittles of its letters as suffused with divine revelation. What the Talmud is saying, however, is that the catastrophe could not have occurred unless God had, as it were, withdrawn divine power from

the world, allowing human effort and testimony to become more central, even decisive.[17]

For Christians there is revealed a relationship between God and His creatures more nearly in line with Jewish Halachic faithfulness than with our idea that all that happens does so solely by God's action. If we are to continue to speak of "by grace alone," then we shall need to allow for the fact that, by the grace of Creation, the grace of Sinai and the grace of Jesus Christ — all and each unfinished events — God has really turned over into our hands the Way into the future which He has promised. We can move ahead in hope, but it will be a hope that calls us to cast our efforts into God's plan for this world. Redemption has been promised. The creation shall be completed. But this is not something which will happen apart from the efforts of God's people and God's Gentile church. What is new in the revelation of our days is that God will not deal with us as a "problem-solver." He is God, and not man; His ways are higher than our "problem-solving" ways and His thoughts are higher than our "problem-solving" thoughts. He wills, apparently, to deal with us as a loving Father who genuinely expects us to stand on our feet and struggle to do our part, which may be the largest part for all we now know, in bringing closer the age of redemption for which we long.

There is an alternative, I may add. It is that of old orthodoxies, Jewish and Christian (and also Nietsche): There can be no new revelation either because, with orthodoxy, God can and will do nothing new, or, more imaginatively, with Nietsche, because the old God has died, so new revelation is impossible. If indeed — that is, in the judgment of the communities of faith — new revelation becomes a reality, then history need not be left in the hands of the *Übermenschen*. It can be taken up by simply *Menschen*, men and women who will act responsibly toward each other and before Him who has given them this responsibility.

---

[17]"Judaism and History: Historical Events and Religious Change," in S. Kazan and N. Stampfer, eds., *Perspectives in Jewish Learning*, vol. I (Chicago, 1977), p. 55.

The Goal of the Way:
The Redemption of Creation

INTRODUCTION

We set out in the face of death to discern the Way in which we find ourselves walking through history. We do so as those already walking, already on what we trust is the Way. On the way to what? Can a Way be discerned whose destination is unknown? If there be a Way, then must it not have a goal? Yet how shall we speak of that which we cannot see? How can we speak of that for which we can only hope? Yet speak of it we have, for without this hope, we could scarcely have kept going. Without speaking of our hope we could hardly speak of the Way. Indeed, without this hope, it is doubtful if we could keep on walking.

The Way which we are trying to discern is one with a goal and, although it is not in sight, we must try to express our hope, in words as well as by the joyful fact of our walking. If we did not agree in the hope, and so to at least some extent in how we expressed it, we could not agree to walk together in the Way, for we could have no confidence that we were in the same Way together. Since we are speaking of our hope, however, not our past and not our present, we should not aim for a clear definition of our destination. Indeed, along the Way we have used a variety of images or figures for our goal. These fall roughly into two groups: one a set of figures for a goal that is within history, the other falling beyond or outside history. The first has pictured a radical change in history and for this earth. The second has presented reality in terms other than those of time and space. Are these alternatives? Should we choose between them? Is it possible to hope for both? And why these two apparently rather different foci — a world of peace and righteousness on the one hand and a heavenly condition on the other? These are some of the questions raised by the way in which those in the Way have carried on their conversations from the beginning and to our day.

REDEMPTION AND THE REDEEMER

Fundamental to further thought on these matters is the question: Who is the Redeemer of whose redemption we wish to speak? Redemption is our basic word for the goal of the Way, whether seen within or beyond history. Redemption is the act of releasing from bondage, of buying back what has been put in pledge. This commercial context of the word's origin was never quite lost, but the term became important in Israel's vocabulary because of the experience of and reflection upon the delivery from Egypt. The *redemption* entry in the *Encyclopedia Judaica* (vol. 14) opens with the summary definition: "Salvation from the states or circumstances that destroy the value of human existence or human existence itself." God is the Redeemer, the one who rescued Israel from slavery. But this God who is the Redeemer has always been known as the Creator. This gives us then a foundation for our reflection on the goal of the Way: The Redeemer is the Creator.

The identification of the Redeemer with the Creator is nowhere in doubt in the Scriptures, but perhaps its clearest articulation is in the writings of Deutero-Isaiah, as in chapters 41 and 42. Isa. 54:5 can stand for many another passage: "Your husband is your maker, whose name is the LORD of Hosts; your ransomer is the Holy One of Israel who is called the God of all the earth."

Redemption, or salvation, has generally been understood by Israel as the fulfillment of God's promises to His people, the realization of that which has been declared in revelation. Since the Redeemer is none other than the Creator, however, it would seem appropriate to say that redemption must be the completion of Creation. So it is often pictured in the Scriptures, the desert bursting forth into bloom and the lion lying down with the lamb. Redemption means Creation come to full term. But what does that mean?

It could mean, on the one hand, following Isaac Luria's idea of the "divine contraction" which made Creation possible, that God will complete what He began in Creation and return to His fullness. This would view Creation and redemption symmetrically, so to speak. At the end there would be God alone, as He was before Creation. Since God would then properly be said to be "all in all," redemption would mean the completion of Creation as its terminus, its *finis*.

On the other hand, if Creation is the gift of otherness as God's act of love, then redemption could not mean the termination of that other without implying a serious qualification of that love whereby He willed an other than Himself. Redemption will then be better conceived as the completion of Creation in some sense that does not bring it to a *finis*. In this way of considering the matter, Creation and redemption are asymmetrical, or in other words historical. On this view one might still make use of the idea of Creation involving a divine contraction, but then this would have to be considered an irreversible self-determination on God's part.

In considering these differing views of redemption, we are reflecting the great variety of ways in which it has been imagined in the Jewish as well as in the Christian conversation. Given this diversity, a coherent or organized presentation of the matter does not come easily and may not be desirable. After all, what is wrong with a variety of views, so long as they are not mutually contradictory or exclusive? What matters is that a hope be defined which can be that of those on a Way through history and so a hope which can help us forward in the path to which we have been called. The hope must be about ourselves, about the company of those who are walking, and also a hope for the context of our walk, the world in which we are actually walking. Just this is assured if we do not forget that the Redeemer is the Creator, and that redemption is of the Creation. This, as we shall see, has been characteristic of Israel's and thus the Jewish people's hope.

ISRAEL'S HOPE FOR CREATION

As Israel was created a nation and a people, so its hope has ever been primarily national and social. Its hope has been in the salvation of the nation, the people. Its hope has been for the restoration, the redemption of the Jews. As George Foot Moore put this for rabbinic Judaism: "What the Jew craved for himself was to have a part in the future golden age of the nation. . . . It was only so, not in some blissful lot for his individual self apart, that he could conceive of perfect happiness."[1] Israel's hope was therefore historical, in the strict sense that what was hoped for was a new condition in the historical future of this actual people on this solid earth.

It should be noted that this hope is for a new condition of this creation, but it is not a hope that God alone will bring this about. Referring to the prophets and especially Isaiah 40f., Moore erred in saying: "The deliverance itself was always the work of God."[2] But in fact the prophet wrote that God, the Creator of the ends of the earth (Isa. 40:28), "gives vigour to the weary, new strength to the exhausted" (v. 29). And for those who look to the Lord (v. 31), God is not said to act for them, but rather that they "will win new strength, they will grow wings like eagles; they will run and not be weary, they will march on and never grow faint" (v. 31). In Isaiah 41, he said: "Fear not, Jacob you worm and Israel poor louse. It is I who help *you*, says the LORD" (v. 14). As to the hills that were to be made low (40:4), here we read: "See, I will make of *you* a sharp threshing-sledge, . . . you shall thresh the mountains and crush them and reduce hills to chaff" (41:15).

If we say, with Moore, that deliverance is to be the work of the LORD, that would appear to be true in just the way that God's Exodus was His work, the Torah is His Torah, indeed all revelation is His. The eye of faith has ever so seen it, for it sees more than the eye of unbelief. The eye of faith, however, cannot ignore what anyone can see! In these events there were always also human beings at work, doing what they believed was the work of God. If we listen with care to the words of Deutero-Isaiah, we hear that God promised to help and be with Israel. It therefore seems more accurate to say that God has promised to be Israel's co-worker, rather than to put it the other way round. Moreover, the location of redemption is clearly here in this world in which Israel lives. Creation redeemed will still be creation. Redemption, in Israel's conception, was to be the completion of Creation, not its replacement. So it was consistent with this hope that man as the capstone of

[1] *Judaism in the First Centuries of the Christian Era* (New York, 1971 [1927]), vol. II, p. 312.

[2] Ibid., p. 330.

Creation would be the agent—of course with God's help—to bring this about, as we saw in Deutero-Isaiah.

Judaism continued in this line of hope of its ancestors. Hope in Judaism has been first of all hope for the people, the end of foreign domination and oppression, the restoration of the Land to the people, an age of righteousness and peace. Coupled with this national hope has been always a universal hope, that all the world would come to serve the one God. This has often been called Jewish messianic hope, but the focus has been more on the conditions of the messianic age than on the figure of the messiah. In some rabbinic texts the messiah (always a human figure) comes to lead the people into the new age. In some texts, he comes only when all Israel is already obedient and all has been prepared; in others he comes only when conditions are at their worst.[3] Agreement lies only in the hope for the messianic age and in the conception of that age as itself covering only some definite span of time. Generally, there is the present time, then the age of messiah, and then "the World to Come," the last being, we might say, such a reordering of creation as to include the resurrection of the dead.

The resurrection of the dead has played an important part in Israel's hope from Pharisaic times to the present, not as the central form of personal hope, as has been so often the case with us, but rather as an expression of each faithful Jew's hope of participating in the future redemption of Israel. The World to Come has often been envisaged as a time when there will be no more death, but death has not been for Judaism quite the fearful "last enemy" that it was for St. Paul and became for our whole tradition. Working from the same scriptural texts as did Paul, the rabbis could say that death came into the world because of Adam's transgression, but they also kept their eyes on other texts.[4] Death, with the Psalmist, could also be seen as the creaturely end of a good creaturely life and in that sense good. By a fanciful exegesis it was even said that the "very" in God's last word of Creation was death (Gen.R. IX, 5-9). Death too was part of God's good creation, so if one lived out one's seventy or so years, then death was a well-earned rest. Only when it came too early, before one had also added one's own bit of walking to Israel's forward movement through history, was death

[3]For a selection of talmudic texts on this subject, see A. Cohen, *Everyman's Talmud* (New York, 1975), pp. 349-56.

[4]See Cohen, *Everyman's Talmud*, pp. 38ff. and 73ff.

to be complained of. Whereas death in Israel's cause, as a martyr to sanctify the Name, was a great reward.

Judaism's greater willingness to accept the fact of death is perhaps connected with the fact that its hope has been so explicitly corporate and historical. If one's hope is primarily for the community, for the people of which one is a part, then one's own death is not the end of the story. One's own life, for so long as it lasts, is only a part of that larger life of the people. If one dies, so be it, just so long as the people prosper. It would of course be fine if one could share in the prosperity of one's people, if one could be there to celebrate along with all Israel when the people come to the great day of rescue and restoration. But that that day come is the center of Jewish hope and individual hope is subsumed within that larger and prior hope.

Israel's hope, Jewish hope, is of the sort that comes from understanding oneself as part of a people underway. Jewish hope means that redemption lies out ahead; creation is far from complete. Israel hopes as a people on the move, whose history is going somewhere, namely toward the fulfillment of all God's promises to His creation which He gave through His people Israel. To believe that Israel's history is going somewhere entails the belief that creation is going somewhere. Its story is not over; we are in the midst. With this hope for the completion of creation, for the whole of mankind coming to serve the One God and so of Israel arriving at the stage of righteousness and peace in its own promied Land, unthreatened by war or foreign domination, Israel has been strengthened to continue to walk in God's Way, its hope never stronger than when the times seemed most hopeless.

When one reflects on the actual history of the Jewish people, of which the Holocaust was the ultimate but by no means the only horror, one can only stand in wonder before the survival of Jewish hope. Irving Greenberg has presented the matter starkly in arguing that Jewish hope has rested in the confidence that one single piece of history, the Exodus, revealed the final truth about reality, *all other historical evidence to the contrary*.[5] Considering how much evidence to the contrary there has been, one can realize how a Jew today can find it difficult to hope for more than survival for oneself and one's children. We are in no position to say anything to the

[5]"Judaism and History: Historical Events and Religious Change," in S. Kazan and N. Stampfer, eds., *Perspectives in Jewish Learning*, vol. I (Chicago, 1977), pp. 43ff.

Jews about their hope; our sketch of the formal outlines of Israel's traditional hope is intended only to help us with our own conversation. As for their conversation, we must leave that to them; only we dare not, on this stage of our Way, stop praying for the peace of Jerusalem and for the speedy coming of redemption.

THE CHURCH'S HOPE

Against the background of the hope of Israel and traditional Judaism, we must now consider the character of *our* hope, first made available to us Gentiles when we were drawn by God into relationship with His son, Jesus of Nazareth, as our King and Lord (Eph. 2:12). The beginning is grounded in Jewish hope, of course, for the proclamation of Jesus as it is presented in the Apostolic Writings was of the imminent fulfillment of that for which every faithful Jew longed. God's reign over His creation was about to break in. The sign of the dawning of the new age was Jesus himself, identified from Easter on as God's messiah. At first, it would seem, the new era was expected immediately, before his disciples could complete their preaching mission, within "this" generation, within their lifetime. A generation later, the conviction remained strong that the new age might arrive at any moment. The faithful were to begin living now in total anticipation of the new era about to begin (Rom. 13:11ff.). Indeed, they already had some of the benefits of the age to come. It was as if it were already beginning.

The hope of the new community, however, was more complex than the Jewish hope and that was due to its conviction that Jesus himself was already the decisive first act of the unfolding drama of God's redemption of His creation. Jesus had come; then he had been crucified; then he had been exalted, raised, affirmed by God; soon he was to return and inaugurate the second and final stage. Time passed, however, and things did not develop as they hoped. What had begun as fairly typical Jewish longing was greatly intensified by the conviction that the moment had arrrived; but the completion of what they were sure had begun never seemed to come. The result was that hope deferred was almost inevitably transformed into a slightly different form of hope. The open, national hope of Judaism was transformed into the inner, personal and spiritual hope of the church. In addition, those who did the hoping were increasingly not Jews, but the new Gentile membership of the fellowship of those in the Way. This transformation of a vital bit of our conversation at its beginning needs to be reconsidered before we can discuss what we now need to say about the goal of our Way, in light of the recent beginnings of a reorientation of the mind of the church of which we spoke in the last step.

Jesus came preaching that the reign of God was at hand. In parable after parable, God's reign was depicted in the terms of this world, yet a world reordered. The reign of God was coming, it was breaking in. It would be a new condition of life here and now among human beings, however differently human life would appear. It would mark the end of one age of this world, and in that sense an end of human history as we have known it. It would however be a new era of history, a new condition of God's creation. Whether he came to the conviction early or late, Jesus is presented as having believed that great suffering would mark this transition, his in any case but also undoubtedly the suffering of many. The arrival of the new age would be marked by catastrophe.

The apostles came preaching that the first great act in this drama of redemption had just taken place. The messiah had arrived, had been crucified and had been exalted, glorified, raised up by God. The second and culminating act was about to take place: Jesus would return and God would complete the transformation of creation into the renewed state for which it longs, the dead would be raised, the reign of God would begin. The present was therefore an interim, a pause in the very midst of the transformation of creation. The moment had come, the night was far gone, the day about to break. This being the case, life was to be lived now on the basis of what was taking place, i.e., in accordance with the breaking day, not the passing night. And, already, the power of daylight, the Spirit, was given to the faithful to strengthen them in this new life.

The expected daybreak, the second and completing act of the drama, however, did not arrive. After nineteen centuries it still has not arrived. What have we said in response to this delay? On the one hand, we have kept on hoping that, indeed, the renewal of creation would still come. On the other hand, we began to shift the way in which we expressed our hope, putting more and more emphasis on the first act of the drama as ultimately decisive. Redemption really had been achieved; the end had already come with Jesus, only it could not yet be seen. The goal of our Way was so to speak already reached in its beginning. As we noted earlier, this

conviction continues in our conversation, as when Wolfhart Pannenberg can say that "with the resurrection of Jesus, the end of
history has already occurred, although," he admits, "it does not
strike us in this way" (see p. 43).

In the last five chapters of his *Refutation and Overthrow of the
Knowledge Falsely So Called* (Adv. haer. V, 32-36), Irenaeus offered a
notable alternative to the tendency of our conversation to turn toward a
realized, spiritualized eschatology. His recurring theme was that redemption must come "in this created order."

> For the righteous must first rise again at the appearance of God to
> receive in this created order, then made new, the promise of the in-
> heritance which God promised to the Fathers, and will reign in this
> order. After this will come the judgment. It is just that in the same
> order in which they labored and were afflicted,. . .they should
> receive the fruits of [their suffering]. . .and that in the same order
> in which they suffered bondage they should reign. (32:1). . .God
> promised [Abraham] the inheritance of the Land, but in all his so-
> journing there he did not receive it." and therefore, said Irenaeus,
> "it must be that he will receive it with his seed, that is, with those
> who fear God and believe in him, at the resurrection of the just.
> (32:2)

Of course he understood "the seed" to be the church. Commenting on
Christ's promise "that he would drink of the produce of the vine with his
disciples," he pointed out that "it belongs to flesh and not to spirit to
receive the drink of the vine" (33:1). For Irenaeus, the Kingdom meant
the renewal of "this created order." It is regrettable that these chapters
remained unknown until about four hundred years ago. By then the
damage had been done.

This transformation of hope from that which is to come into a
conviction that the future is already past, leaves one hoping not for
a new event or change in history, but for a clearer vision of what is
already the case. Insofar as this transformation has taken place,
hope no longer has creation's future as its focus. We aren't hoping
for the renewal of creation but, rather, that we may come to see
what has already happened. It has been a consequence of this shift
that most of us along the road have stopped hoping for something
new to occur, that the road we walk would come to its end, that we
would arrive at the destination. On the contrary, the hope has
been not that the reign of God would begin on earth, as in heaven,
but that we would leave the earth to go to heaven. Not a coming
kingdom, but a going church, going from this vale of tears to be

with Jesus in the heavenly places. Walking here on earth, then, has been conceived as preparation for resting there with him. One could say that our hope has been so to walk here that we should eventually (i.e., at death) get there.

Even in this form, we have believed that this is all of grace, that our walking could never earn that reward. The reward as well as the walking here have been conceived to be — as in Judaism — totally and without condition the free gift of a gracious loving God. So we have always meant it, but of course it must also be added that some of us some of the time — and this is also the case with the Jews — have gotten this a bit mixed up and made it sound as if we earned our reward because of the merit of how we walked.

Also in this transformed sense, hope has therefore been of great importance to our walking. We have walked because we hoped, even when the hope and the walking have in this new form a quite different relationship. At first, the hope was for the Way, that it was going somewhere, that it led on into the day of God's reign. Our Way, history and the whole world was on the way toward its future. In the altered form, hope was for the realization of what has already come. Redemption has come, or so we have said. What we have meant is that redemption has arrived, only not here, not on earth. It is stored up for us in another realm. The reign of God is not to break upon us; we are to go to heaven where redemption timelessly awaits us.

Throughout our long walk and our many conversations, however, there have been those who have raised the old hope, the Jewish one in its early apostolic form, that Jesus was to return, if not soon, then eventually. In all frankness, though, we must admit that this has been a minority position and in our day we tend to dismiss those who hold it as naive. When we do so, we fail to reflect upon the fact that our prevailing reformulation of hope pays the price of dismissing the significance of history. If history has really come to its end on Easter, how can any further history have any significance? If it has any at all, it does so as a training period for those destined for heaven. It loses direction and importance as the locus of God's further history with His creation, His people and His church.

Now, however, when new events in the recent history of Israel are making themselves felt, with history once more reasserting its

importance in our conversation, we need to reconsider the formulation of our hope. Can we continue to ignore history? Must not
history itself be the locus of that for which we hope? Must not our
walking be on a way that goes somewhere? Can we not at this point
learn once more to listen to the Jews and perhaps learn something
from them? And will we not hear from them that redemption still
lies out ahead, that we hope for the renewal or completion of God's
creation, which is clearly not yet here? If we do, then we shall learn
from those recent reorienting events of Jewish history the place of
our own responsibility in bringing about the object of our hope,
the goal of our voyage. In order to do this, we shall have to do some
fresh thinking about that event around which our hope has turned
so centrally for all our history. I refer of course to the resurrection
of Jesus, the event of Easter.

EASTER AND HISTORY

The question that confronts us in thinking about Easter is whether
we can come to see it as an event in history, and of such a sort as to
lead us to look eagerly ahead to further history, to the goal of our
Way, or whether it must remain for us the end of history which
takes away from all further history any major significance. Once
again we return to that central question of our conversation: What
happened on Easter?

One answer that bears reconsideration is that Easter was God's
victory over death, death being held to be "the last enemy." The
ground for this answer lies in the thought of Paul. Paul saw death
as the last enemy because for him everything in heaven and earth
turned around the death and resurrection of Jesus. "He was given
up to death for our misdeeds, and raised to life to justify us" (Rom.
4:25). "Since it was a man who brought death into the world, a
man also brought resurrection of the dead. As in Adam all men
die, so in Christ all will be brought to life" (1 Cor. 15:21-22). In
Christ, God was dealing with all humanity, as Paul saw it. Hence
his history is humanity's history and there can be no other history
apart from his.

If we see in Christ God's marvelous new beginning of a way for
Gentiles to enter into the Way and to come to His service, then we
may prefer to say that much indeed, but not all, turns on this one

event. In which case, we shall certainly consider death seriously, but perhaps not as the last enemy. It is part of the seriousness of creation, even part of the seriousness of our failure to walk as God would have us do. But it is not the last enemy or the worst that can befall us. It can be faced. There is such a thing as a good death, a winding up, a falling asleep after a good life.

By any reckoning, however, the death of Jesus was not a good death. We call the annual celebration of its date Good Friday because of the good that has come from it. The good that has come from Good Friday is not the end of death; death continues, whether good or bad. But by his stripes we Gentiles *have* been healed, by a definable, historical sequence, not by a metaphysical theory. By his death, we *have* been brought near, drawn to the God of Israel and into the Way of hope. By his sacrifice at Gentile hands, it has come about that a door has been opened to us who were strangers to all that Israel knew. Just this positive result of his death is what was announced and made possible by Easter.

If Easter is considered an event in the life or history of the individual Jew Jesus, then I do not see how we can deal with it historically. It is a matter between Jesus and God and we must leave it there. If, however, we take Easter to be an event in that larger history of God's Way with His creation, then we shall see here what we have seen elsewhere when we looked for the "mighty acts of God": We see the actions of Jews. We see Jews going into action, Peter standing up to preach in Jerusalem, Paul taking up his collection and writing his letters. We see, in short, the faith and work of the apostles.

Historians, in our day, have their own conception of history, in which no place can be provided for God's work. In our conversation in the Way, we have access to no facts which the historian has overlooked. If we are going to speak of Easter as an event in history, we ought not think of some other realm than that of the historian's. But as long as our conversation continues, we shall surely continue to say that God too is looking at these facts and that, therefore, we have His concern in mind when we speak of this event for and in our realm as also being an event for Him. With the historian we see beginning on Easter the glorification of the debased one, the exaltation of the humiliated. With the historian we see this glorification and exaltation in the words and actions of the disciples, just as we see Moses and Aaron alone leading the

Hebrews out of Egypt, Jeremiah alone denouncing the sins of his people, Cyrus alone giving orders for the return of the Jews to Jerusalem. But because we see these events as absolutely central in God's history with His creation, so we say in each case that God was at work here, helping, leading, urging on His people and moving ahead with His plan for His creation.

Easter marks the moment in which the disciples came to see great good in the death of Jesus and that Jesus was of immeasurable importance in God's purposes for His creation. As we have seen, the precise definition of that in which this new thing consisted was to undergo change. Today, after nineteen centuries, in the light of recent events in Jewish history, we are compelled to add our own words to the conversation of the past. Our own addition takes nothing away from what others saw in Jesus in the past. They saw what they saw in their day. Further history leads us to see matters from our own perspective. From where we walk, on this stretch of the road, it seems simply wrong to speak of Easter as the end of history. We cannot take God's doings with His people, His church and His world over these centuries so lightly.

We would not see any of this or speak in this way, we would not even be walking in this Way, were it not for the event of Jesus, his death and resurrection and the preaching of his apostles. We Gentiles would be without hope and without God were it not for him (Eph. 2:12). If the cause of historical events is itself historical, then Easter is a historical event. It is the beginning of which our nineteen-century-long walk is the result. It is the door that opened for us the possibility of this walk and so entry into Israel's hope.

We need to say afresh to ourselves, then, that our hope is just the Jewish hope into which we have access through Jesus Christ our Lord. We do not have a different hope, any more than we serve a different God. It stands to reason that our Gentile hope will lack something of the national emphasis of Jewish hope, although it cannot leave it out entirely. How could we who adore the God of the Jews not be concerned about God's own beloved people, from whom is our Savior and our salvation? As those who have actually received the light which Israel has in fact provided, we cannot but be concerned about that light and its future. But, with the Jews, our hope reaches out beyond ourselves and our future. Its goal is one for the world, for the renewal and completion of God's creation. It is first and last hope in and for God and His purposes.

HOPE AND THE WAY

The Way which we walk is one in that its goal is one, but the ways in which we walk it differ. This can be seen simply by watching how we walk, but it can also be seen in how we talk, especially in how we talk about the one goal. We are certainly not the only ones who walk in hope. Many people, perhaps more than we, walk in the Marxist way. They too have a hope, and their hope is for a good society, a world of righteousness and peace. Like us, they too believe that human beings are to an immeasurable extent responsible for reaching the goal. Unlike us, they do not think that our responsibility is to the Creator of this world, and therefore they do not see our human responsibility as itself a gift, as sheer grace. This may account for the fact that their whole view of things in which hope plays its part appears to us to be less personal. But we should not prejudge history. Marxism too is a Way and those who walk it, like us, are also finding their way. The story in which both they and we walk is not yet finished. However much we may differ from them on how the present or next steps ought to be made, we should rejoice whenever we can move ahead with them. After all, many of us can admit that we have been stimulated by some of them to be more attentive to the extent to which we have been called by the Giver of the Way to take responsibility for our walking.

By our very self-understanding as Gentiles who walk in the Way of the God of the Jews, we cannot help but be concerned with the similarity and differences between the way we and the Jewish people walk in God's Way. For both of us agree that there is a Way that is given by the Holy One of Israel and that we walk toward the redemption of His creation. This extent of agreement leads us to express our common hope in far more similar ways than is true of any other group, including the Marxists. The differences between us arise not because one of us is right and the other wrong, but because they are God's elect people whereas we are God's elect church.

Both of us believe that God is with us to support us in our walking, however much He has required that we assume responsibility for the particular stage of the Way in which we find ourselves and so for contributing to the eventual attainment of the goal. This is for both of us our sustaining hope in the Way, that God is with us. Only we have each our own appropriate way of saying this.

Judaism can and should remember and rehearse the word of hope spoken to her as a people in her relative youth: "I am with you,... I help you" (Isa. 41:10, 13), spoken and grasped with that immediacy that marks the intimate relationship between God and His people.

Appropriate to our own election and identity as those Gentiles gathered by God through Jesus Christ into His service, our hope is expressly focused on God's *mediate* way of being present with us. As He has elected Jesus of Nazareth to be the one Jew through whom we can have access to Him, so He is with us to help us in no other way than by the Spirit of Jesus being with us. So the word of hope for us is that of the glorified Christ: "I am with you always, to the end of time" (Mt. 28:20). Or as the author of Colossians put it: "Christ in you, the hope of a glory to come" (1:27); which is to say, our hope for the world and of having a place in the realization of that hope is grounded in and depends on that union with Christ which God has provided for us Gentiles. Paul also expressed the relationship in the reverse order: You in Christ (Rom. 6:11, 8:1; Phil. 3:9; 2 Cor. 5:17). It is our Gentile-sustaining hope in the Way.

When we and the Jews speak of our hope concerning the end or goal of the Way, we have both used the same Hebrew term, or (in our case) its transliteration: *messiah*. Only again there is an appropriate difference. As God's people called to play the central role in the center of the action of redemption, and to do so as a people, the Jews express their hope as communal or national. If it will be well with the Jews, then that means it will be well for the world, for the Jews have never hoped for any goal of the Way that was not a redemption of the whole of creation. Since Israel's redemption has always been thought by them to be conditional upon the redemption of the world, so they could always look to their own situation to determine where things stood with the world. This communal or national focus for knowing when redemption would come finds its appropriate expression in their focus of hope. What they hope for the world and so also for themselves is the days of messiah, the age of redemption which God has promised and of which the messiah is either sign or instrument. Their focus is on the redemption itself, not on its agent or sign.

For us, the focus is far more on the figure of the messiah himself, the agent or sign of redemption. Our prayer is for *his* coming and we comfort ourselves in the assurance that we know his name. He is Jesus Christ, we are sure. When he appears, then we shall appear with him in glory. This shift of focus is proper and appropriate for Gentile hope for, apart from him, we would not have come to share in Judaism's hope at all. As Gentiles who share in this hope through Jesus Christ, his appearance must be central in our hope for the age of righteousness and peace toward which we believe ourselves to be walking.

We need to remind ourselves, however, that behind and through these differences our hope is no other than that of the Jews. With them, we hope for a redemption which has not yet come. Our adoption as sons, as Paul put it, lies ahead. Creation is still groaning, as is the Spirit of God, for the redemption of creation. By his close association with that hope, Christ has usually been called by us the Redeemer, but his task still remains to be done. The age of righteousness and peace is one for which we still wait, hope, pray and work. It is that toward which we walk, the goal of the Way in which we find ourselves.

If we could come to make this clear to ourselves, then the Jews might come to see that our hope really is theirs, although apprehended in a Gentile way. If they came to realize that we too await redemption, then they might be willing to grant that, for all they know, the messiah may turn out to be Jesus of Nazareth. They have never had a dogma or even a settled agreement about the identity of the messiah. What matters is that *the days* of the messiah come. And if we can see why they put it that way, they might be able to see why the identity of the messiah is so important to us Gentiles. Any Jew would do for them, but for us, we share this hope through only one Jew. If on both sides we come to see matters in this way, then we may better blend our prayers and bend our efforts toward the hastening of the day of God's redemption. And that, after all, is what is primary: not our different emphases but the final hope, the hope that focuses on the goal of the Way, the redemption of creation, the completion of God's plan and purpose.

IN THE END, GOD

Franz Rosenzweig remarked that Paul's hope, that in the end God would be all in all, had remained a mere theological phrase for the church, that it had never been incorporated into and made a serious point in our theology.

The remark is generally correct, but at least Origen developed the point with some care, if not in a way that would have interested Rosenzweig (see his *de princ*. III, 6:2-3).

In 1 Cor. 15:24-28, where Paul expressed his hope, he speculated that Christ must destroy all God's enemies, of which the last is death. Having brought all creation subject to the Father, Christ will then "deliver up the kingdom" to God, cease to "reign," "be subject" to God, that God may be "all in all." Rosenzweig developed this Pauline speculation into his thesis that finally God Himself will be redeemed of being Creator, that creation itself, and so God as Creator, must give place to God alone, presumably alone with Himself. The thesis is interesting and has the asset of relieving us of any nervousness about the shifts in astronomical theory concerning the ultimate destiny of the detectable universe. However it may be in an interim that may be of considerable duration, in the end (clearly *not* an end of which the scientific method can or ought to try to take account, for this "end" means also an end to the scientific method—along with everything else) God will be all in all.

To such a piece of daring speculation, I think we can only say that we should leave these matters to the Creator. It seems unlikely, having made the commitment and self-limiting move entailed in having begun this creation that His final goal were to be rid of it; but who knows? Perhaps for God, too, enough can be enough; but of these matters we really know nothing, and neither did Paul. The apostle had quite different ways of expressing his hope as well, in which there is no note of God's being "all in all," whatever that may have meant to him.

One other vision of the end in Paul's letter, perhaps his last, has at least one important point in common with that of 1 Cor. 15, namely the one that ends his major discussion of the relationship between the church, becoming increasingly Gentile, and the Jewish people (found in Rom. 11:25-36). The common point is that there is not a single christological reference in either final vision. And this seems worth our attention. For if Christ's role indeed has been to draw us into Israel's hope and the service of the God of the Jews, then when we have reached the goal of the Way how can it be other than that along with Israel, along with the Jews, but now joined by all of creation, we can join the chorus of Rev. 19:6: "Hallelujah! For the Lord our God the Almighty reigns."

That God reign, that all acknowledge Him, that His will be done on earth as well as in heaven—that is the goal. Note well, that is the goal of the Way which we walk now. This makes our walking a matter of cosmic, theological importance of the highest sort. Ours is a hope which depends for its realization on the walking which that hope may stimulate. And that is why, even as we hope, our first concern must be with our walking, with the Way itself. This is the Way which we seek to discern. From here it becomes clear that before we can think further about the Way ahead for all creation, the Way for the World, we must first reflect upon and perhaps reinterpret the Way in its two great major manifestations or understandings up to our present moment in the continuing story. This we hope to do in coming to a fresh understanding of the Way of Israel, and then of our Gentile manner of walking God's Way.

But now I have made what contribution I can to our conversation at this stage of our journey. Others will have their say while I catch my breath, and the conversation will continue. For we walk in the Way of life.

Index of Biblical References

Index of Names